# DON'T TAKE IT PERSONALLY!

## The Art of Dealing with Rejection

## Elayne Savage, Ph.D.

New Harbinger Publications, Inc.

Distributed in the U.S.A. by Publishers Group West; in Canada by Raincoast Books; in Great Britain by Airlift Book Company, Ltd.; in South Africa by Real Books, Ltd.; in Australia by Boobook; and in New Zealand by Tandem Press.

Copyright © 1997 by Elayne Savage
New Harbinger Publications, Inc.
5674 Shattuck Avenue
Oakland, CA 94609

Cover design by Blue Design, San Francisco, CA.
Text design by Tracy Marie Powell.
Edited by Farrin Jacobs.

Library of Congress Catalog Card Number: 96-66072

ISBN 1-57224-077-6

New Harbinger Publications' Web site address: www.newharbinger.com.

10   9   8   7   6   5   4   3   2   1

To Jocelyn
For her wisdom and inspiration

*But words are more powerful than perhaps anyone suspects, and, once deeply engraved in a child's mind, they are not easily eradicated.*

—May Sarton, *I Knew a Phoenix*

# Contents

# Acknowledgments

I have learned some valuable life lessons during the process of writing and publishing this book. I discovered that the opposite of rejection is not just acceptance—it's also perseverance. And in the six years this project has gestated, I've learned to persevere—with the help of a great many people. I'm grateful to the many hearts, minds, and voices that joined in the creation of this book—you know who you are.

First of all I want to thank clients, students, and workshop participants who have inspired me with their courageous stories, perceptions, and wisdom. Each day brings something new and valuable to learn from them, and this book is the best way I know to give back what I've learned. Their individual stories have become collages, a way of reaching out to many people.

Thanks to my literary agent Victoria Shoemaker who shared my vision of *Don't Take It Personally!* and whose optimism and encouragement kept me going. Thanks to Kimn Neilson for teaching me to become a better writer in the process of skillfully editing my book proposal, and to Farrin Jacobs, my editor at New Harbinger, who has been a delight to work with as she performed magic with the manuscript right before my eyes. I'm indebted to Isaac Mizrahi for his perceptive and thoughtful feedback. I'm grateful to Maire Farrington and Anna Rabkin for their valuable input. Thanks to Habib Douss, Jennifer Miller, Bruce Klein, Barry Berkowitz, Molly Hazen, and Nancy Suib for their important contributions.

Several people have helped fashion my thinking over the years, and the pages of this book are infused with their ideas: Eric Greenleaf, Eliana Gil, Joan Sangree, as well as Norman Fischer, Reb Anderson and the other teachers at Green Gulch Farm.

I'm also appreciative to authors Susan Jeffers, Susan Page, Thomas Farber, Janet Wolfe, and Stuart Hart for their mentoring, accessibility, wise counsel, and encouragement. A special thanks to Sebastian Orfali and Beverly Potter for teaching me about publishing and promotion.

Thanks to Herb Bivins, co-owner of Black Oak Books in Berkeley, California, who believed in this book from the beginning. Every time he'd ask, "How's that book coming?" I'd feel more and more like an author. *Don't Take It Personally!* came to be because of this kind of ongoing encouragement from Herb and others.

I value the long-term sustainment I've received from enduring friendships. Sima Blum and I have known each other from high school days in Baltimore, and Allan Wolfe, another Baltimore friend, was the first person to urge me to get started on this adventure. My friendships with Bette Cooper and Larry Grusin go back to the University of Alabama. In fact, the title for this book (which was just a gleam in my eye at the time) came from a comment Larry made years ago after reading one of my articles. And thanks to John L. Blackburn for figuring sooner or later I'd grow into my capabilities.

I'm grateful to other longtime friends and colleagues who have offered sterling contributions to this project—especially Steven Salomon, Ruth Belikove, Marilynn Denn, Audrey Fain, Mary Gullekson, Lynn Taylor, Richard Friedlander, Gail Glassberg, Julie Kovitz, Harry Pasternak, and Phyllis Gorelick.

There's no question in my mind that I persevered because people thought to ask, "How's that book coming?" I'm especially grateful to the caring and support from the community of people at Green Gulch Farm. Thanks to members of the Emeryville Toastmasters and the Speaking Circle for helping me develop my ideas and skills. And to local members of the National Woman's Political Caucus and the California Association of Marriage and Family Therapists for cheering me on. I appreciate the encouragement from folks at the Mind-Body Connection in Oakland and in and around the French Cafe.

I owe a special thank you to the three muses who sit on my shoulder. First, there is Marcia Blacker, my Omaha Central High School English teacher, the first person to encourage my writing when she entered one of my stories in a contest. I lost the contest, but many years later I found Marcia, and we're still in contact. The other two muses are Drs. Hal Bailen and Raymond Biase, who believed in me and nurtured my physical and emotional well-being for many years. They had so much to give but then it gave out. I miss them and wish with all my heart they could be here—but I'll bet they know this book is happening—how could they not?

Finally, I want to thank the members of my family who have applauded my efforts, especially my daughter, Jocelyn Savage, for her wise insights and ability to offer just the right words of love and encouragement, and my brother, Lee Raskin, for his valuable advice and dedicated support. Hey, we did it!

# Introduction

## *Sometimes You Don't Know What Hit You*

It happens so fast—a barrage of words, a wilting look, an insulting tone of voice—and it's as if a loose board springs up and whacks you on the forehead. You feel stunned. You lose your balance. You can't think straight. And then the hurt starts. You might freeze up and withdraw. You might be reduced to tears. You might explode into a blaze of rage. You wonder, "Where on earth did that come from?"

When someone else's words or actions lead to misunderstandings and hurt feelings, it's because you're taking it personally. *Rejection*. That's what it is and it just takes over. Your knee-jerk response is all out of proportion to the event itself and is most likely a reaction to rejection experiences dating back to childhood. But new hurts pile on top of old ones, and it's as if each cutting remark opens up an old wound that never healed.

Over the years, signs and signals, tones and inflections, words and phrases pile up. These childhood rejection wounds may come from parents, teachers, siblings, aunts, uncles, grandparents, baby-sitters, or neighbors. Maybe they were intended, maybe they weren't. Either way, they become self-rejecting beliefs that can tinge your adult relationships. Anything in that stockpile may trigger a defensive response that ignites into something larger than life.

When people endure a natural disaster such as an earthquake, or hurricane, or when they experience a frightening incident like a physical attack or an upsetting episode like a verbal attack, they may not only be reacting to the shock of the present crisis. They may also be reacting to all previous traumas, going back to childhood. Enduring rejection is similar. You may not only be reacting to the present situation but to past experiences as well. Some of these experiences may have been traumatic, and children experiencing them may have felt violated, betrayed, or rejected, making it hard to trust the world as a safe place. One woman described how she feels overwhelmed and is reminded of childhood experiences whenever she feels rejected. "It's like the tornado hits and I'm Dorothy."

As psychotherapist and researcher Elaine Aron describes in *The Highly Sensitive Person,* some children are especially sensitive to their environments and tend to get overstimulated, overaroused, and overwhelmed. These children feel constantly battered by a multitude of anxiety tornadoes.

Let's talk about two specific childhood anxiety tornadoes: the fear of being abandoned and the fear of losing our identity. What creates these fears? From our earliest years, we learn about relationships from our parents or other caregivers. But because we're so dependent on them for care, these are by necessity unequal relationships. Children are inherently trusting until something happens to break that trust. Lying all alone in a crib, hungry or wet, can seem like an eternity to an infant with no sense of real time. That child might feel vulnerable to the parent's whim—will that parent ever return and give comfort? At times, we worry they'll leave us—and we come to fear the rejection of abandonment. At other times, we might become afraid our caregivers will overwhelm us with closeness, smothering out the spark of our identities—another rejection. How does this happen? They may not let us show independence or creativity or assertiveness or a sense of our own personhood. These dual rejection fears—abandonment and intrusion—often accompany us throughout life, causing no end of trouble in relationships.

Fear of possible rejection has lead many of us to withhold statements of love, acts of caring, sexual advances, or even movie or dinner invitations. We're often afraid to come forward with requests such as asking someone for a first date, requesting a raise, submitting artwork or manuscripts, or asking for favors like a ride to the airport. It's constricting and restricting, keeping us from being ourselves. When we hold back like this, people often misunderstand what our hesitancy is really about.

It helps to understand how adult rejection ordeals are rooted in childhood. Most of us wanted to be loved, cared about, and respected, but perhaps that didn't happen when we were growing up. There were so many disappointments. What if you wanted to be comforted by your mother, but she held back? What if you wanted your father to listen to your stories about the school day, but he just kept reading the paper, not paying attention, not even looking at you? Wouldn't it have been great to be praised once in a while for the times you did something well instead of having been chastised for the times you messed up? Wouldn't it have been nice once in a while to be told you did a good job, even for small things—like the times you successfully carried milk to the table—instead of getting yelled at the one time you spilled it? One man remembers, "I rushed home once to tell my dad I got 92 percent on a math test. He looked at the grade, looked at me and said, 'So what happened to the other 8 percent?' I think in that moment a part of me died—I quit trying."

Many of us encountered rejection messages, even though our parents or teachers may not have intended them. Perhaps we felt laughed at or invalidated or ignored—maybe even disowned or abandoned. Perhaps someone inadvertently discounted our emotions by scoffing, "You're acting like a baby. What's the matter with you, did your feelings get hurt?" Perhaps they were trying to dictate how we should feel so they didn't have to examine their own feelings. But it felt like they were trying to take our feelings away.

Years later, we're still affected by these timeworn childhood wounds. Early dings and dents take their toll, and we're stunned when these old feelings reverberate into our adult lives and relationships, causing even little things to set us off. When we feel easily slighted, when our feelings continue to get hurt by the actions, words, and behaviors of others, or if we unrelentingly blame ourselves for any given situation—we're taking it personally.

A songwriter I know uses musical terms to explain this process: "I picture myself as a harp with all kinds of large and small debris swirling around out there—words, feelings, innuendos. Some float toward me, passing right through the spaces between the strings, and glide on by. But others seem to be hurled at me and hit the strings, striking a chord that reverberates way back to my past, bringing up old hurts. It really jangles my nerves and throws me off balance.

"I'd like to be able to ride out these encounters and not get so unnerved—to reorchestrate and find my balance. First of all, I want to choose whether they stick or pass by. If they do stick, I want to be able to say, 'Okay, what can I do to make this noise musical?' What works best for me is to chant to myself, 'Don't take it personally, don't take it personally.' In fact, it's become my mantra."

There's no question that taking things personally can get in the way of both work and personal relationships. Sensitivity to rejection can be a symptom or attribute of a number of psychological issues: Adult Attention Deficit Disorder, depression, stagefright, eating disorders, highly sensitive nervous systems, shame-based issues, shyness, and abuse. And you may be able to think of others. Rejection, however, is more than just another slice of the pie—it is also the crust that overlays these issues.

# Take It Seriously but Not Personally

We are taking things personally when we get our feelings hurt by misinterpreting the meanings of others. Words or actions feel like rejection even though that wasn't the intention. But sometimes words or actions of another person not only seem rejecting—they actually are. It's important to properly acknowledge this to ourselves. As Harvey Mackay writes in *Sharkproof*, if you didn't get a job, were turned down for a raise, or denied admission to the college of your choice, "don't rationalize away the hurt ... point your head in the right direction and get back in the game. ... It's not a permanent condition. It's a short-term setback." As painful as it may be, maybe we can learn something constructive from what was said or done.

What if there's no question you're being excluded from social functions or work activities by a certain group of people? How can you best deal with the situation? It helps to ask yourself a few questions. For example, "Could I be so supersensitive to feeling left out that I pound on doors to get in?" "Am I overgeneralizing the situation and believing there's something wrong with me because I'm being excluded?" "Could I be putting out some sort of message to people that says 'Go ahead, exclude me, I'm expecting it?'"

Most of us have at one time or another had a really bad day and taken it out on someone else. That doesn't make it okay, but it sure does happen. What if someone said something to you that was especially hurtful? It could be that this person is a rejecting sort of personality, maybe even a bit mean-spirited. But most likely this person was not thinking very highly of him or herself that day and unloaded on you because you happened to be there. Mackay reminds his readers, "Whatever you do, don't take rejection personally. It may have nothing to do with you."

Gathering information about other people in an effort to understand them better may circumvent problems for you in future dealings. In fact, you may even decide not to have any future with that person or persons. You can be selective not only about what information you let into your life, but who you let in as well.

What about those times when a small part of you can acknowledge that something someone said just might be true, but you were overreacting to the way they said it. Can you respect the truth of their words while disregarding their attitude? In other words, can you take it seriously, but not personally?

Then, too, there are times when taking things personally could be useful. When we open up our hearts and minds to include all aspects of the world, we are allowing ourselves to take them in—in a personal and intimate way. Isn't this also taking things personally? What happens when this phrase is seen in a positive way rather than in a negative way? We gain the opportunity to obtain new and different information about ourselves and our world.

## Sorting Out the Facts

The key is to screen input from others and process it appropriately. For example, mail arriving at a large corporation goes to the mail room to be sorted. Then it usually gets sent on to the appropriate department. But what if a piece of mail is routed by mistake to someone in the wrong department, who isn't used to dealing with it? This person might get confused and overreact. However, in the right hands this particular communication could be properly processed and given attention. You, too, can learn to give incoming information proper attention by considering its usefulness. You can learn to toss or reroute the mail.

When I was a child, my processing system didn't work very well; I was always taking something personally. My antennae were always out. I would watch and listen carefully, searching for cues from people around me. I frequently felt I was being judged or compared. It seemed as if almost everything was a test, but nobody told me the rules or if I passed it. I'd try to read their faces, their tones of voice, their walks, their sighs. If someone looked at me the wrong way—narrowing their eyes or raising an eyebrow—I'd wonder, "What's wrong with me? What did I do wrong this time? How can I do it better?"

A few years ago, I was ironing clothes and burned myself. As I blurted out "What's wrong with me?" I remembered the message I'd heard as a child: "What's wrong with you, can't you do anything right?" When I thought about this some more, I realized that most of the time it wasn't even a spoken message. It was communicated by looks and tones of voice. My mom's long sigh clearly said, "You can do better," which to me meant "What you did was not good enough."

It seems I was getting my feelings hurt all the time. I often thought people were laughing at me. I remember my first day at dancing class when I was about five years old. While all the parents watched, the teacher told us to follow her as best we could and she began to shuffle and stomp and kick. Then she began to shimmy, which we just couldn't figure out. Can you just picture all of these little five-year-olds shaking their butts instead of their shoulders? The parents roared, and I, of course, thought they were laughing at me. For many years after that, I would make sure I was in the back row of any dance or movement class, and I never again tried to shake my shoulders or shimmy because I thought everyone would laugh at me.

Then, a few years ago I discovered NIA (Neuromuscular Integrative Action), a highly aerobic (yet barefoot) technique that blends the rhythms and movements of modern, jazz, and ethnic dance; yoga; and tai chi, tae kwon do, and aikido. This is movement without judgment, and it's perfect for self-conscious people like me—there's no right or wrong way. In other exercise classes I'd be mortified if I made a mistake, but now I can stand in the front row—and even shimmy if I feel like it.

In NIA your energy follows the music, and you move from the core of your body. You move with purpose, "taking a stance," developing new body awareness and a sense of your own power.

Participants are encouraged to "personalize their actions to support moving freely and openly, to personalize their thoughts to support fullest potential, to personalize their feeling to discover more about themselves, and to personalize their spirit to support moving about the earth freely and lovingly." I love the idea of making a choice to personalize how I move, think, and feel—it's a nice switch from my usual tendency to personalize other people's messages.

Some beliefs we develop about ourselves can come from misunderstandings. When I was nine years old and visiting my aunt across the country, I overheard her telling someone on the phone, "I'm disappointed in her, she's lazy." I believed she was talking about me and from that day on I thought of myself as lazy. Twenty years later someone said to me, "How can you think of yourself as lazy? You commute to San Francisco, work full-time in Child Protective Services, attend graduate school, run a household, and parent a young child. That doesn't sound very lazy to me." Well, when you put it that way . . .

Maybe I never was lazy. I decided to check it out from the source—my aunt. I even scheduled an appointment with her to talk about it. "Lazy?" She was genuinely surprised when I recounted the story in my memory. "I couldn't have been talking about you—it must have been about someone else. Maybe the housekeeper."

You can see how my supersensitivity as a child has affected my life. Another child might not have been so reactive. Another child might have been more resilient and not so quick to perceive rejection. Another child might have gone about his or her business without wasting time and energy on deciphering the meanings of looks, tones of voice, or laughs. (Chapter 10 takes a look at resiliency.)

From the time I was very young, I put out my antennae, turned the frequency to high, and got very good at paying close attention to what was going on around me. I got so good at it, that I thought I could read minds. Have you ever had a similar experience?

One message I came to "read" was that my parents didn't have much room for me when they disappeared into their own private worlds. Even though I believe my parents loved and cared about me, they often seemed to be emotionally unavailable. My dad worked long hours and I didn't see much of him except on Sundays. My mom seemed preoccupied with her own thoughts and worries. I felt left out, ignored, hurt, lonely. It felt as though I was always knocking on doors, wanting to be let in.

Feeling left out has caused huge problems for me. Back when I wa
married, my husband was planning to move his study to a structure in
the backyard. I overreacted. I had finally gotten used to the many evenings he would go into his downstairs study and close the door to write.
But the idea that he would actually be leaving the house really upset
me. I felt left out just thinking about it. And I thought about it day and
night. I couldn't sleep. Looking back I see how I was interpreting his
plans to mean he was "leaving" me. I felt hurt—as if a door were closing
in my face. Yes, I took it personally!

I began to wonder why this situation carried such a charge for me.
What were my childhood experiences? How often did I feel left out and
alone? What kind of emotional shades got drawn?

The moves back and forth across the country didn't help. When I
was nine, we moved from Washington, D.C., to Omaha, then back east
to Baltimore when I was a senior in high school. Moving my senior year
was the hardest. I had to leave old friends, start a new school, learn new
routines, and make new friends. I remember feeling as if I were on the
outside looking in, as if I didn't belong anywhere.

For me, feeling left out is connected to feeling different from other
people. Both of these feelings are linked to one of the most devastating
experiences of my life. When I was twelve years old my mother and
grandmother died in a plane crash. They were on their way to the Mayo
Clinic so my grandmother could undergo some tests. When my mother
told me she was leaving, I felt left out; in my eyes, my mother had
chosen to leave me to accompany my grandmother. And the next thing
I knew, she was dead.

On top of the grief, I experienced strong feelings of isolation. One
of the clearest memories I have of feeling left out was the first day of
school in eighth grade. Back in those days, families were supposed to be
perfect, like Ozzie and Harriet or the Cleavers—intact and happy. Hardly
anyone had divorced or single parents, so having a mother who'd died
in a nationally publicized accident was not only devastating but mortifying.

I remember, about a week after the plane crash, walking across the
playing field toward the inner school yard where students were clustered
together. As soon as they spotted me, they stopped talking. I knew they
had been talking about me, feeling sorry for me. I remember feeling so
different from everyone else, so alone, as if I was the only person in
the world without a mother. I was the center of attention, yet I felt so
left out.

Feeling left out triggers strong responses for me. These responses
interfered with my marriage as illustrated by the backyard-study story,
and I unwittingly passed them down to my daughter as you'll see in
chapter 7. Yet there are things I have done in my adult life that seem to
perpetuate that feeling—like marrying a writer who was in his own world
so much of the time. You can bet I really felt excluded when he carried

s in his head between his characters! I had a lot of practice
riage learning about my "left out" issues, and a few other
n't it uncanny how we're attracted to the very people
overblown responses from us?

The experience of my husband moving his study outside taught me something important about myself. I realized there was some sort of a process going on here, and I began to pay attention. First, I learned to recognize when those "left out" feelings begin to take over. Next, I would remind myself that feeling like that most likely meant I was feeling rejected—sometimes even abandoned. Putting words to my feelings helped define the situation for me. Understanding this process changed the way I was responding to overwhelming situations. Now it's easier to keep my balance and my composure. It helps to ask some questions here:

- Am I taking this personally? How?

- Is there any cause for me to feel threatened?

- Am I feeling rejected in some way?

- Where did this reaction come from? Is it something "old"?

Next consider for a moment how much energy it takes to worry about something so much. Think about how much energy goes outward, squandered energy that could be used more creatively. Ask yourself, "Do I really want to put so much time and energy into this?"

This process of rejection allows you to make some choices here. At this point you can begin to identify and manage painful feelings of rejection that threaten to immobilize you. It may be an old feeling you recognize. It may be the same one that caused you so much confusion in childhood. Remind yourself that you can choose to stay immersed in this childhood pain if you want to—or you can make an effort to bring in your adult perspective. By reminding yourself that you have a choice, you can begin to feel in control of it, instead of allowing it to control you.

# Reweave Your Tapestry of Experiences

*Don't Take It Personally!* will help put you in control. By identifying childhood rejection messages and the core beliefs you formed about yourself and your world, you can see how you might overadapt to your environment in order to protect yourself from hurt or fear. By reflecting on your childhood, you can learn to make connections between the "then" and the "now," exploring how these obvious, and not so obvious, messages come to be repeated in everyday interactions, in personal relationships, and in the workplace. Next you'll explore how many of these

> ## Remind yourself: I have a choice here.

rejection messages were passed along from generation to generation—and learn how to break the cycle. Finally, you'll learn how to recruit these old messages to work for and not against you. You'll learn to highlight strengths instead of "weaknesses" and to develop tools to manage painful feelings so they don't overwhelm you and cause you to lose touch with your emotional compass.

*Don't Take It Personally!* provides the opportunity to reweave the tapestry of your life experiences by inspiring you to see yourself in a new light, to become more aware of options and personal resources and to use them creatively. This enhances the process of breaking old patterns and moving from self-rejection to self-acceptance.

I wish I could promise that these old unwanted behaviors can be totally extinguished. But in reality they're something like a slow-motion version of those trick birthday-cake candles. They seem to die down for varying lengths of time, then unexpectedly flare up again. But these flare-ups can be useful. (It's really true.)

Whenever this happens it's a reminder that you have a unique ability that has saved your feelings—maybe even your life—a lot of times as you were growing up. Look at it as a method you learned to protect yourself, an overadaptation to an unsafe world. You don't have to discard it just because it's no longer usable in its current form—you can modify it. You can choose to recognize it, appreciate it, befriend it even, like an old friend from childhood who pays a surprise visit. You grew up together, you were once a part of each other's lives. Then your interests changed, along with the way you both view the world. Although you don't have much in common anymore, you've been through a lot together.

You've had a lot of practice taking things personally, so what about taking things personally in positive ways for a change? How would it feel to recognize a caring look on someone's face? What if you could really hear favorable comments about yourself? And take them in? And believe them? And cherish them? What if you could embrace these positive messages in your life, trusting that appreciation really exists out there, that you can absorb it, letting it infuse every part of your being? What if you could accept yourself?

> You learned to overadapt in childhood in order to
> feel safer. Maybe it's time to modify these behaviors
> and make them more usable.

Accepting yourself includes recognizing the various parts of yourself and accepting them. There is usually a child self, maybe more than one. There is probably an adolescent self as well. Then there is the adult self, with all its complexities and a lot of possible players: the reserved self; the spontaneous self; the light self; the heavy self; the carefree self; the responsible self; the good self; the bad self. You may come to recognize other parts as well. One woman describes how she tries to accept herself, "I want to be like a big umbrella over myself, to parent myself. I want to be like a sheepherder, available to all the little parts of me."

The more of yourself you can learn to accept, the less room there is for self-rejection. After all, if you don't like yourself, it spills over into your relationships. I know it seems that some days are filled with trying to avoid the minefields of rejection that appear to be everywhere. Treading so cautiously, dodging and swerving, can be such an energy drain. Why not choose to think of minefields as *mind*fields, allowing yourself fertile ground for changing your mind-sets—your beliefs about yourself and your environment.

## How to Use This Book

We each experience rejection in our own way and so we each will ultimately have to find our own solutions. *Don't Take it Personally!* will help you identify your rejection issues, negative beliefs, and recurring patterns of behavior as well as the sources of all of these. Then it will provide you with the means for change. But don't expect to be able to do everything all at once. That's why this book is broken up into three parts. When you read part one, try to find the situations that most closely mirror your own rejection experiences. If you start paying attention to yourself and when you're taking things personally you'll be better prepared to deal with these situations when they arise. In part two you'll learn to look to your past experiences to see how these dynamics have invaded your present interaction. You'll examine messages that were perhaps unknowingly passed on to you by your family, friends, and caregivers.

Part three is where you'll learn to make a change. You'll read about the possibility of making choices and discover creative ways to transform stumbling blocks into building blocks. You can practice walking alongside yourself, giving yourself enough distance from stressful situations to create options. You can even find the balance of taking yourself seriously enough to believe in yourself, yet lightly enough to laugh with yourself.

The first step involves recognizing the feeling and putting words to it. Are you ready to join me in some teamwork? Let's look at some of the ways you might be taking things personally.

# Part One

# Zeroing In on the Problem

# I

# Maybe I Can't Name It, but I Know It When I Feel It

## The Many Faces of Rejection

Rejection comes in many forms—and none of them is easy to deal with. When you feel rejected, you might be experiencing multiple feelings at once. You may find yourself hurt or overreacting and you don't know why. A simple, and perhaps unintentional, slight might lead you to feel inferior, powerless, ignored, isolated, discounted, humiliated, or not supported. It's not easy, however, to label your feelings in the midst of experiencing them.

One way to do something about taking things personally is to learn to recognize the various forms it can take. Once you identify it, you have a fighting chance to do something about it. In this chapter you'll find some common configurations. As you read these stories you'll get a clearer picture of where you fit into the rejection merry-go-round. You may even find yourself thinking (or even saying out loud) "Aha! I recognize that one," or "That sounds just like me."

## Alex's Story

Alex didn't trust that significant people in his life would stand by him and support him. He expected to be treated as if he were not important. In his marriage, he'd defer to what he thought his wife wanted and agree to almost anything to keep her affection. The same thing happened at work. He'd be upset with some policy or decision, but he wouldn't say anything; then he'd get irritated and resentful that no one considered his needs. The trouble was no one was aware of his needs because he didn't state them. Alex told himself his needs didn't count and if he asked for anything he'd just be rejected.

When his marriage broke up, he felt as if he were falling apart. He told his parents he needed their company and support and asked if he could spend a week with them. When they said it wasn't possible at the present time, Alex was stunned. His immediate reaction was to tell himself that they couldn't be bothered, that he didn't count.

Why was Alex so quick to assume his parents didn't care about him? He remembered all the times his mother was too busy with her students to spend enough time with him. "I'll never forget how hurt I was when I discovered some students were calling her 'Mom.' I was already jealous because I thought they saw more of her than I did."

Then there was the time Alex hand-lettered all the diplomas for his sixth grade class. "I was so proud of my work, I wanted my parents to be proud of me, too. But my dad didn't attend the graduation. He thought it was more important to go to an Eagle Scout ceremony with a friend and the friend's son. My dad was a supportive kind of guy—for everyone else but me."

In a memory that has haunted him from childhood, Alex recalled being seven or eight years old, wanting desperately to talk to his dad. He stood there forlornly, watching his dad get into the car and pull away from the curb, on his way to visit yet another friend in need. Alex cried out at the top of his lungs, "Stop! Come back here!" But the car was already retreating down the street. Now he realized that he really wanted to say, "Please don't go, Dad. I need you more than those other people do."

Years later, Alex often feels like that little boy, expecting people will abandon him because they can't be bothered. When people aren't available to meet his needs, he jumps to conclusions. Because of the way he interpreted childhood experiences, when Alex's marriage broke up he was quick to conclude that since his parents said he couldn't stay with them at that time, they didn't care about him. As it turns out, his dad had been experiencing serious medical problems necessitating hospitalization. His parents were attempting to hide this information to protect Alex at an already fragile time in his life. Alex began to wonder if he had misinterpreted earlier incidents as well and decided to initiate a series of talks with his parents to get a clearer view of his childhood perceptions.

In retrospect, he understood that their preoccupation with their careers was not a measure of his worth to them. Through talking to them about his childhood, Alex realized that both he and his feelings did count, although his parents weren't always aware of them. It proved to be a valuable lesson in two ways: Alex learned to voice his needs and to not take things so personally.

# Louisa's Story

Louisa feared that people would leave her—there was always a sense of impermanence in her relationships. It's really no wonder she felt this way: by the time she was fourteen years old her family had moved from city to city twelve times. This sense of impermanence was also woven throughout the generations: members of both sides of her family had died when their children were young.

Louisa never felt secure. Once, she told me that the only place she really felt safe was in a fabric store. She would find herself heading right for the remnants; she kept piles of material in her closets and in her bedroom. She began to spend more and more time in fabric stores, and the piles kept growing.

Why this fascination with pieces of fabric? Why was Louisa so driven to stockpile? One day, she happened to tell me a story about her security blanket. "I took it everywhere with me when I was a little girl. One day it disappeared. I looked everywhere in the house but it was nowhere to be found. I was so upset. I was inconsolable and my mother finally had to tell me what happened to it. The workmen doing repairs on the street outside our house needed some rags, so my mom cut up my 'blankey' and gave it to them. It broke my heart." The "blankey," too, was impermanent and had disappeared from Louisa forever.

No wonder those piles of fabric were so comforting to her—something to touch, to hold on to. But somehow with the return of this memory and in the telling of the story, the need to stockpile was no longer so great. In fact, on one of her "fewer and far between" trips to the fabric store, she walked past a house where a quilt project was in progress. Several women were making quilts for AIDS babies. Would you be surprised to learn that the next day Louisa dropped off several shopping bags of material? Enough to make quite a few "blankeys."

# Gene and Maureen's Story

Maureen was leaning on the counter reading the paper when Gene walked into the kitchen. She looked so appealing, so sensual, he wanted to touch her. He thought he'd surprise her, she often encouraged him to be more spontaneous, so what the hell! He came up behind her and gave her a loving hug. But Maureen gasped and pulled away from him. Gene, feeling rejected, withdrew in silence. He misunderstood her actions and told himself his advances were unwanted, that she found him unappealing.

So maybe he was a little too impulsive, maybe too aggressive, but he didn't think his actions warranted her overreaction. He accused Maureen of tricking him by urging him to be spontaneous then refusing his advances. Maureen was confused too—she didn't understand why she reacted so dramatically.

In couples therapy they discovered this wasn't about Gene at all. Nor was it about spontaneity. Maureen reacted to Gene because he came up behind her. When they experimented with approaches from the front or from the side, she was much more receptive to his advances. All she needed was some warning that he was moving toward her.

But the direction of the approach was only part of the story. Maureen made a startling discovery about herself. She realized she never feels safe when her back is exposed, and when Gene came up behind her she was caught off guard.

Once she became aware of this, she was able to relate the feeling to other areas of her life. For example, she realized she was extremely uncomfortable in restaurants if her back was exposed to foot traffic. All these years she'd been telling herself she preferred sitting with her back to the wall so she could look out and see people arrive. Not true. She learned she was trying to protect her back from a possible surprise attack.

Maureen's not exactly sure where this fear came from, but she has cloudy memories of being unpleasantly surprised, perhaps even scared, by adults as a little girl. Sometimes in teasing ways, sometimes in ways that disrespected her privacy. She may never know the exact origin, but she knows she was left with the fear.

Now that Gene understands that Maureen can't tolerate sudden movements from behind, he is better able to respect her needs and no longer gets his feelings hurt. He thinks twice now about how he approaches her for a hug and is practicing spontaneity in other ways.

Maureen, too, is changing. It made such a difference to be able to pinpoint her fear, and now she can sit in semiexposed areas if she chooses, without feeling anxious. Well, not *too* anxious. But she still prefers a hug that she can see coming.

# Different Strokes for Different Folks

Cultural experiences can create different styles that lead to taking things personally. For example, families of various ethnic backgrounds may show caring and connection to others by raising their voices, by nagging, through food, by degrees of closeness or distance, or even by the amount of gift-giving. And of course gender differences are another form of cultural upbringing leading to misunderstandings. You'll find examples of these troublesome cultural styles throughout the book.

---

> Sometimes the difference between two people
> is really a matter of style.

---

One woman, an artist, summed it up pretty well when she observed, "Relationships are like color swatches: One color held up to another may look dark and grungy, but put it next to yet another color and it becomes bright and beautiful."

Bernie grew up in a family that showed affection for each other with spontaneous hugs and kisses. His mother and father would walk down the street arm and arm, occasionally giving each other a hug or kiss. Lena's family, on the other hand, was reserved and wouldn't dream of demonstrating affection in public; they believed that sort of behavior belonged only in the bedroom. So, when Bernie and Lena were in a public place and Bernie reached over to kiss her, she pulled away from him. This happened on more than a few occasions, and Bernie was hurt and confused. Because he thought Lena was rejecting him, he withdrew and became less and less demonstrative. She in turn, upset by his withdrawal, became even more unresponsive. A chain reaction started that was eroding their relationship. Once Lena and Bernie discovered it was due to different styles learned in their respective families, they were able to make some adjustments with each other.

For Evelyn and Jordan the style difference seemed to be physical—it was the length of their strides. He took long strides, she walked more slowly and with little steps. He'd walk ahead of her and she'd feel hurt—especially when he'd already be on the other side of the street as she was stepping off the curb. Then she realized, "The more I feel sorry for myself, the slower I walk. The smaller my steps, the smaller I feel, until I almost disappear. I can see I'm contributing to the distance between us. I guess it's time to let Jordan in on my concerns." So Evelyn told him she'd try to walk faster if he'd try to walk slower.

Evelyn began to see that there are other areas in their relationship where she "walks behind" Jordan. For example, if she feels hurt by something Jordan says or does, she drags her feet or takes a step or two backward, and disappears. This intensifies the distance between them. Jordan, whose early childhood experiences were a series of abandonments, perceives Evelyn's withdrawal as another "leaving," and he strides ahead. Both of them metaphorically create protective distance, she by "lagging behind" and he by "striding ahead." The ever-growing space between them becomes filled with misunderstandings and hurt feelings.

## Who's Responsible Here?

It might be that you take things the wrong way. Or you take things the right way but your feelings get easily hurt. You possibly feel people are taking sides—for you or against you. You may get upset when other people don't see things the way you do. You might feel rejected, slighted, or even attacked. As one woman said, "I'm so porous, everything seems to penetrate. I wish things could just roll off. I could sure use some Scotchguard!"

Then there's the responsibility aspect. You might feel blamed or blame yourself. You might take something as a personal failure—thinking it's your fault. You might even run through a checklist of what you could have done to save someone from making a mistake, or what you should have said to keep someone from feeling depressed. It goes something like this: Maybe I should have paid more attention. Maybe I should have paid less attention. Maybe I should have been more entertaining. Maybe I should have been less entertaining. All those "shoulds."

You can choose to take responsibility for your own state of mind, for achieving the results you want to achieve, and for your own part in an action. But, as Judy Tatelbaum observes in *You Don't Have to Suffer: A Handbook for Moving Beyond Life's Crises*, "We can be responsible for our own personal responses, not for the event itself." We don't have to blame ourselves.

Nor do we have to blame others. If we grew up in a blaming kind of family everything's externalized—it's someone else's fault. One woman says, "It was always difficult for me to pick up a phone to tell someone I was running late because that meant I had to take responsibility for my lateness—I couldn't blame the traffic or something. And I've learned something else really important about taking responsibility: Blaming others for upsetting me doesn't change the fact that I'm upset. Dealing with my own upset clearly has to be an inside job."

Sometimes taking things personally results from having trouble separating our own feelings from those of others. We might take something on as our own problem when in fact it has little, if anything, to do with us. When we were young we saw ourselves as the center of our world. Everything revolved around us. Because we were not yet able to see things from the perspective of others, we personalized things, experiencing actions as intentional. How could we not? After all, we were the center of our universe, trapped within ourselves. Taking things personally *does* have a ring of specialness to it, doesn't it?

Once we grew up and approached adolescence, we began to develop a sense of ourselves as separate from others around us. We no longer saw ourselves as the center of all activity. Maybe we began to empathize with others, putting ourselves in their shoes. Maybe we began to figure out that our parents and teachers felt or acted the way they did for reasons that had little or nothing to do with us. We began to take a perspective on situations from a wider view. In other words, we learned to depersonalize the actions of others. But not all of us learned to do this. This important concept is discussed further in chapter 10.

## Playing the Blame Game

Taking things personally can mean expecting to be blamed by others. I've noticed a subtle dynamic regarding taking responsibility in some couples I see. One will maneuver the other to make a decision that would more appropriately be joint. Why? Because then the uninvolved partner can say, "It's your fault, I didn't make the decision."

We get so used to the blame game that we begin to blame ourselves. We're frequently too ready to accept fault and we tend to take on things as personal failures. One woman said, "I came to believe if something went well it was an accident. If it went wrong, it was my fault. 'So what did I do wrong this time?' I'd ask myself, and I'd pull out a whole checklist of possibilities and go over them in my mind, one at a time."

---

**We get used to the blame game and often end up blaming ourselves.**

---

We may feel shamed, even humiliated when something goes wrong. It's hard to take criticism—even constructive criticism. It seems we automatically feel as though we're being branded with a huge "at fault" stamp. Another client said, "I wither like lettuce in the hot sun when someone blames me for something. It reminds me of all the times growing up I heard someone say, 'Look what you made me do.'"

Then there's the gem, "How can you do this to me?" This is the trademark of the martyr, instilling both guilt and blame on the unfortunate child. It's usually repeated frequently, and accompanied with a great sigh. It can make knots in your stomach and have devastating long-term effects.

One woman was exploring the role blame had in her relationship difficulties. "I keep asking myself what I'm doing wrong, how I can do more, so I don't feel so blamed." I asked if she expected to feel blamed. She thought a moment, and said, "Yes, I guess I do. I always have." I asked her if she could give equal time to the portions of relationships where she felt cared about, respected, maybe even valued. It wasn't easy at first, because she had to focus on acceptance instead of rejection, but she was able to slowly explore the possibilities.

Many of these blaming examples have a common theme—they all involve generalizing to mammoth proportions. Yes, perhaps it's true you made a mistake in a specific situation, but when you start to tell yourself you always make mistakes and that you're stupid for making mistakes, this is overgeneralizing. These "mistakes" can become quickly distorted into "proof" of what a bad person you are.

One young woman I know used to berate herself for small infractions. "I used to really be hard on myself when I'd stop to buy a candy bar at the corner grocery on my way to the bus stop. Now I let myself enjoy it, and tell myself, 'One candy bar does not a bad girl make!'"

# It Might Be Time to Readjust Your Emotional Filter

Taking things personally is usually related to feeling rejected in some way. It can come from actions, words, a tone of voice, or "that look." Have you ever felt rejected by a raised eyebrow? No matter if the behavior or gesture is intended or not—your feelings can get hurt. If the experience gets repeated many times and if it involves people you should be able to trust, you begin to start believing that something is wrong with you. You begin to develop core beliefs about yourself, and they are hard to change. In fact, you may let in only the words from others that confirm those negative things you already believe to be true about yourself. You may filter out any and all positive messages.

Think about this for a minute. How many times has someone paid you a compliment that was so different from what you think of yourself that you couldn't even hear the words? It was as if their mouth was moving but no words were coming out. This used to happen to me all the time. Once I noticed I couldn't hear the words, I learned to check in with myself and ask, "Why am I having trouble hearing what is being said here?" A good guess is that the person was saying something nice— maybe even generous. So I would force myself to ask the speaker to repeat the comment.

Of course, it was another story if someone was saying something negative to me, something I had no trouble believing about myself. Then I would absorb it like a sponge. How quick we are to attract any floating negative messages in the air, while at the same time repelling positive ones! Because negative messages are so well known to us, they are comforting in their familiarity and seem to offer a sense of security. Anything new or different, even if it's positive, involves taking a risk. (Chapter 4 discusses this in more detail).

Rejection issues become full-blown when it comes to getting up enough courage to find the words to ask for something you want or need. What if someone tells you "no"? Can you tolerate the "no" or do you feel devastated? Do you tell yourself you are worthless? Do you tell yourself that person doesn't care about you?

One woman I know always waited for her friends to invite her to dinner or the movies. She almost always accepted, but was hesitant to initiate plans with them for fear they would say "no." Her friends, it turns out, felt hurt at her inertia, thinking they were doing all the work in the relationship.

## *"Not Tonight, I Have a Headache"*

Misunderstandings and hurt feelings abound because people are hypersensitive to rejection in sexual situations. What if your partner turns away from your advances? Or pretends to be asleep? Do you take it personally? What if your partner sometimes doesn't get "turned on," or "turns off" in the middle of making love, or doesn't climax? Do you tell yourself that something is wrong with you? Or that you're not attractive enough? Or not sexy enough? There's a good chance your partner's response (or lack of one) says a lot more about her or him than about you. Yet here you are, wasting so much energy letting in all your negative thoughts—and believing them. These were the kinds of experiences Lorna and Kenneth were having around sex.

Lorna came into therapy because Kenneth wanted her to be "more affectionate" and she didn't know how. She knew this was Kenneth's euphemism for saying he wanted Lorna to initiate sex once in a while instead of always waiting for him to make the first move. But he considered it *her* problem and wouldn't join her in couples therapy, so she came in alone. In therapy Lorna figured out that she was afraid Kenneth would reject her if she approached him, but she wasn't really sure why she felt this way.

She remembered she'd been sensitive to slights as a child. She recalled all the times her mother got irritated with her for tugging at mom's skirt, or punished her for asking for something. Then there was that awful time when her father was tinkering with the TV at a relative's house and Lorna impulsively tried to hug him. He pushed her away! She felt so humiliated. She never again initiated hugging her dad because she couldn't take the chance he'd push her away again. Lorna began to link up these childhood rejection experiences to her current fears.

By discovering the origins of her fears, Lorna could begin to move past them. She was ready to imagine taking small steps toward initiating sexual contact with Kenneth. She planned out what she might say to him, ways she might touch him. One evening she dared to try.

Kenneth was stretched out on the bed watching TV. Lorna took a deep breath, and stretched out beside him. Then, without a word, she rested her head on his chest and began to stroke him. Kenneth, thrown off guard, bolted upright and blurted out, "You're smothering me!"

Lorna went ballistic—her worst fears had come true. She told herself, "He doesn't love me, he doesn't want to be with me." She was ready to call it quits. This time Kenneth asked to join Lorna in therapy. He tried to assure her his knee-jerk reaction had very little to do with her; it had surprised him as much as it surprised her. And what might Kenneth have been reacting to? Why was he so afraid of being smothered?

Kenneth recognized the feeling. "When I was a little boy my mother was afraid my crying would disturb my dad, so she'd put her arms around me and squeeze me tight to silence me. I felt my breath was being sucked right out of me, I was gasping for air." Kenneth turned to Lorna, "When you put your head on my chest, Lorna, I felt the same terror I felt as a child." Then he continued, "Even though I've been saying

I want you to be more affectionate, maybe I was also giving you some 'stay away' messages."

Both Kenneth and Lorna began to understand how his childhood experience was a rejection-studded triple whammy: First, there was the underlying fear of what his dad might have done or said to him if Kenneth disturbed him. Then there was the loyalty issue. Even though his mother thought she was protecting him from his father's anger, it seemed to Kenneth that she was putting his dad first. He felt betrayed by her. Third, when she stifled his cries, she robbed him of his spirit, of his voice, and of his selfhood.

Lorna was touched by Kenneth's candor. When she put herself in his shoes she could see why he reacted the way he did to her advances. She no longer felt he was rejecting her. He was doing the same kind of thing she's done many times herself—reacting to something that hurt her in the past and is affecting her in the present. But what about the future? How could Lorna feel secure about approaching Kenneth next time? How could Kenneth feel safe enough to respond to Lorna's advances? They agreed to experiment with ways that felt comfortable to both of them.

Although sexual rejections are not always as dramatic as this one, a lot of couples experience them. Someone initiates an invitation for sex, the other person declines (subtly or not so subtly), and it feels like a rejection—complete with disappointment, hurt feelings, anger, and withdrawal into silence. While men are conditioned to initiate sexual contact in a relationship, many women aren't. It's a big deal for most women to make the first move. And once turned down, they'll usually not risk trying again. Lorna and Kenneth had the benefit of hearing about each others' early experiences, which gave them a context in which to understand the others' actions.

## Feeling Left Out Again?

Melinda had some recurring childhood memories that made her very sad, but she wasn't sure why. She remembered "being banished to the backseat of the car—like I was just along for the ride." She recalled having to walk behind her mother, grandmother, and aunt when they all went shopping. These are not unusual memories for children to have, yet Melinda felt left out of the family circle, invisible, as if she didn't exist. Perhaps she was overly sensitive, but when these things happened, she took it personally.

As she and I explored those early years together, we discovered the existence of many underlying messages of rejection, such as the times her mother was too busy to answer her questions or do homework with her. These things are harder to remember because they are so subtle. The memories about the car and shopping seemed to symbolize the many other feelings of rejection Melinda experienced. These left out feelings have followed her into adulthood.

Melinda told me how she gradually tried to make herself invisible. "I'd dress to blend into the woodwork. I'd speak in a whisper so no one could hear me. When I wanted to pretend I wasn't there, I just wouldn't make eye contact." She came to expect that important people in her life would exclude her—and they did. She now realized that by "going invisible," she was contributing to her feelings of exclusion. She got used to not being noticed and would become uncomfortable when someone paid attention to her.

---

By "going invisible" we contribute to
our feelings of exclusion.

---

I gave Melinda an ongoing homework assignment. I asked her to pay attention to the times when she didn't want to be noticed and the times when she did want to be noticed. An interesting thing happened. She found herself more in charge of her world, and felt safer. She highlighted her hair, and started dressing in more vivid colors. She got contact lenses, no longer needing glasses to separate her from the world around her.

Joann also had childhood problems with being noticed. She remembers, "It was like an internal tug of war. I'd try hard to be good so I could be rewarded, but I always felt passed over in my family. Part of me wanted to be noticed, to be recognized. But I'm realizing another part of me must have broadcasted, 'Don't look at me.' And I find I'm still doing that. I go to the trouble to dress up in a snazzy new outfit for a job interview. I really want to be chosen over the others, yet I make myself invisible by speaking too softly or ducking my head, or not making eye contact. When it becomes clear they aren't noticing me, I get disappointed, feeling rejected all over again."

## It Just Isn't Fair!

When you grow up taking things personally, a lot of things don't seem fair. Somehow it feels as though you get the short end of the deal again and again. So when you feel someone is taking advantage of you or treating you unjustly, you may tend to overreact and lose control.

"I always felt short-sheeted by my parents," laments Marjorie. "It seemed they always favored my younger sister over me. When I was nine years old I saw a beautiful white toy rabbit in the toy store window, and I wanted it so badly. My parents wouldn't buy it for me, so I figured out a way to get it. I took in ironing to earn the money, and I bought it for myself. The next thing I knew, my parents bought my sister an identical rabbit so she wouldn't feel left out. I was stunned. It just wasn't fair! To this day I'm so hurt and angry that I can hardly talk about it."

When Frank feels he is treated unfairly he gets more than just angry, he gets enraged. Anger is related to "now" feelings, but rage comes from past feelings—emotions from childhood experiences that get triggered in the present.

Frank remembers one particularly awful day at work. He was livid after a meeting with his supervisor, Ms. Crawford. Company policy calls for employee performance to be evaluated on a bell-shaped curve. Any ratings out of the middle range require written justification. An outstanding rating or a poor rating means more work for the supervisor. Therefore, even though Frank and his supervisor knew much of his work was outstanding, his evaluation was mostly average. Frank didn't feel validated for work he did well. It wasn't fair. He felt betrayed. He blew up, screaming at his supervisor, "I'm not a mediocre employee. How dare you say I am."

Later, Frank began to realize how old issues of unfairness were being triggered—"My anger is beyond Ms. Crawford." What was familiar about this intense feeling of unfairness? He remembers the time he was passed over for a little league baseball award. When the coach's son got it instead, Frank was a sad, hurt, confused little boy. Then he remembers when he was seventeen years old, working in a hardware store. He was not given recognition for developing a new pricing system. The manager took the credit. That didn't feel fair either.

---

Anger is related to "now" feelings. Rage comes from past feelings that get triggered in the present.

---

We expect others to act the way we act. If we have integrity and a sense of fair play, we expect others to be the same in their dealings with us. When this doesn't happen, we get disappointed, our feelings get hurt—we take it personally.

Jimmy remembers how he worked hard in Catholic school to win a spelling contest. The prize was a religious statue. Sister Sophia told him she'd give it to him in a day or two. The days came and went and she didn't give him his prize. Each day he anticipated getting that wonderful statue. It was three weeks before he worked up the courage to ask her about it. When he did, she insisted she'd already given the statue to him.

Then Sister Sophia did something that would have an effect on Jimmy for the rest of his life: she accused him of lying about not receiving the statue, and punished him. Jimmy was overwhelmed at the unjustness of it all. He will never forget this incident. It still colors his dealings with authority figures in his life. He has a hard time trusting them and feels he has to be on guard against possible betrayal.

Laurie recounts another kind of school incident. Math was not easy for her in middle school. She studied hard for several days for a test. She thought she understood the material, but she got one of the lowest grades in the class. When the teacher read the test scores out loud, Laurie was humiliated. It didn't feel fair to be exposed like that when she tried so hard.

Years later, in college, the philosophy instructor promised he would give class members extra credit if they showed substantial improvement on the final exam. Going into the exam, Laurie's overall class grades averaged a good, solid B, then she made an A+ on the exam. Laurie received the highest grade in the class, yet the instructor gave her a B for her semester grade. When she questioned him about it, he said, "Oh, I meant improvement from a C to a B or even an A. I don't consider going from a solid B to an A very significant." Laurie was furious. It didn't seem fair that she got the same final grade as a classmate who went into the exam with a low C average. She fumed about it for weeks. Could some of her reaction be to her old feelings of being treated unfairly by her teacher in school?

## Don't Judge Me

Feeling judged quickly brings up anxious, childlike feelings. There you are, a very young person again, in the presence of The Authority. And that person seems bigger than life and you feel very small. You feel diminished as a person in the shadow of this big authority figure, whoever it may be.

Keith knows that feeling. Whenever he's around authority figures he expects to be humiliated. As a child, he was often told, "You should be ashamed of yourself for not cleaning your room," or "for not setting the table right," or "for talking back." He would think, "Uh oh, now I'm in big trouble. These people are large and looming and I'm defenseless. I'm waiting to be punished—it's unavoidable. It's out of my control."

Shame and humiliation are overwhelming feelings for many of us. They can take over in a flash. In *Shame: The Power of Caring*, Gershen Kaufman says the central aspect of shame is a feeling of exposure—"To feel shame is to feel *seen* in a painfully diminished sense . . . the piercing awareness of ourselves as fundamentally deficient in some vital way as a human being." One woman portrays it as "bleeding into everything and permeating my being. The feeling of being overwhelmed colors everything."

Once I made a mistake in a coffee store and asked for many pounds more coffee than I wanted. When I realized my mistake, I not only turned red, but I "flooded." Panic washed over me and I couldn't think straight. I was a "bad" little girl again and someone was going to judge me. The coffee people were gracious, and didn't ask me to pay for my mistake. But I paid for it in other ways—my "badness" intruded on my thoughts for a few days, until I regained control.

When I'd flood like that I couldn't sort out my feelings. It was as if they were fine gold chains all tangled up. I once read a household hint that suggested putting knotted chains on waxed paper, adding a few drops of mineral oil, and gently moving them around with two straight pins until they untangle. It not only works for chains, it works for feelings as well. It has been a useful image for me to keep handy. Try visualizing this image the next time you feel all tangled up.

# 2

# I Wouldn't Talk to Someone Else the Way I Talk to Myself

## *Self-Rejecting Messages*

"I'm pathetic. If you really knew me, you wouldn't like me." Bonnie looked stunned to hear herself say it, but there it was, her biggest fear. I guess I was a little surprised when she blurted it out in our first session, because it usually takes longer for clients to confide this secret thought. And when they do, they usually add something like, "I'm really different from other people," "I'm kind of weird," or "There's something wrong with me." One nineteen-year-old was more specific: "I can only allow others to get close to me physically, sexually. It's okay for them to get to know my body, but if they got close enough to know the real me, I would disgust them."

When Catherine gets disappointed or upset with people in her life, she starts hitting herself. On the shoulder, in the face, sometimes leaving red marks. She's very unkind to herself; in fact, she's mean to herself, in much the same way she remembers how her parents and older sisters "all used to pick on me, telling me what to do, what to say, what to wear. Now that I'm grown up it's still the same when I go back to visit. On one visit home I wrapped my head in a silk scarf which was very stylish in California, but I guess not in North Dakota. They picked on me then, too, and kept asking if I had cancer or something, maybe my head was bald and that's why I was wearing a scarf."

Most likely the "picking" was because Catherine was different, not part of the family mold. Her family's unspoken rule of "It's not okay to be different" was interpreted by Catherine to mean, "I'm not okay, there's something wrong with me." And when I hypothesized that perhaps her family's question about cancer was really out of concern for her health, she didn't buy that idea at all. "Nope," she insisted, "it wasn't out of caring. It was out of meanness."

A man I know says, "When something goes wrong, I call myself terrible names. I see myself as some defective thing. I feel flawed, like something's missing."

The issue of how we come to think of ourselves as so flawed and to reject ourselves so thoroughly will be addressed in chapters 6 and 7. For now, lets focus on the way in which these self-rejecting messages manifest themselves in our daily lives and how they've come to control our behaviors.

# "I'd Like Myself Better If I Could Just Be Someone Else"

We often spend our days thinking about how much better life would be if only we could be smarter, more attractive, taller, more witty, and on and on. Are you really saying to yourself that you're not good enough the way you are? Self-rejecting messages come in all shapes and sizes, just like the people who are thinking them.

## How Self-Deprecating Can You Get?

What kinds of things do you tell yourself about yourself? Do you find fault with your looks? Do you think your ears are too big or too small? Your nose? Your chin? Are you always having a bad hair day? The list could go on and on.

Besides the physical messages, there might be a bunch of psychological messages you tell yourself too—such as calling yourself "stupid" for missing a turnoff on the freeway, or "idiot" for leaving home without those letters you meant to mail. Then there may be some social self-rejecting messages, such as feeling socially inept or unsophisticated—the "I can't believe I said that (or did that)" variety.

### The Big Blow-Up—Overgeneralizing

A woman I know sometimes daydreams on the bus, occasionally missing her stop. She realizes her mistake right away but freezes and can't will her arm to pull the cord to get off at the next stop. She chides herself for missing her stop, putting so much energy into it that she rides miles out of her way. In the blink of an eye, she distorts her "mistake" into the "fact" she's a bad person.

Another woman became upset when the date for RSVPing her wedding invitations had passed and only a few of her family, friends, and co-workers had responded. She began to imagine her wedding day with the groom's family filling his side of the room, and only two rows of people on the bride's side. "It feels like they're all ignoring me," she brooded. She "just knew" that no one would be there when the only information she had to date was that they hadn't RSVPed on time. Didn't she skip a step somewhere?

A man I know calls himself names whenever he makes even a small mistake. If he accidentally spills even a small drop of food on his shirt he mutters, "Dunce!" He's overgeneralizing of course—blowing things way out of proportion. One drop of food does not a dunce make, but his reaction is very swift. Perhaps it's true you made a mistake in a specific situation, but when you start to tell yourself you always make mistakes, and that you're stupid for making mistakes, you're overgeneralizing.

## Shoulda, Woulda, Coulda . . .

This brings us to the "shoulds"—those self-critical, second-guessing messages we manufacture. They include messages such as "I should have done it better, differently, more gracefully, more quietly, more quickly, more perfectly." Yes, we do seem to keep trying to do it more and more perfectly, don't we?

According to Susan Jeffers in *End the Struggle and Dance with Life,* "['shoulds'] make us worry. They make us do too much, think too much, plan too much. These shoulds pull us apart and make us lose our center."

What about cutting some slack and lightening up about those "shoulds"? Maybe you can practice telling yourself, "This isn't a should-have-done, it's a might-do-later."

Jeffers suggests writing down "as many shoulds and shouldn'ts you can think of that have become a chore instead of a joy. For example, you don't have to make your bed every day . . . unless you *want* to. You don't have to have a clean car . . . unless you *want* to." And by the way, you don't have to pick up the phone every time it rings, or exercise at least one half hour a day, or answer all your mail either—unless you *want* to.

Hindsight is a great learning tool if you don't flagellate yourself with the "shoulds." Why not ask, "What did I learn from this? How can I do this differently next time?" "Should have" is about the Past. "Next time" is about the Future. As one woman likes to say, "Shoulda, woulda, coulda. The fact is, I didn't."

## Self-Blame—What Did I Do This Time?

In chapter 1 we looked at the Blame Game: when we take things personally, we expect to be blamed by others, and we often end up blaming ourselves.

Messages of self-blame can develop from a child's view of separation or divorce. When a parent leaves the family, the children don't always understand why and often blame themselves. The remaining parent is most likely too wrapped up in sadness and hurt to help the children understand that the parent didn't leave because of them. Andrew remembers being very frightened when his dad left. He was four years old. "I remember sitting on the kitchen floor in front of the stove the day my dad stormed out in anger. I reached out toward my dad, crying for him to come back. But he never came back to live with us again. And he didn't visit much either, he just sort of disappeared." Andrew thought it was his fault his dad left. The reasons why varied from day to day—he did something wrong, or he should have done something differently, or he wasn't good enough. He blamed himself for many years—well into his twenties. He still tries to hold things together for important people in his life—his mom, his best friends, his girlfriend because, "If I don't hold it together for them, they'll leave me too, just like Dad did."

---

> Taking things personally can mean expecting to be
> blamed by others—and we end up blaming ourselves.

---

### Just Say Thank You

The importance of receiving compliments has already been touched on, but I want to make the point here that by rejecting compliments we're also rejecting ourselves. Many of us put a lot of energy into not letting compliments in or pushing them away. We excel at making excuses or habitual self-deprecating responses. Sometimes we can't even hear the words when something positive is being said. Do you remember my story in chapter 1 about how sometimes I'd see someone's mouth moving but no words were coming out. I finally figured out that perhaps something nice was being said to me, but I sure wasn't letting it come in. Ways for you to explore being attentive to compliments is discussed later in this chapter.

## Do You Listen to the Things You Tell Yourself?

As children, when we don't get what we want most—a responsive parent who gives unconditional love and caring—we don't feel accepted. We feel that something is missing, as if there's a huge hole inside of us.

Without a feeling of acceptance in childhood, we can grow up to become needy, dependent adults. While part of us keeps hoping that we'll magically receive the love we want from others, another part still expects that people will disappoint us. If we grew up in an inconsistent and unpredictable world, we come to expect more of the same. It's as if we need the predictability of unpredictability because it's familiar.

> [We prefer] the security of known misery to
> the misery of unfamiliar insecurity.
>
> —Sheldon Kopp

How you explained childhood rejection feelings to yourself, and what you told yourself when these experiences occurred, constitutes the messages you carry into your adult years. These messages become your beliefs about yourself and your world and the people in it. They're an integral part of your being. As ridiculous as it sounds, we seem to hold on to these beliefs for dear life. Maintaining these negative expectations serves a useful purpose, offering a kind of security because they're familiar and giving a sense of order and organization to our experiences. Without this sense of order we feel unbalanced, confused. It is often easier to hold on to an old belief than to change it. As Sheldon Kopp explains in *If You Meet the Buddha on the Road, Kill Him!* we prefer "the security of known misery to the misery of unfamiliar insecurity."

If we threaten the beliefs we've developed about ourselves, it could throw us off balance, so we learn not to allow new information in. New is risky. If we dare to let in favorable stuff from others, we might risk tremendous anxiety. The bottom line is that we're more comfortable with our old beliefs. I know a screenwriter who says he is so used to rejection that he actually gets anxious when a producer likes his work. Acceptance is so foreign to him, it makes him nervous.

Because of this need to be comfortable, we develop a system that filters messages. We become selective about what we take in from others. From the time we're little we learn to filter out messages that could threaten our belief system and upset our sense of order and organization. And how do we filter? By blocking or distorting messages.

Matters can be even more complicated if our parents were afraid we'd embarrass them by seeing things in certain ways. In order to protect themselves, they try to dismiss our perceptions, perhaps telling us we're imagining things or we're crazy. As a result, we learn to question or invalidate our own perceptions. (See chapter 6 for a look at what happens when a child's perceptions are discounted by parents.)

We not only block out positive messages, but we add a constant static of negative messages as well, audio distortions that sound like "you're bad" or "not good enough" or "not smart enough" or "can't read your parents' minds well enough."

For example, if you tried to show your mom a drawing you made and she said she was too busy, did you tell yourself she was too busy *for you?* If you didn't do something exactly the way a parent wanted, did you tell yourself you're no good or not good enough? Now that you're grown up, do you tell yourself some of the same things in your current relationships?

When one woman asked a co-worker to help out with a project, he responded, "I can't do that, I don't have time." But in her head she heard him say, "I don't have time *for you*," and she felt turned down and rejected.

Collecting these kinds of beliefs about yourself is similar to filling an expandable carry-on suitcase. There's lots of room to cram things in, but then you find out it's too heavy to carry. It's a big load. There are no built-in wheels and it no longer fits under the airplane seat. Sometimes it's even too heavy to lift into the overhead compartment without help. In a similar way, messages from childhood pile up, infiltrating every nook and cranny of the soul. They become belief systems and expand into larger-than-life proportions. They get so overblown in fact, that before you know it, you're taking messages personally and you begin to reject yourself. Self-acceptance doesn't have much room to exist in the face of so much self-rejection. What a heavy burden to lug around—and it takes so much energy!

Once we begin to see ourselves as "worthless," "unlovable," "undesirable," or "unacceptable," we tend to get wedged in that space. It becomes difficult to take in positive, affirming messages. Especially in moments of anxiety, it becomes difficult to gain access to the compartment within us that contains the accepting messages. It's as if we know it's there but we just can't get to it. It seems blocked off, closed up, not available.

Gaining access to the accepting part of ourselves is hard because we are so loaded down with encumbrances. Are we too weighed down by negativity to allow ourselves to open up to acceptance by others? How can we let in a positive flow of information, information we can really hear?

So here we are with carry-on baggage that's bulging with old messages and erroneous explanations, and it's slowing us down. Maybe we could strap on wheels that would transform unwieldy negative beliefs into positive self-acceptance, helping our maneuverability immensely. This would streamline our load; we would get rid of the weight of excess "stuff" we have collected over the years and begin to glide.

One of the most basic tools I know for practicing self-acceptance is to practice accepting compliments from others. For example, if someone says, "That's a really nice shirt," out of habit you might respond, "Oh, *this*? It's been in the back of my closet for years." When a compliment is offered to you, what about responding with a simple, "Thank you"? That's it—just "thank you." That's all you have to say. Accepting a compliment from another person whether you agree with it or not can be difficult to do. It's worth practicing until you get good at it. Accepting a compliment is an important first step toward self-acceptance. Would you consider giving it a try?

Mirrors are another key to self-acceptance. When you walk by a mirror do you look at yourself? Do you actually notice your reflection or are you faceless? A lot of adults who have felt rejected or invalidated as children become invisible to themselves. They are unable to notice their reflection much of the time. Or they focus in on separate parts of their faces, perhaps their lips, or one eye, or just their hair, as if they are just part of a person. As they learn to gain access to and accept the different parts of themselves, they report seeing more complete images in mirrors. Then they know they're becoming a real person, a whole person. They're learning to reject their self-rejecting messages.

# 3

# Tiptoeing through Minefields

## Communication Breakdowns

Jane didn't like to drive. When she had to run errands to the supermarket, the bakery, or the cleaners, she'd hint, "Larry, I just don't know how I'm going to get all of my errands done today. (*Huge sigh.*) It's just too much driving to even think about." If Larry guessed what was on Jane's mind and picked up her hints, this "proved" his love. Better yet, Jane knew he *really* cared if he offered to drive her even before she put out hints. She had it all figured out—different responses meant different degrees of how much he loved her. She saw these exchanges as tests of his affection. But the reality is that no matter how much she wanted Larry to be clairvoyant, he really wasn't, so Jane was often disappointed and hurt.

To complicate matters, Larry had trouble saying "no," even if he had other plans. Instead of being up front about his own needs, he would disappear into his study, get involved in some task or project and "lose track of time." Jane's feelings got hurt when he retreated to his study to work. Larry would not only physically disappear, but he emotionally disappeared as well.

When Jane took Larry's actions personally, a downward spiral would begin. She'd go into the bedroom and sulk. After about ten minutes of feeling sorry for herself, the anger would build. Then she would go to the study and scream at Larry. As he retreated even more by "disappearing" inside himself, Jane would become enraged. Larry would try to talk to her, to calm the situation, saying, "It just isn't worth it to fight." Jane, because she is so vulnerable, would tell herself he really meant that *she* wasn't worth it. Things began to deteriorate severely in their relationship. But they recognized the need to get some professional help. Larry phoned me for couples counseling.

In the couples sessions, Larry's willingness to try to understand their process together gave Jane encouragement. She felt supported by him. Larry listened as Jane described the emotional pain she experienced when she wanted attention and he closed off. She recalled her childhood, when her parents often pushed her outside the house to play on Sundays, locking the door behind her. She would sit for hours in a "sad little heap" on the front porch. Jane laughed as she realized the real reason they shooed her outside: "They just wanted to have some sex!" But she didn't know that then, and she felt unloved and unwanted, lonely and shut out. I could see by the look on her face that she had just made an important connection: that's how she felt so often with Larry—lonely and shut out. The same way she felt when she was a child.

When Larry "disappeared" it was as if he was closing a door on Jane. Open and closed doors were so confusing to her when she was a child. Though her parents often locked her out, Jane herself was not allowed to close her bedroom door. And a closed bathroom door could be opened by anyone. Because there was no right to privacy for her in her family, being alone didn't feel like a choice, it felt like a punishment. It's no wonder Jane had trouble understanding Larry's desire for "alone time." She interpreted it as an act of rejection—a punishment. She took it personally.

Larry recalled his own childhood—how his mother was always "in his face," demanding that he keep her company and entertain her. She was always intruding on his privacy. No wonder he reacted so strongly to Jane's manipulations. He commented, "If I open the door to Jane just a little bit, the whole herd might come stampeding through." Finally, Jane began to understand his need for more breathing room.

Both Jane and Larry have been rehashing these painful childhood rejection messages in their marriage. Jane remembered how she would sit those long, lonely hours on the front steps, repeating to herself, "I'm tough . . . they can't hurt me . . . I'll show them . . . they'll be sorry!" Yet all the while feeling like "a puddle" inside—very fragile, very vulnerable, very hurt. Since that time she has been afraid she will appear weak, so she hasn't expressed her needs directly to anyone. If she did, someone might reject her like her parents did. Larry might reject her. Jane has come to expect that doors will be shut in her face. And they are, because who did Jane choose for a partner? Larry, who learned to close doors to protect himself from the intrusion he expects in life.

And what is this all about? In the sessions, Larry recalled how he used to swear to himself that he'd "never get manipulated by some-one's wants or needs again." As a young child, his "job" was to read his mother's mind and cater to her whims. It was a full-time job because no matter how he tried to please her, it was never enough. His mom's needs were so huge that he felt overwhelmed by them. He reiterated his fear that "the whole herd might come stampeding through." So he had to draw the lines of protection carefully around himself by disappearing. He had to get those doors closed right away. He felt six years old again.

Larry was coming from that same little boy place when he over-reacted to Jane's unspoken needs. Unspoken demands were being made on him in a way he did not understand. When Jane didn't ask directly for what she wanted or needed from him, he felt manipulated, just as he did by his mother. Then he began to feel overwhelmed—invaded, assaulted, violated. It's as if a life-or-death situation had been re-created for Larry. When he felt manipulated by Jane, it actually seemed like a personal threat to his well-being. He took Jane's actions personally and protected himself the only way he knew how—by disappearing.

In the couples sessions, Larry practiced identifying his level of comfort—how open or closed could he allow the door to be? Maybe it didn't have to be all the way open or all the way closed. He began to realize there can be in-between situations that are tolerable for him. Larry practiced communicating this comfort zone to Jane.

Jane's task was to keep reminding herself that even though the door appears closed, it most likely is not locked. Closed doors can be opened. She does have the ability to gain access. She doesn't have to remain outside. She can ask to come in. Jane recognized that these are all choices she can make. She realized she could choose to bring herself into Larry's world by being more direct about her needs. Neither Jane nor Larry had to continue to have hurt feelings. Unless, of course, they chose to.

Larry and Jane's story illustrates an important factor of taking things personally—miscommunication. When you take something personally your emotions are controlled by what others do or say or what they don't do or say. You tend to see things more subjectively than objectively. As Judy Tatelbaum points out in *You Don't Have to Suffer*, "Personalizing tends to single us out as special and to separate us as wronged or misunderstood." She goes on to say, "Singled out we are victims and life is always harder from the vantage point of a victim." You may believe there is intent whether there is or not, personalizing impersonal events—interpreting words or actions in a negative way as if they are directed at you. One woman described, "When I accidentally punched in the wrong number during voice-mail menu instructions, I thought I detected a slight irritation in the computerized voice!"

However, there is more to the role of "victim" than meets the eye. Sometimes the victim appears to others as a persecutor or rescuer.

## Trading Roles

You may have noticed in these first chapters there are several examples of feeling resentful or victimized, of pushy or bullying attitudes, and of caretaking or rescuing behaviors. Sometimes we may find ourselves switching from role to role from one moment to the next. This concept has been described in the Karpman Drama Triangle, where the three points are represented by the roles of Persecutor, Rescuer, and Victim. The roles are interchangeable, with each person playing one of them at one time or another, and seeing other people in them at one time or another. Sometimes a person may switch from Victim to Persecutor to Rescuer in a flash, other times it's a slower process.

First of all, I want to point out how easy it is to become a "victim" when we take things personally, especially if we feel singled out. But we take on other roles as well.

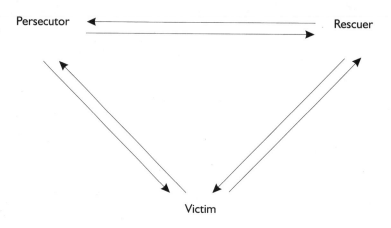

## Figure 1: The Karpman Drama Triangle

The story of Jane and Larry has numerous examples of these alternating roles. Jane, in her Victim stance, depended on Larry to drive her on errands. When he neglected to read her mind, she felt disappointed (Victim) and saw him as the "bad guy" (Persecutor.) However, when she got angry and blamed him, her own role changed to Persecutor and Larry saw himself as Victim.

In addition, when Larry saw her tactics as controlling (Persecutor) and felt manipulated by her (Victim) but couldn't say "no" for fear of hurting her feelings (Rescuer), he felt sorry for himself (Victim) and tried to take care of himself (Rescuer) by disappearing into his study. But Jane saw him as Persecutor. Jane would feel hurt (Victim), and scream at him (Persecutor), and Larry would feel victimized by her. These role changes happen so fast, it's hard to keep up with them. Did you catch any I missed?

The classic "martyr mother" offers a good example of the triangle in action. She usually complains of doing so much for other family members (Rescuing) that she feels unappreciated (Victim). She may frequently be heard to say, "Oh, poor me, look at all I do for you and look what I get in return—nothing." But this martyr happens to be the most powerful person in the family because other family members keep trying to please her or feel guilty and responsible for her feelings (Rescue). Until they get resentful, that is. Then they begin to feel victimized by her. If they retaliate by acting rebelliously or procrastinating or making empty promises, they take on the role of Persecutor in her eyes, because she is feeling victimized by them.

This martyr's process of traveling from spot to spot on the triangle is much like any other codependent—rescuing by infantalizing (victimizing) other people, then anger and resentment build up, leaving the hurt feelings of a victim.

Notice how the Victim spot is on the bottom of the triangle. But, because of the power the "victim" holds in the family, it might as well be on the top.

Abusive family dynamics are also good examples of the triangle interplay. For example, a parent who bullies or hurts a child (Persecutor) is often hurting inside and feeling vulnerable (Victim). Sometimes the parent's rationale for abusing the child is to keep him or her from making the same mistakes the parent did (Rescuer). (More about bullying behavior in chapter 5.)

One man characterizes his role in his family of origin this way: "I'm either somebody's hero or the bad guy. When I say things in their best interests [Rescuer] sometimes they don't want to hear them. Other family members call me a troublemaker [Persecutor] for speaking out, and they turn on me. That's when I feel like a Victim."

It doesn't have to take another person to play out the triangle. Each of us can easily slip in and out of all three roles ourselves. For example, we might feel badly about something we did or didn't do (Victim) and call ourselves names like "stupid idiot" (Persecutor), but by telling ourselves to shape up, we're rescuing ourselves as well. As one woman said, "When I feel like a victim I give myself a big kick for feeling that way, but sometimes I turn around and rescue myself from that thought."

Isn't it astounding how one person may see him or herself in the role of Victim (or Rescuer), and another person may see that person as a Persecutor. And we wonder why people get upset with us!

In the twenty years I've been using this theory, recognizing how roles are interchangeable has made a remarkable difference in my understanding of personal and work relationships. "I thought I had discovered fire," enthused author of *Codependent No More*, Melody Beattie, when she first applied this concept to codependent relationships. That says it all. Awareness of how this process works between people can help stop interactions that lead to hurt feelings, misunderstandings, and taking things personally. Most especially it can help curb that destructive cycle of feeling personally attacked, and needing to defend by mounting a counterattack.

# A Matter of Upbringing

Gloria's family has talked to each other in loud, shrill voices as long as she can remember. Her grandparents did the same. In some cultures, speaking in raised voices is a way of being connected to other people. In Mack's family, raised voices meant something different: they meant "You'd better watch out, you're gonna get it." So when Gloria raised her voice, Mack felt threatened. He would react to her shrillness by withdrawing from her. She wasn't even aware of the decibel level when she spoke. She was stunned when Mack would react to her like that.

Gloria grew up in a family where fights were exciting, and often family members picked arguments for fun. It gave her a charge to pick fights with Mack because it made her "feel alive." Although she probably didn't realize it, she was expecting to feel as connected to Mack through their fighting as she had to her family in childhood. However, Mack's childhood experience of fighting was very different. Fights were serious and someone was usually out to hurt someone. On top of that his dad beat him; family fights felt like a matter of life or death. As a little boy, he feared for his life because he had no idea how badly his father might hurt him. So, while in Gloria's family fights were life-affirming, in Mack's family they were life-threatening. As you might guess, much of the time Gloria and Mack didn't understand each other's experiences. They were walking around with hurt feelings that they weren't able to talk about with each other.

# Acting Out

When we're unable to put words to feelings of pain or anger, anxiety builds up. In order to get some relief, we often act those feelings out. The term *acting out* is used to describe inappropriate or excessive behaviors such as sulking, giving the silent treatment, provoking or antagonizing, slamming doors, or flying into a rage. Acting out also includes excessive spending, gambling, extramarital affairs, destruction of property, and self-destructive behaviors, including abuse of substances such as tobacco, alcohol, drugs, and food. Many of us release the pent up energy of anxiety by starting fights. Trouble is, before we know it, this kind of quarreling can get down and dirty, becoming a dumping ground for unresolved feelings.

---

"Acting out" is a way to express feelings we aren't
able to express in words. Try talking them out
instead of acting them out.

---

How does someone come to act out his or her feelings? When Jason was growing up he had to be a "good little boy" and that meant keeping his emotions to himself. No matter how hurt or angry he felt, he went quietly to his room and cried silently to himself. Now, whenever he got upset with his girlfriend, Kerri, he became uncomfortable and anxious. But Jason couldn't communicate his distress, so he did things like making promises he didn't intend to keep and showing up late for special occasions—or not showing up at all.

Yet, Jason says, "when Kerri told me she couldn't continue to be with me because she couldn't depend on me, I was hurt. It was as if she was saying her needs are more important than mine. It felt like it was a contest between my needs and her needs, and there was no room for anything in between. I felt rejected, so I rolled over and ignored her." When couples act out with each other, rejection begets rejection. Everyone gets a chance to take it personally.

## Did They Really Mean What You Think They Said?

What people mean to say and what we hear them say may be very different. Even when the message is unclear, it often doesn't occur to us to check out the meaning of the message. We may have grown up with garbled messages and been confused about their meanings. But we couldn't ask about them—asking such questions may not have been accepted or encouraged in our families. Maybe our parents even said, "That's none of your business!" We were supposed to try to maneuver around the issues, to try to guess the meanings. Often we guessed wrong. Often we got our feelings hurt because we never learned how to ask someone what they meant.

You may still maneuver around issues. You may still take things the wrong way. Have you worried for days or even weeks about what someone meant when they said something to you? Have you noticed how much energy it takes to think about it so much?

Besides reminding yourself that you may be hearing someone's message through your own special filter, also remind yourself the message may be more about the other person than about you. When people seem critical or judgmental, they may be struggling with their own issues. Because it often doesn't have to do with you at all, it can be helpful to remind yourself, "This is most likely not about me. They are probably talking about themselves. What might they be saying?"

When Judith was packing for the return flight home after visiting her mother, she wrapped some slightly damp lingerie in plastic bags and put them into her suitcase. Her mother was aghast and ranted, "How could you do such a thing? Why didn't you think ahead to make sure the lingerie was dry in time?" And then came the zinger, "This is why

> ## The message most likely says more about the person giving it than it does about you.

you failed in your marriage." Judith was devastated, although this certainly was similar to the "you're stupid and inadequate" messages she had heard from her mother since childhood. And this time was no different from the others—Judith felt rejected. On the flight home, when she had a chance to reflect and was able to stop fretting about her own inadequacy, she instead wondered what on earth had gotten into her mother?

What about if a friend or acquaintance stops calling you and doesn't return your phone calls or answer your notes? You would most likely feel confused and hurt. Would you grill yourself about why the person could be upset with you—what you might have said or done or what you didn't say or do? The truth is that some people use other people, and you might be less useful to them than before. But do you translate "less use" to "useless"? Do you further translate that to "worthless"? Remember, this may not be about you at all.

> ## The other person's reactions may be more about self-protection than about rejection.

Keep reminding yourself that most likely other people's reactions are more about protecting themselves than about rejecting you. Ellen learned this after a lot of anxiety and hurt feelings. She had been wanting to go out with Jerry for a long time. He finally asked her out and she really enjoyed the evening with him. She was feeling good about the prospect of having a relationship with him. He was attentive and seemed excited to be with her. She was feeling special and desirable. The next day, Ellen fantasized most of the morning at her desk about running into Jerry after work. Maybe he would even invite her over and cook one of his special dinners for her. She had heard he was a great cook. She did run into him after work. To her surprise he seemed only minimally friendly—in fact, somewhat aloof. She was crushed that he had not greeted her as if he was glad to see her, since she certainly was glad to see him. But he never would have known that: because his attitude confused her, she became quiet and withdrawn.

Then it got worse. He not only didn't invite her to dinner, he excused himself, saying he had to meet friends for dinner. Ellen felt so disappointed—this was not at all like her morning fantasies. She felt hurt and very unspecial at that moment. So she handled the situation by protecting herself with a quick departure. The rest of the day, and the day after, she analyzed and reanalyzed all the reasons he might have acted so cold to her. What a long list she was able to invent!

Maybe I was too eager—said or did something that turned him off.

Maybe I came on too strong. Maybe I was too coy.

Maybe I talked too much. Maybe I didn't talk enough.

Maybe I seemed too needy. Maybe I seemed too independent.

Maybe I was too funny. Maybe I was too serious.

Maybe he changed his mind about me and was no longer interested.

Notice how each of these thoughts is a self-blaming, self-rejecting message. Ellen took it for granted that the problem was her own inadequacies. It had not occurred to her that Jerry's behavior may have to do with Jerry. The truth is, as she later got to know Jerry better, she learned something important about him: Jerry was distant because he has some problems with closeness. Jerry had allowed himself to feel too close to Ellen the night before, so he pulled back, creating the distance he felt he needed. And Ellen took it as a rejection. Then, in turn, she backed off and began to protect herself, putting on her own mask of indifference. And how did Jerry respond to Ellen's coolness? Even though he would have liked to stay and talk with her, he excused himself by saying he had dinner plans when he really didn't.

## Reality Check

We want other people to value us and our opinions, and sometimes we get far too invested in this. One woman felt hurt because her adult daughter didn't read a book she sent her. A man I know got angry when his friend didn't take his financial advice. A therapist I know was upset when his client didn't do a "homework" assignment. Sometimes it seems the more invested we are, the more we take things personally. We find negative meanings and intentions where there may not be any.

A few years ago I attended to a party to celebrate a classmate's Ph.D. When I walked in, a former instructor of mine showed surprise at seeing me. He asked, "What are *you* doing here?" I couldn't enjoy the party. I kept asking myself, "What am I doing here?" If you remember, one of my big issues is feeling left out. So I told myself, "Maybe I don't belong here." I couldn't think clearly, I wasn't able to comment or check out his meaning. I spent a lot of energy and time trying to figure out what could have have made him dislike me or what he might have meant, rather than asking him.

It's easy for misunderstandings and hurt feelings to happen between parent and child, even when the child is an adult. Sharon's mother gave her a gift of a statue of a mother and child. "I hated it," said Sharon, "I saw it as a mother pulling her daughter toward her, needing to lean on her. Mom could tell I was upset, so she returned my gift to the store without asking me. Then I was even more hurt." Years later, the statue story was retold when the mother joined Sharon for a therapy session. Sharon told her why she'd disliked the statue so much. Her mother expressed real surprise, "I didn't see it that way at all, I saw it as the child leaning on the mother."

It's easy to personalize messages at work, too. Imagine that you discover your supervisor received a complimentary letter about your work. However, he kept it in his desk for over a month, without showing it to you. What do you tell yourself? Do you think he's deliberately withholding positive information from your personnel folder? Do you think he has something against you, or doesn't like you? Could it be that withholding the letter has nothing to do with you? Maybe it didn't cross his mind that sharing the letter with you would have been a nice thing to do. Checking it out with him may shed new light on the situation.

Diane's situation at work was a series of misunderstandings. She was the office manager for many years for a small company. It was sold to new owners who brought in some of their own people. This presented a situation ripe for difficulties. To make matters worse, they had all the old employees fill out forms to apply for their old jobs. At the onset, Diane felt that because they were late in giving her an application form, they really didn't want her to apply. So she didn't, until they said, "Aren't you going to fill out the forms?" There was probably never a question she'd get the job, but she didn't know that.

Diane kept on running things the way she always had because they didn't give her any guidance. She was punctual, coming in at nine and leaving at five, and she got the job done. But they soon began to shuffle some of her work over to one of their own people, and she found she had time on her hands. Because it was hard for her to feel the same loyalty to the new owners that she'd felt to her longtime employers, the new owners felt she had an "attitude." One day they called her in and said she didn't have "a passion for her work," she wasn't being "a team player," and complained that she only worked nine to five. Her feelings got hurt, and she presumed they were telling her they wanted to fire her. So she decided to tell them she wanted to quit.

Could it be they were really saying she wasn't being loyal enough to them? Could it be they were hurt by her "attitude" and protected themselves with a "We'll leave you before you can leave us" attitude of their own? Did Diane know what they meant by "passion"? No. Did she know what they meant by "team player"? No. She could only guess. Yes, it might be a good idea to ask them what they meant before she quit—at least it might clear the air.

The process of searching for cues and hidden meanings often leads to communication problems between couples. We're very quick to make up a story of what our partner's behavior means—and even quicker to take it personally. Seldom does it cross our minds to check out the reality, or perhaps we never learned how. For example, three months into dating, Tom told Lucy that he thought they had "an imbalance" in their relationship. Based on her image of herself as unworthy, she spent hours worrying about what dark meaning "imbalance" may have. Those dreaded red flags of criticism and disregard cropped up from childhood. Before she knew it childhood fears flooded in, and she was feeling negative and helpless, unworthy and rejected. How did Lucy translate "imbalance"? She heard Tom saying that she cared more about him than he did about her. So to protect herself from rejection she told herself, "I'll leave him before I lose him."

When Lucy had brought this experience into the therapy session, we were able to do a "reality check" on what had happened. She began to see how she presumed his message was a reflection of her unworthiness, saying, "you mean he actually could have meant something else?" She rehearsed ways in the session that she might bring it up again to Tom and check out what his actual meaning might have been.

She finally asked him what he meant by "imbalance." Apparently he didn't mean anything negative. In fact, Tom, a musician, had been using musical language to express his hopes for more intimacy. He wanted to see them "fine tune" their relationship to make it even better. In Tom's ambiguous way, he way saying he valued their relationship, but Lucy had missed that completely, fearing the worst.

How did Lucy stop these fears from taking over? How did she stop taking it personally? She gathered up her courage and checked out Tom's meaning. In doing this she was able to clarify an important issue in her life and regain self-respect.

One day when I was in class, someone started coughing and couldn't stop. The instructor said, "I just hate it." The look that came over my classmate's face was terrible to see. It was as if she'd been struck in the face. What was going on here? Later she told me she took the instructor's comment to mean, "I just hate it when you do that." Her older sister used to say that to her all the time. When she finally got up the courage to ask the instructor about it, she found out that she had been trying to commiserate and meant, "I just hate it when I start coughing like that."

Isn't it extraordinary how often we misunderstand each other? These misunderstandings lead to hurt feelings unless we find a way to communicate clearly, to check things out with the other person.

Clear it up. Clean it up. The best way to do this is by exploring someone's meaning or intent. This isn't about confronting people—it's about confronting situations. Lonnie Barbach and David Geisinger, co-authors of *Going the Distance*, remind us: "Be curious, not furious." They

> Misunderstandings lead to hurt feelings. By communicating clearly we can avoid misunderstandings.

recommend replacing accusation with inquiry, and castigation with education. In other words, give the other person the benefit of the doubt.

## How to Check Things Out with Someone

Too often we find ourselves reacting to something but are hesitant to talk about it because we still believe the admonitions we were brought up with, the ones about "rocking the boat" or "hurting other peoples feelings." If you've wished you could check out the intent of words or actions and didn't know how, here are some helpful steps.

> Checking things out is not about confronting people—it's about confronting situations.

### Try Naming Instead of Blaming

First, keep in mind that finger-pointing doesn't work very well here, but by using *I statements*, instead of *you statements*, you can reflect your perception and feelings and send a nonblaming message. An *I statement* is a statement about how something affects you, your interactions with the other person, and the relationship. It's a statement about how you feel rather than being critical or complaining about what the other person did wrong. For example, saying, "You idiot, how dare you scream at me" isn't going to get you very far. But saying, "I'm upset you raised your voice to me" is a clear statement of the speaker's feelings, said in a nonblaming way. There's a big difference between blaming and naming the issue or feelings. Remember, your feelings belong to you and it's not easy for someone to argue with them. Saying things in a nonblaming way gives the other person a chance to be open to hearing what you have to say without becoming defensive. It also gives the person a chance to validate your feelings by repeating back what he or she heard you say. Remember, when you validate someone's feelings you are recognizing that it's okay for that person to have feelings—it doesn't mean you have to share them.

> ## Validating someone's feelings doesn't mean you have to share them.

These steps for checking things out are somewhat flexible. Experiment with them, tailoring them to your needs. And don't hesitate to tell someone you'd like to go through these steps without interruption. There's plenty of opportunity for the other person to respond.

**Step One:** Describe the behavior in observable, nonblaming terms. "Yesterday, I noticed that while I was talking with you, you seemed preoccupied with something else." (This frames the interaction from your own perception in such a way so that the other person feels less defensive and less likely to argue.) After you state your perception of the behavior or interaction, you might want to ask, "Am I correct about that?" or "Do you agree that's what happened?"

**Step Two:** Describe how you felt about the behavior. "I felt hurt (angry, upset, confused)."

**Step Three:** Describe how you explained the behavior to yourself. For example, "When you walked out, I told myself 'I'm not worth listening to.'" In certain appropriate situations you might want to add how the behavior re-creates old messages from childhood. "This is the same thing I used to tell myself when my mom dozed off as I was talking to her." (Use this step selectively—only in situations where it feels safe. For instance, maybe with a romantic partner or friend, but probably not with an employer.)

**Step Four:** Describe how you would like the interaction to go next time. "Next time I would like you to give me your full attention."

It's helpful to add active listening steps to make sure the other person understands your meaning: Ask the person to repeat back what she or he heard you say to make sure your meaning was clear. Ask the person to not just repeat your words, but to also include the meaning she or he attaches to it.

If you describe a problem in terms of it's impact on you and on the relationship, you're actually validating the importance of your relationship with the other person. Chances are he or she will be more receptive to what you have to say.

Practice being empathic—put yourself in the shoes of the other person. This is an important key to active listening. Sometimes it's useful to try to hypothesize what might be going on with the person. What might she or he be feeling? Remember, hypothesizing does not mean analyzing. Putting yourself in someone's shoes is different from putting yourself into someone's mind. Yes, I know you may automatically attempt to read minds because it's second nature to you from your childhood days. Back in those days you thought you had to stay one jump ahead of everyone else to protect them or protect yourself. But remind yourself you no longer have to try to speculate because you're developing new skills you can use to check things out.

---

**Putting yourself in someone's shoes is different from putting yourself into someone's mind.**

---

These steps are not easy and might involve taking a big risk—especially for those who are supersensitive to rejection. You may find that getting the other person to first agree to a discussion helps cut the risk factor. For example, you might say, "I have something important to say. Is it okay if we talk now?" Once you get the person to join you in taking responsibility for the discussion, you will find you can say just about anything.

Notice I said *cut* the risk factor, not eliminate it. There is no denying this is shaky territory, especially if you're new at it. Communicating directly about your feelings means sharing a vulnerable part of yourself. Yet isn't this what trust is—sharing the innermost part of yourself with another person, allowing vulnerability?

By making the choice to show the soft inside part of yourself, you're actually coming from a position of strength. *Allowing* vulnerability is very different from *feeling* vulnerable or helpless and needing to defend or armor yourself. Vulnerability includes your tender side as well as your sensual side, your hurt side, and even your angry side.

Let's take a look at the angry part. It's pretty hard to not feel vulnerable when you take the risk of communicating angry feelings to another person. And is it any wonder? Anger was so loaded for many of us when we were growing up. Walter speaks for a lot of people when he observes: "I grew up believing if someone was angry at me, it meant they hated me and they might leave me. I'll do anything so people won't be angry at me. Anger frightens me. I could never express anger as a child and I can't express it now."

Many families had special rules for expressing or not expressing anger. In some families, the (usually unspoken) rule was you could never be angry—you just had to stuff your feelings. That anger had the potential to turn into stony silences. In many families those stuffed feelings exploded in out-of-control rage. In other families you couldn't say you were angry, but you *could* act "crazy," throwing tantrums, or screaming, or slamming doors. In my family I used to bang my head against the dining room wall next to the brass doorchimes. I found a way to both act "crazy" and also feel the pain I was unable to speak of.

Kendra and Bert both had childhood experiences with anger that were causing major problems in their relationship. Bert remembers, "My dad was relentless. If you gave an inch you were dead. So now when Kendra's upset at me, my immediate response is to hide—protecting myself like I did when I was a kid. Because I'm so overwhelmed and can't respond rationally to her in the moment, I need some time and space to go off by myself, sort it all out, and consider my response."

However, Bert's need to be alone triggers an angry reaction from Kendra. She takes it personally and gets furious at him for walking off when she's upset. Not only does she feel ignored by him, but as she waits for him to return to finish the discussion, anxiety creeps in. The longer she waits, the more sick to her stomach she feels, and the more she panics.

Where did Kendra's apprehension come from? As a child she was warned time and again by her mother, "Just you wait, you're gonna get it when your father gets home." And after waiting and worrying, Kendra did "get it"—with a strap. Bert's need for time to sort out his feelings turned into another waiting game for her.

How could they work out a system of resolving conflicts where Kendra didn't have to wait indefinitely and anxiously, yet Bert could have the space he needed to gather his feelings and respond to her concerns? In couples therapy Kendra learned how to use the step-by-step guide for communication to tell Bert how she feels when he walks off. She first describes his behavior in observable, nonblaming terms: "It seems that when I try to talk to you about a problem we're having, you walk off." Then she describes how she feels about the action: "When you do that, I get angry because I feel ignored." Kendra goes on to describe how she explains this action to herself: "I tell myself you're leaving because you're angry at me, and I dread what will happen when you return to finish our talk. It reminds me of when my mom used to say, 'Just you wait, you're gonna get it when your father gets home.' I get such a sickening feeling in the pit of my stomach."

How would Kendra like their interaction to go in the future? "Next time," she tells him, "I'd like you to try to stay present with me while I'm talking about my concerns." And that's what Bert experimented with in couples sessions. He explored ways he could stay in the moment long enough to validate Kendra's feelings. He found that the active listening technique worked best. He let her know he heard and understood her by repeating her concerns back to her. Then he reminded her he needed time to collect his thoughts and he set a time within the hour to continue their discussion. Feeling "heard" made all the difference to Kendra. Once her concerns were validated, and there was an end in sight, she could allow Bert the processing time he needed.

Timing caused problems in a different way for Michelle. "I'd always try to figure out precisely what to say and then wait for the 'perfect moment' to talk to my boyfriend. But it never came." Now she zeros in on the problem and doesn't wait for the perfect moment. The first time she tried checking out something with him, it didn't go nearly as smoothly as she would have liked. But once she made the decision to talk to him, she felt relieved, even pleased with herself, "I felt so much better afterwards. The usual horrible, burdensome feeling was gone. In the past I would dwell on something for days without trying to discuss it with him."

I always ask clients and workshop participants to state aloud their worst fears about what the other person might say or do. Then I ask, "Could the real life response be any worse than the conjectures?" Probably not.

People are astounded to realize how much energy goes into unnecessary worrying about an imagined outcome. Why not put this energy into checking it out in a straightforward way. Once you've done this, you might even say to yourself, "You mean that's it? That's all there is?"

---

**Don't try to wait for the "perfect moment" to discuss a problem. Just do it.**

---

And think of what all that built-up anger does to our bodies. Where does that energy go? Some experience it as a neck ache, or a stomachache, or a headache. Lonnie would hold his anger in until it exploded in accusations—either toward others or toward himself. The negative self-talk would sometimes last for days.

During one session, I directed his attention to how he points his finger and shakes it as he relates his irritation about someone at work. Then I asked him to describe what was happening elsewhere in his body as he was pointing his finger. "My arm is tense, the muscles in my chest tighten and so does my throat, and I speak with a rasp in my voice."

I asked Lonnie to think back again to the situation at work and role-play saying to his co-worker, "It really upsets me when you borrow something from my desk without asking me and when you interrupt me while I'm on the phone." His voice was smooth with no rasp, and he was surprised to realize, "I feel relaxed, like I'm floating. I'm amazed." Putting words to his frustration helped Lonnie make it more manageable.

Practicing helps, even after the fact. And there *are* ways to go back and redo a missed opportunity. Also, if you want to modify or clarify something you said earlier, you can do something about that as well. Just say, "I'd like to return to what we were talking about" or "I'd like to add something" or "I want to make sure my meaning is clear" or "I didn't exactly mean what I said—let me correct it now."

As you explore ways to tailor these steps to your needs, communication begins to flow more easily. When I first tried it out, I even listed the steps on a "crib sheet" to help me out. One day I noticed I didn't need to think it through anymore, it just seemed to flow.

When you check out someone's meaning, or confront a situation, you are being proactive. If you are proactive, you won't feel so boxed in, so stuck. You can make choices here. You can choose how you want to check something out. You are the one choosing the course of action. You are taking the initiative, allowing the situation to glide into healthier communication patterns. You, too, may come to Michelle's realization, "Whenever I finally talk to my boyfriend I feel powerful, centered—even though sometimes it's not the 'perfect moment' or I don't get exactly the response I want. Now I try to hold on to that centered feeling and keep it with me. It's a good reminder for the next time I want to check something out with someone."

When you learn better communication skills your relationships will go more smoothly. Try asking "What is it that you want from me? What can I do to make the situation better?" Then, *really listen to the answer.*

Think for a moment about when you get frustrated or angry in relationships—personal or work-related. Chances are it's either because your needs are not being acknowledged or because they are not being met. Or both. But there's also a good chance that you're not voicing your needs. Good communication in any relationship depends on consideration of needs—yours and others. If you want a gold star in communication do these three things: pay attention to your own needs, clearly state them, and ask about the other person's needs. You'll see how often it works. Practice trying the steps in spite of the fact it feels risky. Once you try something new, it's in your repertoire of behavior, and it becomes easier to try again the next time.

## Troubleshooting

But what do you do if the situation starts getting out of hand? What if you raise your voice or one of you starts to lose control? Calling for a "time-out" can defuse the situation. One way of having a time-out is to excuse yourself and leave temporarily. Going into another room or

Good communication involves paying attention to your own needs, clearly stating them, and asking about the other person's needs.

taking a walk around the block can be helpful. As a child you believed that you could not leave. But as an adult, you can, and if you're feeling overwhelmed by old childhood feelings, leaving is a great way to gain some perspective. As one woman says, "I want to come back later when it's not a charged moment and revisit it."

But let me caution you: Try not to just stomp out and disappear—it will only fuel the other person's anxiety, especially if the person has a history of sudden leavings in her or his life. Remember to assure the person that you'll be back shortly, and give a specific time frame for continuing your discussion.

Counting to ten (slowly) is another way of leaving. (Yes indeed, the very same countdown our parents used to threaten us with.) It gives you some distance from the situation and a chance to cool down. If you can control the angry words, maybe you won't have to take things so personally.

Another way to attempt some damage control is to have a prearranged word or phrase to use as a cue that both of you understand—perhaps one with a touch of humor. One couple experimented in the session with witty phrases. He wanted to say, "Put up your dukes," accompanied by appropriate posturing and gestures. She, because she felt six years old when they fought, wanted to respond, "Oh, yeah! Sez who?" Another couple decided to call out in unison in pig latin, "Ixnay isthay itshay!"

A breakdown in communication can be avoided or mended in almost any situation. When you're feeling upset and you think rejection might be the culprit, take note. Don't reject your own feelings by ignoring or hiding them. Instead, use your feelings as a means to opening up the lines of communication.

# 4

# If You Care about Me You'll Read My Mind

## Expectations and Disappointments

A surefire way to plummet into overwhelming disappointment is to expect too much from relationships. We're programmed to have unrealistic expectations from movies and TV, from romance stories all promising better than wonderful experiences with better than beautiful people who can anticipate our every wish. We want someone to be always caring, always considerate, always loveable, always giving. But these romantic illusions too often leave us feeling cheated and disillusioned—betrayed by our own ideals.

Part of the problem stems from the fact that we don't know how to ask for what we want or need. Society has shown us that people who directly state their needs get labeled as pushy or needy, so we find other methods to try to get our needs met and we usually end up disappointed. We want others to read our minds or give us a specific sign that proves they care for us, so that we don't actually have to ask for anything. We imagine how a situation will turn out or how a person will act and are disappointed when things don't go as planned. We may even find ourselves repeating these patterns of expectation and disappointment.

One woman often found herself getting annoyed at her boyfriend because he didn't tell her how much he missed her when he was traveling on business. After all, isn't that what boyfriends were supposed to do when you'd been dating for over five months? She'd find herself fantasizing about things he might say to her on the phone—how he loved her, how he thought about her. Although he'd call "just to say hello," the conversations were brief and words she wanted so desperately to hear never passed his lips. She'd tell herself that he really didn't care about her as much as she cared about him, because if he did he would tell her.

I'm reminded of another business-trip story. Claire and Andrew were seeing quite a bit of each other even though both were still dating others. They were still finding their way in the relationship, not quite knowing what to expect from the other. When Claire had to fly across country for a week of meetings, she told Andrew where she'd be staying, hoping he'd call. Meanwhile, he wanted to call her but held back, telling himself, "If she's thinking about me she'll call me." In fact, she missed him a lot but was waiting for him to call first because that would mean he was thinking about *her.* It turned into a waiting game, each one thinking the other one didn't care enough to call. If only one of them realized, "Wait a minute here. I care and I'm still not letting myself call first. Just maybe he (she) cares, too."

A woman I know would get irked because her teenage daughters would never ask what they could do around the house to help out. It's not that they wouldn't help out if she asked, but she really wanted them to read her mind and say something like, "Mom, is there anything we can do in the house for you today?" Or better yet, wouldn't it be wonderful if they would just change a lightbulb or scrub the shower tiles of their own volition? This would be a sign that they cared about her.

# Repeating Patterns Can Get Tiresome

"We're a perfect fit—the rocks in *my* head match the holes in *his* head." A client made this comment as she recounted how she repeatedly gravitates toward people and situations that re-create childhood experiences. It's as if there's a powerful force that draws us to the same situations again and again. And our expectations that things will be different this time are simply setting us up for disappointment.

For example, someone who tends to be dependent on others will hook up with a person who needs to take over and control situations. Someone who has learned to think of himself or herself as a victim might become involved with a victimizer, either in work or personal relationships. There are many examples of these "fits" depicted throughout this book.

What is the attraction here? Why do we repeat old behaviors again and again? What makes us unwittingly choose situations that deal with our old issues? There are two basic reasons, and they are not mutually exclusive. Both situations can exist at the same time, in the same situations, with the same people.

First, there is a familiarity about the situation. It is comfortable because it is known, even though rationally it may not be desirable. We think we know what to expect, so we kick off our shoes and settle in—I guess you could say it feels like home—maybe we even get a little homesick for it when it's not around. Something that is known feels more secure that something unknown. The unknown is scary.

Secondly, we tend to repeat our past in an effort to understand it, learn something from it, and overcome it. We tend to repeat an old pattern in an effort to come to terms with it. If we do it enough times, maybe we'll finally get it right. Each time we dance the same dance, we can get better and quicker at recognizing the dynamics.

You can choose to berate yourself for circling around the same predicament or getting involved in the same old kind of relationship for the second or third time, or maybe even the fourth or fifth time. Or you can pat yourself on the back, and say, "This time it only took me four months to notice what I was doing!" If you can look at it as a challenge and ask yourself, "What did I learn from this?" you can hopefully move on.

## Scratch the Surface of Complaining and What Do You Find?

While unfulfilled expectations can be a cause of disappointment, complaining is a sign of disappointment. Have you ever found yourself feeling disappointed about what someone did or didn't do, then getting on their case about seemingly insignificant things? Complaining can take may forms: nagging, grumbling, fussing, scolding, whining. Come to think of it, all these behaviors are a way of making contact with someone, aren't they? There's a good chance you'll get a reaction from that person—maybe a negative one, but at least it's some attention. And if you've been feeling discounted or invalidated because someone disappointed you, any attention seems important.

Let's take a closer look at the complaining. If you scratch the surface, what would be under the protective covering? The harshness of complaining often hides the softness of yearning—a hope or expectation that didn't get met, a need that didn't get fulfilled. Perhaps something you really wanted didn't happen. One way to get results is by saying, "This is what I need from you, this is how I'd like it to be next time." If you can eliminate the hard edge of complaining to the other person, he or she probably won't get defensive in return.

## Do You Expect Too Much of Others?

We often set people up to be icons. We don't want to to look at the real them—we only want to look at our "pin-up." Disappointments result from having unreasonable expectations or too much anticipation; looking for "proof" of love; or having partners who can't say "no" but can't follow through on their promises either. Disappointments also develop from one-sided "secret contracts" that are based on a presumption that the other person will cooperate in a plan that was not discussed beforehand. And as we saw in chapter 2, there certainly can be disappointments from misinterpretations or miscommunications.

Disappointments are related to needs—needs that exist but don't get verbalized. Growing up we may have been told that our needs didn't count or we were selfish if we needed something. As a result, we never learned to put words to our needs. Instead we'd just cross our fingers and hope beyond hope that someone would read our minds. Most likely they didn't or they couldn't or they wouldn't and we'd get disappointed. And we were slow learners, too—we'd just keep crossing those fingers and keep getting disappointed. (Chapter 12 takes a look at how to change this pattern by learning to express needs clearly and directly.)

## An Apology Is Just Icing on the Cake

Expecting or making apologies is fertile ground for disappointments. When you feel wronged getting an apology from the other person is very important to you. But you may not get it, and if you do, it may feel flimsy or insincere. When an apology is important to you, don't just cross your fingers and hope. Try asking for what you want—and be specific. The steps for checking a problem out in chapter 3 will work here. Step 4, in which you state how you would like the situation to be, is a good place to say, "I'd like you to apologize. It's important to me."

Knowing what kind of an outcome you want, what's most important to you, and what's realistic is not easy. The wishful thinking part, the "it would be nice if they'd say ..." part gets in the way. I call this the Principle of Cake and Icing. The cake is the solid part—it has substance. The icing is extra—the fluff. If you were hungry you could fill up more easily on the cake than the icing.

Let's look at this in terms of the apology issue. Often the act of clearly stating how you think the other person wronged you is most important for closure (the cake), but eliciting an apology (the icing) may not be realistic. It's important to understand that you may never get an apology from certain people. This is especially true regarding childhood abuse or neglect where we try to get the person who wronged us to apologize years later. One woman reluctantly agreed to rethink her unrealistic expectations, but she sadly observed, "Maybe I can do without the 'icing' but I would at least like some 'glaze.'"

What about when we're on the other side, when we've hurt someone and it becomes our turn to make the apology? If we feel strongly about being right about something, we may have a hard time apologizing. Yet, to save the relationship and prevent further damage, we sense we must at least bend a little. I'd like to share with you one way of handling this kind of situation that generally works for me. (Of course it may never work for me again now that I've gone public.)

There were times when I felt so strongly about being right I couldn't bring myself to apologize for my actions. Yet sometimes I knew I had to say something to calm things down. I began to experiment with how to say "I'm sorry" without feeling I was selling out my principles. I came up with the idea of saying I was sorry that the situation occurred, even though I couldn't bring myself to say I was sorry for something I *did* or *said*. For example, I might say, "I'm sorry this happened, things got out of hand," or "I'm sorry if I hurt your feelings—I didn't want that to happen." I *was* sorry for the bad feelings, because those kinds of interactions don't feel good for either party. I could say these things and mean them, thereby averting a further deteriorating situation.

## Magical Thinking

As children, many of us learned to be alert to the meanings behind words, to watch our parents' faces or listen to their footsteps in order to guess their moods. It's as if our antennae went up and we developed a highly refined intuitive sense about our parents. Sometimes it meant staying out of their way if the mood was sour. But often it was a way of gauging our parents' needs, a way of taking care of our parents. We became experts at speculating about them and at reading their minds.

As adults we come to expect that the people who care about us will be able to intuit *our* unspoken messages and take care of our needs, because after all, we made it our job to read our parents' minds when we were little. But we're not little anymore and the world no longer operates by magical thinking.

> As children we became experts at reading our parents' minds and moods. Now we think other people should be able to read ours.

Magical thinking is part of normal child development; it is a time when a child lives midway between the world of magic and the world of reality. "In the fantastic world of a two-year-old, all things are possible," says Selma Fraiberg in *The Magic Years*. Fact and fantasy are confused because they're fused together in the child's mind, and their thinking style is dominated by fantasies and wishes. The child feels he or she is the center of the world, believing that wishful thinking will make things happen. In this magical world the child also attributes various wondrous powers to other people or objects.

With the arrival of secondary process thinking, at six or seven years old the child begins the age of reason, developing the ability to follow the rules of logic and taking external reality into consideration. But sometimes, even though we're grown up, we revert to magical thinking, and this leads us to repeated disappointments in life. We feel rejected by the people we care about because they didn't, or couldn't, or wouldn't read our minds. And then we take it personally.

Caroline liked to be held. She wanted Jeff to hold her close and stroke her arm before they drifted off to sleep, regardless of whether they made love. So she'd hint around by snuggling up to him, making barely audible moaning sounds. Sadly, she just couldn't muster enough nerve to ask for what she wanted. She kept hoping Jeff would guess. And hoping. And hoping. Every night Caroline went to sleep disappointed.

## Proof of Affection

For many of us there were a lot of childhood disappointments. Virginia would hope with all her heart that her dad would offer protection when her mom was being unpredictable and abusive, screaming "Wait until your father comes home!" As a little girl she'd fantasize about how her dad would come home from work and protect her, making her world okay again. She'd sit for hours and wait for him by the door. As soon as he walked in, she'd take a flying leap into his arms hoping to get some comforting and love.

But at that moment the mom would appear, shrilly reciting Virginia's "offenses of the day." The dad would say, "I'm disappointed in you, Virginia," and immediately take her to the basement, remove his belt, and spank her for "being such a bad girl to her mother." Virginia kept hoping against hope that her dad would listen to her story just once, but each time he took the mother's side. To make matters worse, Virginia would catch a glimpse of her mother on the basement landing listening to the beatings. Was she smirking? Did she have a glint in her eye?

Her dad would take her mom's side without hearing what Virginia had to say and couldn't, or wouldn't, protect her from the abuse heaped on by her mother. Virginia felt betrayed from all sides. Her mother seemed to be getting some sort of pleasure from watching the beatings from a discreet distance. These feelings of rejection and betrayal have stayed with Virginia. Is it any wonder she still expects to feel disappointed by important people in her life? She continues to have trouble trusting that people won't hurt her so she finds herself testing them—and they usually fail the test.

Virginia, so sensitive to possible betrayals, continues to test loyalty and devotion. She makes unreasonable requests of important people in her life. She in effect says, "Prove to me you care about me by promising you'll take me to the jazz festival even though you don't really care for jazz." The situation she sets up invites disappointment and recreates her childhood feelings of betrayal.

Have you ever found yourself making unreasonable requests like this? What if the other person made the promise, then had a change of mind or simply didn't intend to follow through? Would you interpret this as a message of not caring enough about you? Would you take it personally because they failed your test of love? Maybe it's important to look at why you might set up a test like this in the first place. Doesn't it invite disappointment? What kind of old, familiar feeling might you be restimulating? This process of replicating early childhood experiences in adult relationships is addressed throughout this book.

People concoct very creative tests as proof of love and caring. One woman favored time tests. If a new boyfriend called her by Tuesday or Wednesday after a Saturday date she told herself that meant he was thinking of her and he cared. If he waited until Thursday, she began to doubt his interest in her, and started building up a counteroffensive, which included not answering the phone or being "busy" the next time he asked her out. The poor guy was doomed to failure because he didn't have a clue about her relationship rules.

I want to make an aside here. If you are interested in pursuing a personal or business relationship, it's validating to the other person to make contact within one or two days. If you wait too long, the person might start feeling rejected by you, and the relationship wouldn't get off to a very good start, would it?

One man devised his own way of measuring whether he was on his partner's mind. He sat home alone some evenings while she was at meetings. "I'd become increasingly aggravated as the evening went on and she didn't call me to check in." By the time the woman unsuspectingly walked through the door, he was livid, "She flunked the test because I'd decided, 'If she doesn't call, she doesn't care about me.' I need reassurance that she's thinking of me—she should know that by now. The sad thing is, I almost always expect people will fail me and abandon me. I guess I pull for it until they finally say, 'You're right, I don't want to be with you anymore.'"

A woman I know became upset at her boyfriend when her car was in the shop for repairs for several days. "He doesn't care about me at all, she complained. He didn't even think to offer me a ride to run errands. *I* always offer him rides when he doesn't have his car." Might she be equating "not thinking" with "not caring"?

---

### "Not thinking" doesn't mean "not caring."

Elizabeth had a different measure of caring: how much thought someone puts into picking out a present for her. She told me about what happened in December when her family exchanged gifts during Kwanzaa. "I was surprised and felt misunderstood by my daughter's gifts to me," she said. "Tracy has a good job now and when she kept asking what I wanted, I told her to pick out something that she thought I'd like. I was hoping she'd choose something that represented my tastes, something that was 'me.' My son guessed exactly what I'd like and bought me a satin robe. I guess I expected something like that from my daughter as well.

"She gave me three separate presents, and not one of them reflected who I am. Her gifts seemed so impersonal; it felt like she didn't understand me at all. Personalized gifts are so important to me that I get disappointed if a good friend gives me a book without inscribing it."

What were the gifts? "Two wine glasses, a Michael Jackson video, and a pair of knitting needles. It was the needles that confused me the most. Why would she give me knitting needles, when I haven't knitted in over twenty years? I was hurt because I thought she was hinting she wanted me to be more motherly or matronly or something when she said, 'Maybe you'll take up knitting again.' Tracy can't possibly remember back to when I used to knit sweaters for her. She was only four years old. I didn't know what to do with the needles so I tucked them away in a drawer."

I was very touched by Elizabeth's story. She took the meaning of Tracy's gift personally, thinking her daughter wanted her to be a different kind of mother. This prevented her from seeing how much caring went into all three gifts. Was it possible that Tracy purchased three presents in hopes that one of them would please her? Elizabeth at first had difficulty looking at it this way, but as we continued talking she said, "Well, yes, now I can see that Tracy put some thought into buying the gifts. Actually the glasses were handblown and quite lovely and Tracy and I have enjoyed them when we drink wine together. And it's true that Michael Jackson is one of my favorites—Tracy's, too." But what about those knitting needles? "Yes, in fact, they were very nice knitting needles, probably expensive and, yes, most likely from a specialty knitting store."

I wondered if those needles may have been a gift of love that symbolized fond memories from long ago? Elizabeth again proclaimed that Tracy was too young to remember the days when she knitted those little sweaters. But when mother and daughter talked about this in a joint therapy session, Tracy did indeed remember those days, "There's a knitting shop I sometimes pass, and each time I walk by, I remember how you used to knit me those soft, warm sweaters when I was a little girl. And Mom, I also remember hearing you say over the years how you 'really should take up knitting again.' So I decided to buy you some needles."

Tracy's choice of gifts seemed to be a metaphor for how the past, present, and future were energetically bound together. I found myself caught in a fantasy, envisioning mother and daughter holding those wine glasses high, recalling memories from the past as they shared the futuristic, high-tech effects of the Jackson video.

The reality, however, was different. For six months Elizabeth had felt misunderstood and hurt about the presents, but hadn't expressed her feelings or checked out her daughter's intent. Both Elizabeth and Tracy had leftover hurt feelings from the giving and receiving of these presents. Tracy's good intentions somehow got lost when she didn't explain the intended special meanings. And Elizabeth's quick jump to conclusions led her to misunderstand the nature of the gifts.

From the beginning, Elizabeth set herself up for disappointment when she suggested Tracy buy her a gift that would please her because Tracy couldn't read her mind. And Tracy presumed the significance of her choice of gifts would be crystal clear to her mother. But Elizabeth couldn't read Tracy's mind either.

---

## Caring is not symmetrical.

---

Caring is not symmetrical. There are probably as many ways of showing it as there are people—and just as many ways of missing someone's intentions because their style of caring is different from our own.

Sometimes promises that seem insignificant can cause disappointment. One woman took it personally when her partner promised to move her exercise equipment from the damp garage to the spare room, but didn't follow through. Might it be she was telling herself, "If he moves the equipment for me it proves he loves me?" Bingo. She immediately saw the old pattern and recognized that his love for her didn't have to be contingent on his willingness to move equipment around. How could she take care of herself here? She decided to hire a neighborhood teenager to help her move the equipment.

A woman I know was often getting hurt and disappointed when her partner didn't say or do things to show he cared. "Some of the things he does are silly—not very significant," she complains. "For instance, on our recent trip to France, one morning Gary stopped the car, went into a patisserie, and came out with a huge piece of cake that was mostly icing. He handed it to me, saying, 'I thought you'd like this.' Well I ate it, even though 9 A.M. seemed a little early for all that icing." This story illustrates their different styles. She's practical and likes to know what's going on. She doesn't like surprises, it reminds her too much of growing up in an unpredictable family. He likes to plan small surprises. His dad used to do the same with his mom. Gary's surprises are his way of giving to her, it's the only way he knows to show he cares, and he can't understand why she gets upset with him. In their relationship, he provides a lot of "icing" when she has "cake" in mind. "I can't believe I used to get so upset," she says. "Now I realize how he does things in his little Gary ways to make me happy, and I've been overlooking his intentions all this time."

## What Did You Expect?

It's helpful to remember that the style of one person may be different from the other, especially if one grew up in a very different type of family from the other person.

In chapter 2, we saw how different upbringing can lead to communication problems. Here you'll see how it can create different expectations.

> **Growing up in different types of families leads to different sets of expectations.**

Sometimes early family experiences lead to such different expectations that it causes confusion in a couple's relationship. Mary's big family did just about everything together. Even when the children reached adolescence, they were still expected to join the rest of the family for all activities. There was a lot of "we-ness," and not enough personal space. Since five out of seven family members had birthdays in the same month, they celebrated with one great big joint birthday party every year. Because individual dates were not celebrated, the five people with June birthdays began to forget their own actual birthdates.

Mary's partner, Fred, came from a very different kind of experience. Family members were on their own, with their separate interests and activities. It was as if the family members were disconnected from each other; even many meals were solitary because of everyone's busy schedules.

So what happened when Fred and Mary became a couple? Mary expected what she was used to—relationship "togetherness." Fred expected to pursue separate activities. For example, he liked to spend time after work unwinding with office friends before going home. But Mary wanted him home with her even if they had no specific plans. She told him, "I want you to be with me." Fred told Mary, "I want to do my own thing."

The relationship became really strained when Fred suggested he go camping with his buddies. In Mary's mind, vacations were supposed to be for being together. After all, families are supposed to do things together, aren't they? She was hurt that Fred even thought about leaving her at home while he went off with his friends. She felt like she didn't count.

Mary wanted more from Fred than he could give. Because she didn't get enough from him, she felt rejected, then she withdrew and distanced herself from him. Fred in turn felt rejected and "not good enough." Because they had such different experiences of what "togetherness" meant from their respective families, there was a huge disparity in their expectations for their relationship. They became disappointed by each other and this led to hurt feelings and misunderstandings.

Gift-giving also has different protocol from family to family. In some families it may be desirable to give checks or gift certificates ("Oh wow, I get to buy what I want!"). In other families that may seem like a slight ("Didn't she care enough to go shopping for me?"). Some families may feel fine about exchanging a gift that's "not quite right." But in others, people wouldn't think of returning a gift—they keep it even if they'll never use it, because taking it back to the store feels disloyal or rude. So what happens when a "gift-exchanger" hooks up with a "gift-keeper-no-matter-what"? Does someone end up with hurt feelings? Can they talk about their differences and work it out?

### Don Juan, the Seducer

Alice Miller, in *Thou Shalt Not Be Aware*, details some other ways early family experiences can lead to misunderstandings and disappointments. She describes a type of fellow she calls "Don Juan, the seducer," who deceives women in the name of protecting their feelings. Miller theorizes that as a child, "Don" was probably the apple of his mother's eye, and was rewarded for his dependence on her. He soon learned it wasn't okay to say "no" to his mother because her response might have been, "I'm really disappointed in you, Donny." Because she needed him to need her, she wasn't able to foster his independence by encouraging him to say "no." He came to believe that by asserting his independence and going against her wishes, he'd lose her love. He feared she might withdraw from him, totally reject him, or abandon him.

So what happens when "Don" reaches adulthood? He still can't say "no" to the women in his life because he believes saying "no" might disappoint someone. Women are attracted to "Don" because initially he appears sensitive, kind, and caring. He makes them feel important, giving them the same kind of admiration and affection that he loved receiving as a child. Because he knows how to please, he "seduces" them into believing he means what he says when he can't say "no." But by being deceptive in the name of kindness, he arouses hopes that he can't meet and he ends up disappointing them anyway.

As a child, "Don" couldn't be honest and openly express himself because his mother couldn't tolerate this kind of openness. Perhaps she took it personally, and he was trying to protect her from hurt feelings. Now that he's a man, he's still trying to spare other women's feelings, so he still can't say "no" to them. Miller emphasizes that because he's unable to say "no" at the decisive moments of his life, each relationship becomes a lie and he loses his authenticity. So "Don" goes from one woman to another, like a bee flying from flower to flower, awakening expectations, then disappointing someone. Because his actions often provoke women to be cruel to him, this gives him an excuse to leave them in good conscience and move on to the next woman. Each new relationship seems to re-create the patterns in his childhood.

"Don" is in big trouble if he happens to become involved with a woman who has unrealistic expectations about the relationship. Perhaps someone who secretly wants a man to make her happy by reading her mind and surprising her with things she hints about, such as gifts, trips, outings. And what does she get in "Don"? She gets a man who ambles through life, disappointing women because he can't say "no."

What a match these two are! She's an expert in expectations and he's a wiz in disappointing. She sets herself up for disappointment and she chooses the right guy for the job. When she suggests an upscale restaurant or a weekend at a bed-and-breakfast, he can't bring himself to tell her he's not interested. "Don" can't say "no," so instead he says something like, "okay, sure"—but he'll find some excuse not to go there with her. After the fourth or fifth time of reminding him that he promised (of course, he sees it as nagging) she may begin to tell herself that he doesn't care enough about her. After all, if he cared he'd do whatever makes her feel good. In fact, if he *really* cared, she wouldn't even have to tell him where she wanted to go, he'd be able to read her mind. Wrong. He doesn't have a clue. So she takes it personally.

He may not have intended to reject her. But he has, in fact, invalidated the relationship by not being candid about his feelings. Honest statements might include, "I don't want to spend the money," or "It bothers me when the prices are so high and there's so little food on the plate," or "I really don't want to go out of town for a weekend, I feel more comfortable at home." None of these explanations would be easy to make or easy to hear, but it would give honesty and context to the situation. With an explanation, she might not feel so disappointed and hurt. (More about the importance of saying "no" in chapter 11.)

## Don't Get Carried Away with Anticipation

Another setup for disappointment is having too much anticipation. Certainly anticipation is an important ingredient in successful relationships. It's that "walking on air" feeling, a spirit-lifter, an energizer, a high. To be sure, it's a charming part of the process of planning. But too much anticipation or expectancy of an upcoming event can lead to disappointment if plans go awry.

Anticipation can play a role in work situations as well as personal. What if a friend suggests you apply for a job with a firm run by some friends of hers? She can't tell you enough about how wonderful these owners are and how you'll be "just perfect" for their firm. So you show up for the interview with high expectations because she was so sure you and the owners would click. But that's not what happened. At the interview they looked at you blankly, as if they couldn't see you. There were a lot of long pauses. Obviously *you* were not what they'd expected—they must have visualized a different personality type or body type or haircut or something—sort of like a blind date that went badly.

When anticipation in relationships becomes so important that it takes up an exorbitant amount of time and energy it becomes an addiction, a driving force that creates anxiety. What happens if this anxiety begins to take over? For example, when one man told his new girlfriend he'd call her Monday evening, she looked forward all day to his call and spent a lot of time daydreaming about their upcoming conversation. As the evening wore on and there was no call from him, she became consumed with thoughts of whether he'd call at all, and she got more and more anxious when the phone didn't ring. She felt let down, disappointed, and angry. She began cycling between feeling he was no good and feeling she was no good.

Some people find themselves immediately jumping into fantasies about the future when they begin a new relationship, and they lose sight of the "now." I see this more with women than with men, although I've known a few men who admit to getting caught up in it. Perhaps it has to do with those romantic novels and TV dramas mentioned earlier.

Enjoying dinner together, holding hands, hugging, kissing, even making love doesn't necessarily mean that a long-term relationship or marriage is in the future. When so much energy gets put into the possibility of a future, it can turn into unnecessary anxiety and it takes away from the joy of the moment. This is similar to fussing with camera settings in order to capture a beautiful sunrise on film, but actually missing the experience of the dawning of a new day. As Susan Jeffers observes in *End the Struggle and Dance with Life,* "We diminish the present as we worry about the future." This goes along with one of my favorite sayings:

> "NOW is a gift. That's why it is called the PRESENT. To be
> fully enjoyed it must be unwrapped from the mistakes and
> guilt of the past and the worries of the future."

Anticipation is fine when it's upbeat and optimistic and appropriate, but when that line gets crossed into magical thinking our expectations become unrealistic and can crash and shatter. This is what happened when Valerie and Brenda were in couples therapy to try to work out ways to make time for each other in spite of their busy schedules. They worked out an arrangement where they would have dinner together two days a week, alternating who would prepare the meal. As they planned the logistics of all this, Brenda reminded Val that she works long and unpredictable hours and the lengthy commute could be a problem. In fact, there may be times Brenda might not make it home in time for dinner. Valerie looked stunned at the thought. She confided that she had just been sitting in the session already anticipating the romantic dinners they would have together, visualizing how the table would be set, what candles she would use, how the flowers would look. Then Brenda had to ruin it for her by foreseeing a possible problem. Valerie felt as if her wonderful plans had already been canceled. Her face fell in disappointment.

Brenda only saw it as unavoidably having to work late, but Valerie saw it as a rejection—a message that work mattered more than she did. Then an interesting thing happened in the session: Valerie saw what she was doing. She saw that she was taking it personally. She reminded herself that this wasn't about her, but, in fact, Brenda had a problem with the stressful demands of her work. The moment was helpful because by noticing her process here and gaining some objectivity about her feelings, she made an important gain toward breaking patterns of the past. And Brenda learned a little about empathy—the importance of understanding Valerie's feelings.

Anticipation can shift into high gear in new relationships if one person is just a little too quick to tell the other: "Oh, baby you're wonderful," "I want you to meet my friends," "I think I'm falling in love with you," "I can't wait to go somewhere romantic with you, let's plan a trip (or two or three)," and on and on. Hopes get raised for the person on the receiving end of all this delicious attention, but before there's even time to take a drive into the countryside, the one with all the romantic ideas bolts or otherwise disappears. I call these people the dream weavers—spinners of fantasy who catch some unsuspecting person in their web of promises. It's as if they wade out into the water and all of a sudden hit a six-foot drop and panic, forgetting how to tread water. Poof! Gone—perhaps they scared themselves away. These relationships usually end quickly and badly.

## Romanticizing or Catastrophizing

Sometimes we romanticize a situation. Then, if it doesn't turn out the way we hoped, we take a nosedive. This romanticizing can turn into catastrophizing—seeing the worst aspects of the situation—which then becomes magnified and out of control. For example, this happened to Maggie when her romantic fantasies turned sour. She had been having such a wonderful day with Ralph. They'd spent hours together, walking for miles, sharing a picnic lunch. She kept thinking how comfortable they seemed together. Then they went back to her house and made love for the first time. Afterwards, they cooked and ate a late dinner together. It had been such a romantic day, Maggie expected it to continue. She expected Ralph to spend the night. But he surprised her by going home after dinner.

Maggie was so disappointed—and felt rejected. She told herself he really didn't care about her, that he was only interested in sex with her. She told herself he was no good. Then she told herself she was no good. When he called the next day, she was able to gather the courage to tell him how she had hoped that he might have spent the night. Ralph told her he'd sensed her change of mood as he was leaving, but he had no idea what it was about. Now he realized he most likely had been a little anxious about their first lovemaking. The security of his own house had seemed appealing to him at the time. He wanted to go home and he did.

## Hidden Agendas and Secret Contracts

Expectations regarding "secret contracts" can also lead to disappointments. These are one-sided unspoken contracts between two people. They are based on a presumption that the other person will cooperate in a plan that has never actually been discussed between the two. People often enter into personal or business relationships with different agendas. But they never discuss these plans and somebody gets a big surprise when it's time for the event to happen. For example, what about the father who assumes his children will take care of him when he retires? Or the administrative assistant who presumes his boss is putting in a good word for him so he can get a promotion?

Couples get caught in the web of these undiscussed expectations all the time. When Marvin and Monica married, he took it for granted that she would continue to work to support him. His plan was to stop working and write a novel. Unfortunately, she didn't have a clue about his expectations, because he didn't think to tell her.

Marvin's resentment kept growing as years went by and Monica was not agreeable to supporting him so he could stop working. He came to believe she was intentionally holding him back from his writing on purpose. He got it in his head that she was reneging on their (undiscussed) agreement. Yes, he was taking it personally. Monica, needless to say, was quite surprised to learn in couples sessions that Marvin had expected her to support him. She had no idea of the reason for his growing resentment and anger at her. But now she knew.

One man was dumbfounded when three years into the marriage his wife announced that it was time to buy a house. He'd presumed they would continue to rent for several more years, at least until he was promoted to the managerial level at work. She was shocked at his attitude and screamed at him, "Why are you so stubborn? All of my friends have their own houses by now. What's wrong with you?"

Amy expected her live-in boyfriend to contribute his share of groceries and other household expenses. Sometimes he did, but not consistently. Being a gardener, what he did do was redesign her yard, planting some exotic foliage. He saw it as his "contribution" to the household, but didn't tell her that. She saw it as a "gift" and had no idea it was in lieu of money for expenses. It turns out he thought he was bartering services—something he was used to doing in his business.

And what about indoctrinated sexual expectations? Especially that old myth that foreplay is the appetizer on the lovemaking menu and the main course is supposed to be "the real thing." One couple came into counseling because as the years went by their lovemaking had lost its excitement. The man sometimes couldn't maintain an erection during intercourse, and his partner would get disappointed and feel hurt. Then she'd roll over with her back to him. They'd lie side by side in the darkness, each retreating to a deep internal place to nurse the hurt. Two people suffering in silence. No discussions, no contact, just silence until an uneasy sleep finally came. Each was so immersed in private disappointment that neither could begin to talk about their feelings. Nor could they suggest exploring how to pleasure each other in other ways. The silences became filled with hurts and resentments that kept building up.

## Problems Don't Disappear on Their Own

Nikki took it personally when her lover Neil would busy himself with chores or work projects when she made overtures about going to bed early to allow time to make love. After all, he has a right to sometimes feel like not making love, but it would be so much more effective to find a loving and direct way to say that to her, instead of ignoring her by focusing his attention on tasks. So, with some coaching, he practiced saying, "I love making love to you, Nikki, but not tonight, thanks." When he touched her arm and said that to her, she found it pretty hard to feel rejected.

Psychologist Janet Wolfe addresses this discrepancy between partners' desires for sex in *What to Do When He Has a Headache.* "How much is too little, anyway?" she asks. "Our era is so preoccupied with sex that almost all of us feel we have an inadequate sex life." "Stay out of the Orgasm Olympics," she cautions, "try to stop worrying about the kind of sex life you think you *should* be having and what you think others are having."

Attempting to overlook the problems in a relationship and keeping your fingers crossed that the other person will change is just a setup for disappointment. If you make someone your "project," you could wait a very long time for that purpose to undergo a metamorphosis. One woman in her late thirties sighed, "I always fall in love with men who have a boyish charm about them, but I get so disappointed when they don't act very mature. My current boyfriend is like a seventeen-year-old with a good job!"

Another woman learned the hard way by supporting her boyfriend both emotionally and financially. She would joke to friends that he was a "high-maintenance kind of guy, a real 'fixer-upper'," but when he wasn't developing into the potential she saw in him, she began to blame herself. She told herself, "I must be doing something wrong. If he loved me enough, he'd change." But in fact, he didn't want to change. Why should he want to be "fixed" if he wasn't broken?

---

## "I'll never get involved with 'potential' again!"

---

It took her five years to figure this out. When she finally broke up with him, she was surprised at how relieved she felt. "I'm not even lonely now, compared to how miserable I was all those years I spent being lonely for the person I wished he could be. I'll never get involved with 'potential' again!"

Are these stories familiar to you? Do you often engage in wishful thinking? How often have you had high expectations of something happening? How often have you come crashing down to reality, feeling terribly dejected? How often have you felt depressed after this kind of disappointment? Yes, these unfulfilled expectations can lead to depression. If you consider that depression is connected to experiencing loss, take a look at how many ways the unrealistic expectations and resulting disappointments in the previous examples could lead to one loss after another.

When a woman I know discovered an old college boyfriend was living in her city, she contacted him. They began a whirlwind relationship, taking up where they had left off fifteen years ago. Each was in love with the memory of what the other used to be like back in college. It felt deliciously real for a little while. Then she realized the relationship could go nowhere, it was based on a memory from the past. He was no longer the earnest young man she used to know, nor was she the same sweet young girl he remembered. When the fling was over, she came back to reality and went into a depression that she didn't understand. Slowly she began to realize her sadness was not just over the breakup—it was also about what might have been but never could be. All the energy that went into the anticipation of a future was gone, and she experienced a huge loss.

> Sometimes there is great sadness over
> what might have been.

# Do You Expect Too Much
# of Yourself?

What if your unrealistic expectations are directed at *yourself?* What if someone's illusions about your capabilities are not met? What kinds of messages do you give yourself about yourself?

## *Struggling to Live Up to "Potential"*

"I just want to scream whenever anyone says, 'You have so much potential,'" Paula sighed. "I've heard that all of my life. Whenever my parents talked to me about my 'potential' I always felt I wasn't good enough, that I didn't fulfill their expectations and they were disappointed in me. They probably thought they were challenging me, but I guess I was just too sensitive.

"It's like the coach who keeps the bar a little higher than the participant can jump. It's often a setup for failure because you don't have permission to work up to something. My situation at work is like that. It seems as if my managers push me, and when I can't perform, they talk to me about my 'potential.' I get angry and rebellious, and one of these days I'll probably get fired unless I do something about this."

Paula has come to expect that other people will expect a great deal from her. Her parents had an unrealistic agenda for her, but although she tried hard to meet their expectations, she couldn't. There always seemed to be a gap between what they expected and what she could give to them. As this space expanded it became filled with constant anxiety, which has stayed with her to this day. She's constantly asking herself, "What do people want from me?" She has lost perspective on her own abilities, thinks she's not good enough, and ends up convincing others this is true. If she doesn't believe in herself, how can anyone else? And if they happen to, she seems to find a way to prove them wrong.

## *Perfectionism: The Most Unrealistic*
## *Expectation of All*

We have unrealistic expectations of ourselves as well. Some of us can never be perfect enough to please ourselves—yet we keep trying. Having these unrealistic expectations often contributes to our failure. We fall off of our own pedestal.

For example, how can we admit to ourselves or others that we might have set up an unrealistic goal? Have you ever sat in a classroom or meeting, not understanding what the lecturer is saying, but unable to ask questions for fear of appearing imperfect? Perfectionism doesn't allow for mistakes or questions.

This need to be perfect or perform perfectly can lead to a sort of paralysis—not doing anything for fear of not doing it well enough. Susan Jeffers writes in *Feel the Fear and Do It Anyway*, "Our need to be perfect and our need to control the outcome of events work together to keep us petrified when we think about making a change or attempting a new challenge."

Look at how much energy it takes to try to appear perfect and not vulnerable to others. As one woman said, "It's a lot to keep track of, trying to remember who I told what, trying to cover myself if I made a mistake. Sometimes it can be exhausting."

By trying to be perfect you are trying to protect yourself from rejection, because if you do something perfectly you don't leave space for someone to tell you, "It's not good enough." But what if you're one of these people who has to give 200 percent so you don't take any chances on making mistakes? What happens if your mate or co-workers are only giving 89 or 91 percent? Does this feel lopsided to you? Do you feel disappointed in their performance? Do you consider them disloyal to you? Do you feel the situation is unfair and get resentful?

---

**Perfectionism doesn't allow for mistakes or questions.**

---

In families where the children are expected to conform to parents' expectations, the children are not validated for their spirit or their uniqueness. Sometimes there's a designated "good" child and a designated "bad" child, the bad child often being the nonconformist or feisty one. Since there's no room in the family to be different, this child is singled out for verbal or physical abuse. "I used to cower in the hallway, listening to my dad beat my sister," says one woman. I thought "'Oh my God, this could happen to me too if I make a mistake, if I'm not good enough.' With each beating, I'd try harder to be perfect." (See chapter 7 for more about "good" and "bad" family roles.)

"There was a hole in my family and I was always striving to fill up the space," another woman recalls. It's true that some children try to be perfect in order to fill the void that exists when other family members think of themselves as inadequate. Usually one of the children will step in to "fill up the space," a pattern that continues to haunt that child into adulthood. But filling up space in this way—by being so perfect—doesn't leave space for anyone else. And this need to fill up space sure doesn't leave room for mistakes, does it?

Sometimes, no matter how hard we try, it seems we can't be perfect enough. In families that demand perfectionism we find ourselves in a no-win situation. If our parents or grandparents or siblings keep telling us nothing is good enough, how can we ever hope to be perfect? In fact, how do we know what "good enough" is? How do we know when to stop trying? It seems like that hole will never get filled. But we keep on trying, and keep on falling short, and the little voice inside our heads gets louder as it reminds us, "Not good enough, not good enough, not good enough." That old message of inadequacy keeps replaying, "You can't do anything right no matter how hard you try."

## Torn between Two Voices

Maura had developed two contradictory voices inside her head. If they simultaneously blasted at her in stereophonic sound she became confused and distressed. She felt caught between her belief about herself, "I can't do it on my own," and her expectation of herself, "I can do it all by myself—perfectly." It left her feeling trapped and unable to get anything done.

Where did these opposing voices come from? "My parents expected me to be perfect, and it felt like I was constantly disappointing them. Yet at the same time they were giving me the message that I wasn't capable of doing things for myself. Instead of letting me do my homework alone in my room after school, my mom would sit at the dining room table with me every day from three to five, helping me with my school assignments. Looking back, I bet she wanted companionship from me in those hours before my dad got home. But I didn't know that then, and I came to think of myself as helpless and incapable. These days I'm constantly disappointing myself because I don't know what my strengths are—or my limits for that matter."

Life became an either/or situation for Maura. She flipped from a state of learned helplessness into an inflated view of herself and there seemed to be nothing much in between. In this inflated state it was as if she put herself on a pedestal, then came crashing down at the slightest disappointment. Maura was caught between the belief that she couldn't do anything and the expectation that she should be able to do everything perfectly. I asked her if she wanted to learn some alternatives. Could she imagine a continuum, with her "can't do" belief on one end and her "perfectionism" expectation on the other end? We drew a continuum using Maura's dilemma of trying to pass her statistics course.

Could she choose some place along the continuum line that represented another possible perspective? She seemed to be struggling with that challenge. At first she could only see the either/or possibilities: either studying so many hours that her other coursework would suffer or dropping the statistics class. She couldn't think of any other possibilities. So

I suggested the possibility of letting the instructor know she was having difficulty and asking for suggestions. Then Maura's face lit up—she'd thought of another idea as well. She could look into a tutor for this class. She could put another mark on the continuum to designate this other possibility.

## Figure 2: Maura's Either/Or Thinking Continuum

Now that she saw the possibility of asking for help with her statistics class, could she consider doing this in other situations as well? For example, she'd been putting off assembling bookshelves for her new apartment and attempting to put together a budget because she believed she couldn't do these things well enough. Could she try for a "good enough" success, allowing room for a small imperfection? "Maybe," she said, "I'll have to accept a little less than my ideal. Then I don't have to be constantly disappointing myself." Maura knew she was beginning to control her need to be perfect the day she was able to see how much stress she was feeling over planning the perfect dinner for her new boyfriend. So told herself, "Maybe I'll just plan a dinner for myself and invite him over." And she did.

Some of the most powerful expectations and disappointments we struggle with are the ones we create in ourselves, because they turn into self-critical, self-rejecting messages. As one woman said, and the next chapter illustrates, "I took over where my mother left off—beating myself up!"

# 5

# I Never Want to Be Hurt Like That Again

## Avoiding the Pain

In a recent "Don't Take It Personally!" therapy group, we made an intriguing discovery. Several group members kept three or four tubes of lip balm handy—in the kitchen, in the bathroom, in the bedroom, in the car. The group figured out they all seemed to be using lip balm as a protective barrier against feelings, including feelings of rejection. One man explained, "One way I know I'm having a feeling is when I reach for the Chap Stick!"

Protecting ourselves from feeling rejected becomes a primary mission in life because we will not risk experiencing that kind of hurt again. Yet at the same time, we keep expecting rejection just around the corner. So we avoid asking for what we want or need; sharing warm, loving feelings; meeting new people; becoming involved romantically with someone; seeking new jobs or promotions. Yes, we expend great amounts of energy protecting ourselves from the possibility of pain. In order to do to this we muster every coping skill we can, often building armor or erecting walls. Frequently we invent ways to dull pain by shutting off feelings. Some people use drugs or alcohol or work. Some people use Chap Stick. All of these ways can help us to emotionally survive when the environment doesn't feel safe.

## Expecting the Pain

Not only do we protect ourselves by presuming rejection is out there waiting to happen, but sometimes by magnifying the drama of it as well. Perhaps if we worry about it we won't be caught off guard. Maybe by expecting the worst, whatever happens won't seem so bad. It's as if we're rehearsing what to do in a difficult predicament. Psychology books call it catastrophizing but I like the term one of my clients uses— *awfulizing*. By looking at all the awful things that can go wrong and being prepared to avoid them, we try to feel safer. This behavior becomes automatic, without conscious awareness. But you can see how much energy it takes to be always on the lookout, always prepared. Not to mention the energy it takes to deal with the worry and anxiety that goes along with it.

Expecting emotional or physical pain to accompany love is a common experience of many clients. One woman summed it up, "We were the little kids and our parents were supposed to be taking care of us. But sometimes the grownups didn't do their job very well. In fact, sometimes they were nasty and unpredictable, so when my parents told me, 'No one will ever love you like we do,' I got so confused. What can I expect from anyone else?"

Even though parents may have nurtured their children in some ways, at the same time the children may have felt abused, betrayed, or abandoned, and came to believe, "Those who love me also hurt me." These contradictory messages caused immense confusion back then and led to great anxiety in relationships both then and now. It's not a question for them of *if* they'll get hurt, but rather, *when* it will happen. So, since childhood, they've been wary, on guard, just waiting for it to happen again. (Chapter 6 will address how the origins of these messages are rooted in children's attachment styles.) One man told me, "I can't give up the hurt. The hurt substitutes for love—it fills up the space. There always seems to be room for more hurt, but I don't seem to be able to let love in."

Expectations of rejection are further complicated when we interpret behaviors of others in the same negative ways we recognize from the past. For example, we tend to hear or see only the parts that support what we already believe, reinforcing our negative expectations. We see things as if we're looking through wavy lenses—there's an element of distortion here and these preconceived notions from the past affect our perceptions in the present.

Misperceptions happen all the time, especially when we have some sort of preconception. If we expect people to be hurtful and if we expect to experience rejection, we just might miss a loving, caring message. Recently I scooped up my cat, Rufus, into my arms while I was talking to a friend. I commented on how he's so standoffish, and tends to push me away when I hold him and that he's been that way for fourteen years. My friend said, "Elayne, just look at your cat. He's absolutely melted into your arms. He doesn't look at all standoffish to me." And sure enough, Rufus was relaxed and content and purring. I looked down at the cat in my arms and realized I was holding on to history. How long have I been presuming he's so unfriendly? When had he changed? How had I missed that? My perception was truly lagging behind reality.

Sometimes when we expect that other people will disappoint us, they are all too willing to oblige. It's as if we are equipped with radar that seeks out folks who'll let us down, and they are not hard to find.

> Sometimes our perception lags behind reality.

A couple I know found this to be a problem in their relationship. He craved time to himself and liked to take off alone for the day. She felt left out and hurt when he went off by himself. When these emotions amplified into feelings of rejection and abandonment, she started feeling a desperate need to protect herself and would threaten to pack her bags and leave. He could tell by the terrified look in her eyes that this wasn't only about him taking off for the day. This was about something old. Where did this overwhelming reaction come from? When had she felt this desperate before?

When she was young, her mom used to tell the kids, "If you don't like what I tell you, you can just pack your bags and leave." She joined with her sisters in making a joke of it, chanting, "PYBAL, PYBAL, PYBAL," short, of course, for "pack your bags and leave." But it's not a joke anymore. The expectation of abandonment is as real for her now as when she was thirteen years old, imagining herself being cast out into the world, struggling to carry a suitcase with all her belongings. Where would she go? Where would she sleep? How would she eat? And now, twenty years later, she lives out this fear almost every day. Except now she tries to stay in control of the situation by threatening to pack her bags and leave her partner—before he can leave her.

We tend to overlook positive input from people, too, because it doesn't conform to our expectations of rejection. Sure, we want acceptance and nurturing, but it's so scary to risk the unknown that we often find ways to avoid this risk—especially if we believe the pain of rejection might be lurking out there somewhere.

## Taking Pains to Avoid the Pain

With repeated experiences of rejection, abandonment, or betrayal all of our energy goes into avoiding this excruciating pain at any cost. Many of us learned this skill as children. Children of divorce become especially sensitive to being disappointed by one parent or another, and learn to protect themselves. For example, it seems that twelve-year-old Jason has been "busy" with his friends whenever his frequently busy father tries to make plans to spend the day with him. And his dad gets hurt because Jason is so involved with his friends all the time. But Jason is only protecting himself from the pain of past disappointments, when his dad has canceled or postponed their plans because of a "work emergency." Jason may grow up to find ways to protect himself from possible pain of relationships by staying "busy" all the time.

Children like Jason not only grow up avoiding relationships, but they often avoid having children, not wanting to expose children to the same pain they experienced as children. Adults who were abused as children are especially sensitive to this issue because they want to end the cycle of abuse. "I don't want to have children. I'm so afraid that I'll treat them the same way I was treated," Rachel told me. What was she most afraid of? "That I'll get out of control and rage at them. That I'll see them cringe the same way I used to cringe. I don't want them to grow up with the same kinds of problems I have." I reminded Rachel that she has already done something important about ending that cycle—she is investing in the future by reading books for adults who were abused as children and by initiating therapy. It's a great start.

This is also an issue for adults who grew up in homes where there was violence between the parents. One man gets upset with his mother who likes to say, "Well at least you weren't an abused child. Your father and I never laid a hand on you." He was livid as he told me, "What about all the nights I cowered in my room, worrying that one of them would kill the other? That felt like abuse to me. I'm afraid of getting into a long-term relationship with anyone who wants to have children."

Then there's the avoidance practiced by adults who felt scarred by their parents' divorces when they were young. They come into psychotherapy in their thirties or forties wanting to talk about how their parents divorce has affected them all these years. "I don't want to get married— I'm afraid it won't last, I would get hurt, my children would get hurt. I can't take that chance."

The story I hear most often has to do with issues of loyalty—feeling obligated to choose one parent over the other. These children would feel disloyal if they spent more time with one parent and would worry about how the other parent might get upset, resulting in constant balancing, constant worrying, constant juggling. It was especially complicated when one or both parents remarried—what would happen if the child actually liked the stepparent?

Another often-told divorce story involves the parent who moves out of the house and tends to pretty much "disappear" from the children's lives. There is often little or no contact. It's especially heartbreaking for children who had a pretty good or even great relationship with that parent before the divorce—then all of a sudden, Poof! Maybe there'll be a few phone calls but few or no face-to-face visits. Children can't understand what happened and, of course, blame themselves. Most likely, the fact is that the departing parent misses being a part of the family so much that he or she can only deal with their pain by avoiding contact altogether.

One man talked about being five years old when his parents divorced. He had clothing at both houses, and separate sets of toys, but he felt he belonged nowhere. He had a succession of stepmothers as he watched his father remarry several times. And what kind of message did he learn? Well into his forties, he's afraid of getting married because, "What if it doesn't last? I don't want to be like my dad. And if I made a mistake and married the wrong person and had children, I couldn't stand causing them the kind of pain I experienced."

As adults we may try to avoid pain by numbing ourselves with overwork, self-medicating with drugs or alcohol, or cushioning ourselves with overeating. Or we might put out our antennae, trying to spot rejection from a distance, presuming that everything out there is a potential source for rejection or abandonment, trying to sidestep it before it can hurt us.

When we're afraid of the possibility of rejection, we just won't put ourselves out there. This is not only true about personal relationships, but of job-related situations as well.

For example, a woman I know has not applied for a job since she was fired five years ago. She cringes at the idea of actually submitting a résumé and having a face-to-face interview. So to avoid this anxiety, she works for a temp agency, taking a series of jobs.

Asking for raises or promotions is another area ripe for avoidance. All kinds of anxieties abound here, especially authority issues. The very thought of approaching a supervisor or manager makes many people cringe. It's easier to not ask for anything and hope somebody will notice the good work you do.

Then there's Darryl, who was always so afraid to ask his boss to clarify things, that he pretended he understood how to approach a task or project when he really didn't have a clue. The reason? He was petrified someone would think he was stupid if he asked questions. He avoided asking questions because it seemed safer and easier, but spent enormous amounts of energy trying to figure things out and worrying about how he might screw up.

A woman who was psychologically abused by her father can't stand being around her manager. "I don't know what it is about her but I have a strong reaction to her—there's a nastiness about her that reminds me of my father. I use the woman's restroom on another floor, just so I won't have to run into her and feel cornered. A couple of times I've even walked down the stairs because I was afraid I'd have to ride the elevator with her."

Sometimes fear of rejection squashes our creative abilities. We're so worried about what others will think that we create something such as a painting, poem, or short story, and never show it to anyone. So it sits on a shelf somewhere or is stashed in a closet. A man I once knew confided that he'd completed a novel several years earlier but had never shown it to anyone. I asked him why not. He responded quietly, "What if no one likes it?"

This dynamic of avoidance is pervasive. It can start in infancy but becomes entangled in our adult relationships. That includes relationships with national pastimes such as baseball.

After the year-long baseball strike of 1994 ended, the question on everyone's mind was, "Where were the fans?" Sportswriters scratched their heads and speculated about why the stadiums were only half full. Were the fans angry? Was it a retaliatory "I'll show you" attitude? Was it a case of "out of sight, out of mind"?

I think the fans were taking it personally. Perhaps they felt betrayed by both management and players and felt manipulated by something they had trusted. They did not want to get hurt like that again so they stayed away.

Baseball has been a longtime companion to many people. Play-by-plays have provided a comfortable backdrop while working around the house or in the yard or driving a car. Baseball is good company if some-one is alone, and it's always been a great reason to get a group of people together.

For many people their relationship with baseball was comfortable and secure. They trusted it would always be there for them. They never dreamed this cozy relationship would end. But then the strike happened. No baseball. It evaporated from their lives, leaving an empty space that nothing else could fill in the same way. When you get right down to it, it felt a lot like an abandonment. Trust was shattered. People felt hurt, rejected, betrayed. Quite a few took it personally.

Is it any wonder that fans were cautious about letting baseball back into their lives? They didn't throw open their arms and say "It's okay, I forgive you." No way. They were tentative. Even though they loved the sport so much, they avoided reinvolving themselves with it. Perhaps they were avoiding the emotional pain of another rejection.

## The Ecstasy of the Agony

One of the most popular ways of protecting ourselves is to cling to old ways of being. It's like a Greek drama: we end up seeking out the very forms of rejection we try to avoid. We may fear rejection, but we seem to welcome the comfort of its familiarity at the same time. How can such uncomfortable behavior feel so comfortable? Earlier in the book I made the point that something that's known feels more secure than something that's unknown. This is because the unknown is scary. Rejection feels especially secure because it's so familiar—after all, didn't we learn it in our families? The words "familiar" and "families" even have the same origin.

Just as we did when we were children, we may still wish with all our hearts someone would be there to soothe the hurt, to comfort us.

Yet, ironically, it's the soothers and the nurturers that we tend to avoid. We choose the distancers instead because it feels safer, it's known, it's familiar. We may not know exactly what we want or need, but whatever it is, the people we choose sure aren't able to give it to us. How many times do we have to knock our heads against the wall of rejection, before we realize it only leads to sore heads?

Familiarity is one reason we tend to repeat behavior and relationship patterns, but there's a second explanation as well: the challenge of mastering the behavior. Some part of us seems to believe if we repeat something enough times we'll finally get it right. Hopefully we learn to recognize our patterns sooner or later—maybe even acquire some objectivity about them. That's when we can begin to notice that we are doing some things differently, that something seems to be working.

## Building Barriers

One man goes into work every day, sits at his hub, and focuses on the work in front of him. Office mates have tried a few times to be friendly, but since he wasn't responsive, they gave up. "I watch as the others walk together, talk together, go to lunch together, but I just stay to myself. For a long time I told myself I *like* being alone, but you know, sometimes secretly I wish I could join them. I've stayed to myself so long now, that they just sort of ignore me, so it seems that will never happen in a million years." Joining the group seems like such an overwhelming thought to him, but what about a small step? Is there maybe one person he finds himself wishing he could get to know a little better? He thought a few minutes. "Well, there's a woman who has a great smile. She actually reminds me of my favorite aunt. Sometimes I wish I could smile back." Would he be willing to try a little smile the next time she smiles? He said he'd think about it, but probably not. Within a couple of weeks, though, he did smile back and she smiled even more broadly. "It wasn't easy but it was sure easier than I expected. Maybe I'll say hello to her sometime."

One woman is so afraid that any leave-taking may be final that she freezes up, becomes distant, and abruptly turns away with a curt good-bye. Her boyfriend doesn't know what to think when she switches so quickly from warm to cold. He thinks it's something he did or said or didn't do or say. He has no idea her coolness to him is to protect herself from being hurt, because a part of her believes that when she says good-bye, she may never see him again.

Another woman also learned to avoid pain at great cost to herself. She grew up in a steel mill town. As early as she could remember she heard townspeople say, "You can't hurt steel." While her mother raged, she would chant silently to herself, "You can hit me but you can't hurt me 'cause you can't hurt steel! You can't hurt my spirit 'cause you can't hurt steel!"

And steel she became. "I developed a steel plate of armor around myself; I steel myself against any kind of hurt. Trouble is, I armored myself so well that no one can get close to me. I jump to conclusions and inflate situations in my mind until they become huge. Now I see why I reacted so strongly to my partner's plans to go alone to a reunion and reacquaint with old friends. I presumed I wasn't wanted and felt terribly left out, just like when I was a child."

She had a tendency to awfulize, too. "Before I knew it, I found myself thinking, 'Okay, the relationship is over. Which one of us will move out? How will we divide up the stuff?' Now I realize how I steel myself from hurt—'You can't hurt my spirit 'cause you can't hurt steel.'"

When taking a "tough" stance gets carried to the extreme a person may engage in rageful or bullying behavior. This, too, is a way of protecting oneself from feeling too vulnerable. While the person on the receiving end is fearful of the bully, it would probably help to remember that under that aggressive exterior of the bully is someone who is also scared or hurting. Blustery behavior is usually a cover for emotional pain and helps keep people away.

I once heard comedian Robin Williams poignantly describe what it was like to finally get to know his father. The quote went something like this: "It's like in *The Wizard of Oz*. Don't look behind the curtain—behind it is a terribly fragile man." I immediately was transported back to my childhood and how scared I was during the movie—with that huge booming voice and the billowing bursts of smoke—a smoke screen.

There are a number of "stay away" messages we may put out in order to try to protect ourselves from the anxiety of friendships or romantic relationships. But, if we guard ourselves against contact with others we may not establish relationships at all. So what do we do? We tell ourselves we don't want any relationships. And a big part of us really doesn't because we might get hurt again. A frequent refrain is, "I don't want to get involved with anyone right now. It's not worth the pain it might bring." If we do allow ourselves to take a step or two toward romantic involvement, we hold back from taking that leap because we don't feel secure enough. As one man says, "I want to run because I don't know how to stay. I'm afraid to depend on anyone because I know they'll let me down, so when a relationship warms up, I bolt." In the name of safety we'll hold back from displaying vulnerability or showing trust.

Oh yes, trust. So fragile. So tentative. So important. So complicated. Part of us wants to trust other people and part of us expects them to fail. That old familiar belief wins out again—if we trust someone we could feel hurt, rejected, betrayed, maybe even abandoned. It's especially difficult to restore trust if it was injured in childhood. Throughout life, even small disappointments seem like betrayals, and acts of betrayal can seem like the end of the world. So we learn to test the water before jumping in, but the testing never seems to stop. We don't really trust that others will pull through for us so we set up situations where they're supposed to prove to us that they're trustworthy. They usually fail because they have absolutely no clue it's a test. Remember the woman in chapter 3 who set up a timetable when she met a man she was attracted to, telling herself, "If he's interested in me, he'll call by Tuesday"? And the man who expected his partner to call from meetings to prove she was thinking of him? These kinds of tests are one way of saying, "I'll show you how rejectable I really am—I'll reject myself before you can reject me." Just another way of avoiding the pain of rejection by others.

One of the most frequent problems couples face is how to regain trust once it's been damaged. If there's one predictable repercussion from rejection or betrayal, it's damaged trust. Is it repairable? Can it be mended? Is there hope? It depends.

Sometimes it helps if the person who broke the trust can find a mutually acceptable way to "make amends." Amends can take many forms ranging from washing the other person's car weekly for a specified length of time, to performing a least favorite chore, to paying for a series of special dinners, to saying "I love you" on a regular basis. They can be serious or whimsical, but each form has one thing in common—each one represents an act of caring.

A few years ago a couple came to see me after a crisis occurred in their relationship. He had a one-night liaison with another woman two months earlier and had just told his wife about it. She was hurt and didn't think she could stay with him because her trust had been so badly damaged. She felt he had been "living a lie" from the time the event occurred. She felt betrayed.

I suggested making amends. What could he do for her so that she'd feel cared about? She decided to ask him to make her lunch every day for two months. This necessitated his getting up fifteen minutes earlier than usual and he isn't a morning person. But he did it, with love. Some days he even tucked little notes into her lunch bag.

When good friends have a falling out, amends might be just the thing to get the relationship back on track. Penny got involved in some political projects and didn't have much time for her friend Martha. Penny was so preoccupied that she wasn't even aware that her friend was upset. Martha, who tends to be pretty passive, didn't tell her, until the day she blew up and said some hurtful things. When they came to see me to try to work things out, I suggested creating amends that each could do—little acts of caring. Penny wanted Martha to take her to lunch at a new, pricey restaurant. Martha wanted Penny to call her twice a week for three months, which is the amount of time she felt ignored by her when she was working on the political campaign. And what was Penny to say on the phone? "Hi, I'm thinking about you."

Amends can also be a creative way to deal with teenage discipline without having to resort to the usually nonproductive measure of grounding the child. Because teens need peer support in times of stress, cutting them off from face-to-face or phone contact with friends is often counter-productive. One fifteen-year-old came up with the idea of mowing the lawn or weeding the garden for an amend. The parents were receptive and had other suggestions as well such as cleaning out the garage or washing the car.

## Oops—Too Close for Comfort

What happens if we *do* allow ourselves to get close to someone? For many of us, because we fear getting hurt again, anxiety builds. We learn to avoid the anxiety by creating distance. Picking fights, blaming, screaming, and slamming doors are all ways of pushing someone away. Other ways include retreating to another room, leaving the house, and withdrawing by freezing out the other person. Instead of expressing our feelings to the other person, we act them out through these distancing behaviors. (There's more about acting out in chapter 3.)

Danielle and Greg were experts at these behaviors and came into therapy to try to find a place they could come together instead of battling so much of the time. "I don't want to do this fighting anymore," Danielle said during the couples session. "I want to learn about my part in it." But Greg wasn't hearing her. He was still smarting from the anger she had just unleashed on him. Only a few minutes earlier, he'd tried to acknowledge his own role in the fighting. But she was so fired up about blaming him for never taking any responsibility for their clashes, she couldn't hear him. Neither Danielle nor Greg were feeling heard by the other.

How did Danielle's childhood experiences contribute to her belief that he couldn't hear her? She described what it was like growing up: "The truth was always disguised in my family. My side of the story never got heard and sometimes I was beaten for trying to tell it. With Greg I feel just as powerless as I did in my family. When I feel blamed, I feel trapped—like there's no way out. I believe if I make one little mistake I'll be punished, because when I was a child my parents' anger was so unpredictable. They didn't always explode at me, sometimes they'd freeze me out with long silences. But sometimes at the end of those silences I'd get hit. Now, whenever someone gives me the silent treatment, I think they're angry at me, and I can hardly stand the tension, the not knowing. When Greg walks away and retreats to his room, I freak out. I try to remember to tell myself, 'Silences don't have to mean anger, Danielle,' but waiting makes me nervous. I need a response right away." Danielle's early family experiences have been re-created in her marriage. She expects to be hurt instead of heard.

I watched Greg struggle to take in what she was saying, but he seemed to space out when some things were hard to hear. Danielle, quick to presume she wouldn't be heard, zeroed in on the few moments he wasn't able to hear her. She became indignant, "See, you never listen to me, you don't understand me." This is her old behavior pattern and she recognized it, "When I think he's not listening to me I scream at him or slam doors to make myself heard." And what did Greg do when Danielle raised her voice like that? He seemed to disappear—it was as if he folded in and over himself.

Why does Greg need to protect himself like that? "My parents always wanted something from me," he remembers. "They were always in my face. I had a sick, needy mother and a demanding, authoritarian father. No one paid attention to *my* needs. I tried so hard to do things the way they wanted, but I always seemed to disappoint them. My mother was like a huge cavity, nothing I did for her seemed to be enough. And my dad would always say, 'All I ask is one little thing from you and you can't even do that.' The pressure to be perfect was so great. I always felt so ashamed, so defective—like a huge failure. As the pressure built, I'd get anxious and withdraw because I felt trapped. I had a desperate need to escape, so I'd go into my room and go inside my head for a rest. I find myself doing the same thing now in my marriage. I just want to bury myself in my cave to sort things out and digest them."

Danielle was astounded, "You mean you run off to *sort things out?* All this time I thought you were trying to get away from me." Now she was able to see why he needed some space, but what could she do when her own anxiety built up as she waited for a resolution? So they made an agreement that might help in the interim. Before Greg retreated to his study, he'd try to remember to first validate her concerns and feelings and then set a time for when he'd return to continue the discussion.

Then we went to work on diagramming the reciprocal nature of their pattern together. We arbitrarily chose a place to start, looking at which behaviors came before and which came after. We selected an interaction—a moment when they had both felt close and connected. They were both able to acknowledge how difficult it was for them to trust that moment. Greg experienced pressure building from the intimacy. As it built he felt like a bubble about to burst and started pulling back. Danielle, sensing him pulling back, blamed him for not hearing her. He became more anxious and she misinterpreted his anxiety as anger, expecting him to explode at any moment. Greg, uncomfortable with the rising pressure, tried to create some breathing room for himself by picking a fight with her. She, in turn, tried to protect her hurt feelings by lashing out. When she angrily accused him of not hearing her, he perceived this as blame and himself as inadequate. His old "never good enough" issues were triggered and he felt trapped by her demands. In *his* eyes she inflated and he diminished.

But Danielle wasn't feeling very big. Her pain was overwhelming and she tried to even the score by zeroing right in on his sore spot. She piled blame on him. Now it was Greg's turn to try to even things up, "When I get backed into a corner I start to pull back and disappear, so

I puff myself up and get harsh." As he became more and more fierce, she perceived him as threatening. In *her* eyes he inflated and she diminished. At this point they became emotionally entangled, and a struggle for space took place. Before things got out of hand, Greg turned on his heel and left the house (as he often did) "to sort things out." It took her a while, but after he returned Danielle eventually reached out to him and tried to make peace. Figure 3 illustrates this scenario. This led to an intimate moment or two—and then the cycle began again.

The childhood experiences of Danielle and Greg cause them both to feel trapped in the relationship. Feelings of desperation overcome Danielle when she can't get into Greg's private space long enough to feel heard. He sees her attempts at contact as "smothering," and he panics when he thinks he can't escape. So he escapes by leaving. She feels trapped if she

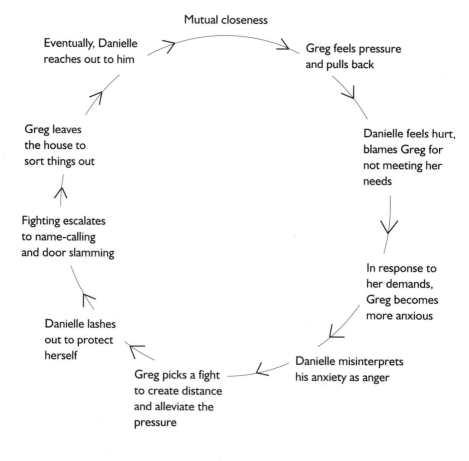

Figure 3: The Anxiety Circle

doesn't have a "way in," while he feels trapped if he doesn't have a "way out."

When Danielle and Greg feel threatened like this they both try to protect themselves by fighting. When she felt invalidated, she would fight to be heard. She'd hammer away at him, trying to get his attention. When he felt trapped he'd create distance the fastest way he knew—he'd pick a fight. "Picking fights helps the anxiety bubble come to the surface," he acknowledges, "I guess I learned to do that at a young age."

Adults who pick fights with their partners often learned this technique in childhood in order to protect themselves. Many abused children discover how to provoke abuse in order to control it. Waiting for the abuse to happen is so nerve-racking that many children learn to "arrange" for it. This way they feel more in control of the time and place it occurs. Getting it over with alleviates their anxiety because there are no surprises. As strange as it sounds, provoking abuse helps children feel safer in an unsafe world—it makes life more manageable.

> **Some children learn to avoid anxiety by provoking abuse—that way there are no surprises.**

Provoking abuse can be helpful to children in other ways, too. Some families have a rule that expressing feelings is not okay, and the children learn to deaden feelings, to cut them off. So they stir things up by inciting a little trouble in order to feel alive again. Is it any wonder that they continue this behavior into adulthood? Picking fights is a twofer: it not only allows them to feel in control and but more alive, too.

Giving mixed messages is another way of creating more comfortable distance. A fight takes place here, too, but an internal one. The conflict comes from our two opposing voices, the part of us that craves closeness and the part that's scared to death of it. When this ambivalence surfaces you might find yourself doing "the approach/avoidance dance," which Lillian Rubin describes so well in *Intimate Strangers*, giving out mixed messages such as, "Go away a little closer." It's as if someone is holding up one hand in a beckoning gesture while the other hand is signaling, "Stop—don't come any closer." It's maddening and it's hard to say who's more confused, the sender of the message or the receiver.

Sometimes we assume an "I don't need you" attitude. One partner may unconsciously pull back, sending the other partner messages like "I'm not willing to emotionally invest in you," "I'm not sure you're going to be here for me and that scares me." When people get scared in a relationship they get very creative about creating distance. One man "called in the troops," when he found himself caring too much about someone.

Perhaps he emitted some sort of scent or sound that filled the air with a plea for help. As if on cue, several old lovers began to demand his attention, day and night. And it worked—it didn't take long for the present relationship to break up.

Some people operate from a place of "I'll reject you before you can reject me." Usually this translates to, "I'll leave you before you can leave me." And the "leaving" doesn't have to be physical. Withdrawing and giving the silent treatment can create a relationship crisis as well. This can be devastating if one or both people have abandonment fears, such as John and Mindy.

John remembers his dad as a "cyclone," devastating everything in his path when he was angry. When John was only seven years old, he'd leave the house and walk around and around the block in order to feel safe, out of the cyclone's path. Neither parent was accessible to him. The father was often preoccupied in his own workaholic world. His way of making contact with his son was through criticism and anger. His mother did nothing to protect him from his father. He felt rejected and ignored; he began to believe he was worthless and inadequate.

Mindy's mother was frequently drunk and constantly threatened to abandon the little girl. Her mom would walk out of the house and drive around for hours, leaving a young and very frightened Mindy home alone. She worried that her mom would die in that car because she was so drunk. She took her mother's actions as a personal rejection, believing she must be so bad that her mother wanted to leave her. She grew up with vivid fears of abandonment that would be reactivated with important people in her life.

Now whenever John and Mindy wanted attention from each other, things snowballed. Mindy often approached him at the wrong time, for example, when he was in the middle of writing a report. John, wanting to escape from her questions, would snap, "Leave me alone now." She heard this as a reflection of her "badness," and felt rejected. She got frightened and created distance by raising her voice and escalating the conflict.

True to his old pattern, John reacted to her fury by leaving the house to walk the dog. Sometimes he slammed the door in the process. Her abandonment fears escalated because she took his words and actions personally and felt vulnerable. She dealt with her anxiety by collapsing on the bed and pulling the covers over her head, which reminded him of how his parents also withdrew from him. Then it was his turn to feel rejected.

Sometimes Mindy got enraged at him but couldn't put words to it so she acted it out by flailing at him. Once she threw a pitcher of water on him. She unknowingly re-created John's abusive "cyclone" father. It's no wonder he reacted so strongly either in fury or by needing to vacate the premises immediately.

John developed his expertise at vacating premises in childhood when his family would pick up and move from one town to another without warning. Once he had to sit through Sunday morning church services knowing the family would be moving to another state as soon as services were over. Since he was forbidden to tell anyone of the impending move he sat in the pew next to his best friend, knowing he'd probably never see him again. He was not allowed to say goodbye.

Is it any wonder his adult history with friends and lovers consists of sudden leave-takings, no goodbyes, and truncated relationships? Sudden departures have been a way of life for him. It's not surprising that he walked out on Mindy because this is the way he has learned to fend off anxiety. This behavior functioned in two ways for him. First, he recognized the need to leave a chaotic environment just as he did when he walked around the block as a little boy. And second, he felt more in control when he initiated leaving Mindy—not like when his family forced him to suddenly leave his friends in childhood.

Although John and Mindy had been together for over four years, they'd never talked to each other about these painful childhood experiences until they began couples therapy. In the second session, Mindy was able to tell John how vulnerable she felt when he left the house. She told him how, when she crawled under the covers, she really wanted to say, "Please hold me. I need you to be with me." And for the first time, John became aware of her needs and tried to respond. He also learned to put words to his feelings instead of acting them out. He recognizes that while "leaving" is a fine way to take care of himself if he needs a time-out, it's best to let Mindy in on his experience and his need for some space. So in order not to fuel her abandonment fears, he tries to remember to assure her before he leaves that he'll be back soon. It's true that in the heat of an argument it is hard to remember you have the option of taking a time-out, much less to try to reassure your antagonist that you're not leaving forever! But it works if you can remember.

How does someone with such huge fears of abandonment hook up with someone who threatens to leave? How do couples manage go find each other and make such a fascinating complementary fit? It's as if they're wearing a sign proclaiming, "I'm looking for someone to tap into my abandonment fears, my fears of rejection and invalidation. No others need apply!"

John and Mindy triggered childhood feelings of invalidation and rejection in each other. They each interpreted actions of the other as statements of personal rejection, when in fact each of them was on automatic pilot, responding to painful feelings from their own childhood experiences and trying unsuccessfully to avoid those feelings.

# Part Two

# Identifying Those Old Hurts

# 6

# You're More Trouble
# Than You're Worth

## Subtle and Not So
## Subtle Messages

Since taking things personally is usually connected to rejection messages, it's important to learn to recognize these messages. Rejection is a type of psychological maltreatment and can take a myriad of forms, sometimes obvious, sometimes subtle. Physical, sexual, severe verbal abuse, and neglect of children are observable, obvious acts. But it is not only the obvious acts that cause lifelong damage. Underneath each of these acts is a message of rejection to a child. Keep in mind that the forms of psychological maltreatment may not be as obvious as physical or sexual abuse, but it is still abuse and can be just as devastating. Some of the subtle behaviors described in this chapter may seem inconsequential and indeed they might be if they just happened once. But rejection, hurts, and disappointments usually don't just happen once. They repeat over time, each incident becoming superimposed on another. Children are so imprintable, so impressionable, that acts repeated again and again can cause long-term damage to adult behavior. These early experiences influence how people respond to life events.

## Fear, Anxiety, and Rejection

Abused and neglected children see the world differently from other children. It's as if they are looking through a wavy lens resulting in some distortion and confusion. Occurrences that seem insignificant to others can take on huge and frightening magnitudes. Children may feel in danger where there appears to be no provocation, yet to these children the situation takes on life-or-death proportions. As one woman said, "When I was growing up, if I made a misstep it could mean my life."

> **Abused children see the world differently and are exquisitely tuned to danger.**

Dr. Bruce Perry of the Baylor College of Medicine in Houston describes how abuse affects children's brains, where neural circuitry helps regulate responses to stress. Since these children are exquisitely tuned to danger, at the slightest threat their hearts race, their stress hormones surge, and their brains anxiously track the nonverbal cues that might signal the next attack.

Fear and anxiety are constant companions to abused children. They live on edge, just waiting for the abuse to come again. It's not a matter of *if* it comes, but *when* it comes. So they're always holding their breath, waiting for the next blow to fall, trying to protect themselves at any cost. Children learn to live with this ever-present anxiety. It becomes a part of their identity and follows them into adult relationships.

"It's as if I'm addicted to anxiety," said one woman. "It's like a high, it gets my energy going. I get obsessed with thoughts of each new romantic involvement. I think about how the contact will go, what they'll say, what I'll say. But the anticipation is more of anxiety than of joy."

Another woman put it this way: "A little bit of anxiety actually leads to more discomfort for me than a lot of anxiety. When I was little, I lived and breathed massive amounts of anxiety all the time. So when a small problem comes along, I get all revved up and build it into a large problem with lots of tension. This kind of drama actually makes me less anxious because it's more familiar."

Waiting for a partner or child to come home when he or she is very late and hasn't phoned can lead to big-time anxiety. And the minute the person walks through the door, it can be a dramatic moment. I remember when I was little and a friend and I would walk home from dance class together. It was a long walk on a busy street, so, looking back, I can imagine how uneasy my mother might have been. However, I didn't consider her state of mind when my friend urged me to stop at her church with her and light candles. She even taught me some prayers. We were there quite a while. When I arrived home, my mother began screaming at me, but she never once told me she was worried. Only angry. Real angry.

I hear similar stories from couples I know. It's hard not to take it personally if, when you walk through the door, your partner is angry at you because you're late and didn't call. It's hard not to get defensively angry right back. Try to remember that underneath the anger is most likely concern and worry—for *you*.

Dramatic moments seem to be necessary in the lives of some people. "I'm an invent-a-crisis kind of person," said one man I know. "I like the rush of adrenaline—it makes me feel more alive!" And so he creates one crisis after another in his life. Unfortunately he often does this by picking fights with his partner, who overreacts to these provocations, taking them as a personal attack.

Another man is a nervous wreck whenever he has to sit with some anxiety. The anxiety sometimes crescendos into a panic. He recognizes the feeling from his past, "It's like waiting for my dad to come home to beat me. So whenever I'm anxious I do everything possible to control it. I do this by trying to control the people in my life."

So now, when fear or anxiety gets triggered, it's as if we put on those wavy glasses again. Situations seem inflated, even gargantuan. Sometimes we find ourselves overreacting to subtle actions of others and we ask ourselves why. The answer is: Rejection.

## Acceptance

To better understand rejection, let's talk about its opposite: Acceptance. Growing up with acceptance means growing up feeling that all's right with the world—feeling loved and cared about, safe and secure, knowing early on that needs are going to be met. Acceptance is feeling validated for who you are and what you think. Acceptance means receiving verbal and nonverbal messages that say: "I accept your separateness, your differentness, your uniqueness. It's okay to be yourself. I don't expect you to think, feel, or see things the same as I do."

Acceptance means parents recognize and respect the differences between their own needs and the needs of their children. They don't confuse their own thoughts or feelings with those of their children. They respect the physical and emotional space of their children, enabling children to develop a well-defined sense of themselves—with good personal boundaries and adequate self-esteem—that can be carried into adulthood.

In an optimal parent-child relationship, the parent recognizes and meets the child's physical and emotional needs by

- Offering love, patience, understanding, empathy, praise, acceptance, and a sense of self-worth

- Participating in the child's experience

- Responding to the child and providing encouragement and direction

- Giving the child opportunities for learning and mastering skills

- Providing a sense of security and safety

- Supplying warmth, cleanliness, and nourishment, and care when the child is sick

- Offering stability and continuity of care

- Providing an adequate standard of reality

- Teaching the child appropriate behavior, limits, and inner controls

- Establishing consequences for inappropriate behavior

- Supplying social experiences outside the family

- Accepting who the child is as an individual and encouraging the child's expanding independence

- Preparing the child for life, instead of protecting the child from life

In this optimal relationship, children flourish, developing a realistic sense of themselves and learning to trust and feel safe. Children develop the capacity to love and be loved, cope with frustration, experience a range of emotions, and communicate these feelings. Through feeling accepted by others, children learn to accept themselves, they learn to take themselves seriously. From self-acceptance springs self-confidence, self-reliance, self-assurance, self-esteem, self-respect, and self-satisfaction.

What happens when children grow up with a lack of acceptance? They learn to invalidate themselves, to reject themselves. When children's sense of self is diminished, they feel more and more like nonpeople. Self-worth, self-assurance, self-confidence, self-respect, self-esteem, self-regard, and self-acceptance all become nonexistent. They begin to feel they have little control over their environment and see the world as rejecting and inhospitable. Sometimes they may begin to see themselves as the target of outside forces and they may start to take things personally.

In discussing acceptance it's helpful to look at early attachment behavior. Much has been made of the importance of a sustained gaze between parent and infant. In *Intimate Worlds,* Maggie Scarf refers to this sustained gaze as "eye-love." Many observers have commented on how a newborn appears to be fascinated with the face of the caretaker, and there are various speculations as to why. Allan Schore's *Affect Regulation and the Origin of the Self* discusses these various theories. One theory is that objects about ten inches away from the infant are most clearly in focus, and this is the distance between parent's and infant's faces. Another fascinating speculation is how the source of the infant's attraction might very well be due to a flash of light processed by and reflected off the parent's eye onto the eyes of the infant. This sparkle in the parent's eyes stimulates the baby to gaze into the parent's face, and hopefully the parent reciprocates the gazing.

"The human soul *feeds on light,*" states A. H. Almaas, in *The Point of Existence.* "This light is awareness . . ." and in order to grow, the baby must be seen with "love, value, openness, compassion, strength, intelligence, joy, satisfaction, peacefulness. . . ." Does the parent "see" the baby and return the gaze? Or is the parent preoccupied or looking away? What happens when the baby becomes excited and averts his or her eyes to avoid overstimulation during these intense periods of interaction? Is the parent attuned to the child's alternating need for attention and withdrawal? Or does the parent take it personally if eyes are averted? (I once heard a story that illuminates the power of this gaze: A local wildlife refuge instructs volunteers *not* to make eye contact with rescued baby birds because the birds might become attached to humans and have trouble returning to the wild.) It seems as though some of us are always seeking out that light in the eyes of others but don't always find it. In fact, there may be times in our perpetual search to bask in "the gleam," that we stumble over "the look" instead. You know the look I mean—the raised eyebrow or the narrowed eyes signifying criticism or judgment, impatience or indifference.

It's not uncommon for infants or children who are sensitive to their parents' actions to feel rejected and turn away. They become unwilling to again risk the parents' coldness or inattention. So they may turn their heads or push their parents away, refusing a bottle or food. An insecure parent may be convinced a child is purposefully avoiding him or her, when in fact, the child is really avoiding the pain of another rejection as we saw in chapter 5. And so rejection begets rejection, becoming a protective maneuver to avoid getting hurt again in a world that has become unsafe and untrustworthy.

---

Sometimes we look for "the gleam" in someone's eye only to find "the look" instead.

---

How do we learn at all costs to avoid putting ourselves in the position of being rejected again? This reciprocal nature of rejection was researched by University of California, Berkeley, psychologist Mary Main and anthropologist Ruth Goldwyn. In a study of attachment behavior, infants of twelve months were briefly separated from their mothers in a laboratory situation in order to study their responses at reunion. Most infants responded by being glad to see their mothers, actively greeted them, and wanted to reestablish contact. However, a few infants didn't seem glad to see their mothers at all, and responded with distress at the reunions. These infants avoided the mothers by moving away from them, turning their heads or their bodies away, or ignoring them.

Why did some of the infants avoid their mothers upon reunion? The researcher believe the answer lies the the degree to which the mother accepts or rejects the child's attachment to her. The mothers of these avoidant infants had repeatedly rejected their children's attempts at physical and emotional contact. So when the mothers were separated from their infants in the laboratory setting, the children appeared to perceive these absences as another rejection by their mothers. The researchers hypothesized that the avoidance behaviors were an attempt by the infants to try to avoid the further emotional pain of rejection. If this is true, then avoidant behavior could be a stance children take in order to avoid a repeat of painful rejection feelings—a way of protecting themselves.

How do children come to see the world as so treacherous? What goes wrong? Let's look first at how healthy, enduring attachment develops. Children have basic dependency needs for food, comfort, and protection. This includes predictable feedings, relatively dry diapers, and a safe environment. They depend on parents or other adults who they see as better able to cope with the world. Children need to feel connected to their parents and develop a feeling of safety. When these basic needs are met, it promotes attachment, a sense of well-being, a secure feeling that all's right with the world. According to British psychiatrist John Bowlby, the child comes to trust that the parent can provide "a secure base from which the child or adolescent can make forays into the outside world . . . [and can] return knowing for sure that he [or she] will be welcomed . . . nourished physically . . . emotionally comforted if distressed, reassured if frightened." In other words, the child feels encouraged and validated for being inquisitive because the parent is supportively giving permission for the child to wander off, explore the world, and then return to the security of the parent.

Researchers find that whether children feel secure or insecure depends on how responsive their parents are to them—whether the parents are sensitive to their children's signals, or whether they block or reject attachment behavior. Children who feel secure in their attachment to parents, generally grow up to be secure adults. They learn to risk asking for what they want and need from others. They learn to accept themselves, as they have felt accepted by their parents.

Suppose however these needs are not met or are met only now and then. Depending on how responsive their caregivers are to their needs, infants develop three basic attachment styles: *secure, avoidant,* and *anxious/ambivalent.* If parents are responsive and emotionally available, children feel trusting and secure and this continues into adult relationships. If parents are nonresponsive and unavailable, children also become nonresponsive and avoid emotional connection in relationships. If parents are sometimes responsive and sometimes not, children become both anxious and ambivalent in relationships. The anxiety comes from not knowing what to expect at any given moment from a parent, and the ambivalence comes from not daring to care for fear of being disappointed. These early attachment styles are similar to styles of adult interactions, although most certainly adult relationships can be more complex. A fourth attachment style, *insecure-disorganized/disoriented,* is described by psychologists Mary

Main, Nancy Kaplan, and Jude Cassidy. The child shows strong avoidance behavior and acts confused, dazed, and apprehensive. For more information on recent studies of how adult attachment is similar to infant attachment, see chapter notes.

Sometimes certain attachment behaviors are not what they seem. Bowlby makes a distinction between enduring attachment and attachment *behavior.* Attachment behavior can be various forms of behavior the child may use to obtain a desired closeness with a parent. Although the attachment behavior may be heightened or intensified in certain situations it doesn't necessarily mean that the attachment becomes stronger. Is a child who clings to his or her parent necessarily more attached than a child who clings less? Or simply more insecure? Parents often misjudge this dependent behavior. When children are sick or anxious and exhibit clingy behavior, parents may reward the children's overdependency and mistakenly encourage more clinging. This kind of behavior may be anxious attachment, resulting when young children don't develop trust that a secure base exists. They're afraid that parent or other caretaker might become inaccessible or unavailable, or disappear altogether—abandoning them. There it is, that *A* word that so many of us dread.

Abandonment is certainly one of the most powerful fears of rejection we can have. The anxiety that surrounds it is familiar to many of us. We lose confidence that significant people can be accessible to us. We are afraid they will not be here for us when we need them, they might disappear from our lives, they might stop loving us. This childhood anxiety stays with us into adulthood and can dominate our relationships, leading to anxious, clingy behavior with people who are important to us.

Psychologist/anthropologist Dr. Ronald P. Rohner has studied acceptance and rejection in over one hundred cultures. He defines acceptance as the expression of parental "warmth and affection, indicating support and approval" and rejection as "the absence or significant withdrawal of warmth, affection, or love." He suggests "the warmth and affection each of us received as a child can be placed on a continuum from a great deal to virtually none." This "warmth dimension" of parenting is marked at one end by parental acceptance and at the other end by rejection.

What kind of experience did you have growing up? Close your eyes for a moment and imagine a continuum with acceptance at one end and rejection at the other. Now visualize along this continuum the many subtle and not-so-subtle hues of parental words and actions. Add to this the many shades of parental indifference or emotional unavailability. Picture yourself with all the important people in your life. What was your experience with your mother? Your father? Siblings? Grandparents? Teachers? Neighbors? Did you experience a solid connection with them? Did you feel valued and loved? Were your experiences closer to the "great deal"—the acceptance—end of the continuum? Or were they on the "virtually none" end—where you consistently felt invalidated and discounted?

It doesn't matter whether words or actions are active or passive, direct or indirect, latent or blatant, intentional or not. Parents might be emotionally unavailable and ignore a child, or they might tease or blame and belittle, or throw things, or threaten abandonment or harm. Either way, the child perceives the message as: "Nobody cares about you, nobody loves you." This perception then gets carried into adulthood, affecting all areas of life.

For instance, take the example we discussed in the Introduction of an infant left unattended in the crib. A woman I know had this experience. She'd cry for hours, but no one would come to feed or change her. A message was imprinted from that time and has colored most of her adult relationships: "No one will be there when I need them."

So, what happens if we believe we can't depend on the important people in our lives? How can we ever trust that anyone will be there for us? When we feel rejected or neglected by the people we depend on to meet our needs, it's so confusing—how can people who are supposed to love us be so neglectful or hurtful? In fact, sometimes the people we want to love and trust, the people we want to protect us, are the ones that we most need to be protected from. So we try to make some sense of the confusion and give ourselves reasons for it. We may tell ourselves something like, "If our parents don't care enough about us to take care of us, we must not be worth loving or being taken care of—therefore, we must be bad." This kind of thinking is natural for small children, who see the world in terms of "good and bad" and "black and white" because their thinking hasn't developed enough to see shades of gray.

So for the children it comes down to making a decision about who's good and who's bad—themselves or their caretakers. Because they depend on their parents and need them to be "good," they'll usually designate themselves as "bad." They're not big enough to take care of themselves, and they depend on their parents, even if the parents are not very dependable. The children may not get fed when they're hungry, but if parents don't provide the food, who else will? Even though they may not get their diapers changed often enough, who else is there to change them?

Some children learn to fend for themselves, however. One woman recalls how she'd often get a fresh diaper from the container in her bedroom and carry it to one of her parents when she couldn't stand being wet any longer. What a brave little girl! At two years old she had the presence of mind to know to get her own diaper. She somehow knew in order to survive she had to look out after her own basic needs because no one else would. And as she was experiencing this painful rejection, she was learning a dangerous lesson. Because her parents were treating her needs as unimportant, she learned to reject herself as worthless and insignificant as well.

If you've ever taken an introductory psychology class, you might remember Dr. Harlow and his experiments with monkeys and attachment behavior. The most well-known of these experiments involved cloth and wire mesh "dummy" mothers. Infant rhesus monkeys were separated from their mothers at birth and placed with replicas of mother monkeys. Some were fashioned from terry cloth and some from only wire mesh. The terry cloth monkeys provided a source of "contact comfort" to the baby monkeys, but they could not provide nourishment. The wire mesh monkeys could mechanically squirt milk, and this was the only nourishment the infants could receive. Most of the babies would forego their milk, choosing instead to cling for hours to the terry cloth monkeys for comfort.

The more creative infants managed the best of both worlds. They would hold on desperately to the cloth monkey "mother." At the same time they would stretch their bodies backwards toward the wire mesh monkey, grasping for the mechanical bottle of milk. Can you imagine the desperation and frustration these babies felt?

Karen knows that feeling well. "When I was little I'd cling to my father, but like the cloth monkey, he couldn't return my hugs. He didn't know how. But my mother was another story. She was cruel. She wasn't just a wire monkey, she was a barbed-wire monkey." Karen perceives her mother's belittling as a purposeful action. She sees her father's unresponsiveness as an unintentional inaction. Yet, she feels equally rejected by both parents. The intent doesn't have to be purposeful for children to feel unloved and unappreciated. At issue here is the long-term effects of the message, even if the action seemed inconsequential at the time and even if there did not seem to be any damage to the child at the time.

Some people were lucky enough to begin to learn self-acceptance in childhood, but things didn't go quite that well for many of us. What happened that made us experience rejection as a way of life? Let's take a look at the kinds of rejection messages that touched us when we were children. Especially the subtle ones, because they're the most insidious.

## Parental Inaction

I want to emphasize again that many messages or acts of rejection or other abuse are more subtle than obvious. In fact, many are not acts at all, but rather inaction, inattention, or inaccessibility. Many are not intended to hurt, but the hurt can last a lifetime. For example, let's look at the parent who treats the child as a second-class family member. One woman recalled how her mother only had time for her when her father wasn't around. "She couldn't even comfort me when he was around. She was always warning me, 'Don't disturb your father because he's in bed, sick.' (He was in bed alright—not sick, but very drunk.) I had to be so quiet that I learned to contract into a pinpoint, withdrawing from everybody and everything. I went invisible. I still do."

Then there's the parent who "turns off" to the child. Andrea tells about how her earliest memories of clothes shopping with her mother affected her for years. "We'd wander through the aisles, and Mom would pick out clothes for me to try on. If I didn't agree with her choice of clothes for me, her face would turn off. She'd withdraw and turn her back to me. After a few very long minutes she'd say, 'I don't know why I even bother taking you shopping.' Now I can see she was taking it personally, but back then I didn't know that and I blamed myself. I wanted to say, 'Mom, what's wrong? What did I do wrong?' It was like she thought I'd crossed her somehow. Now I'm afraid to disagree with people that I depend on for love. They might turn their backs on me. They might leave me. And I guess because I expect it to happen, it usually does."

Sometimes parents emotionally "vacate the premises." When they're not there, children feel discounted—so they tell themselves they don't count. When parents emotionally "disappear," there is little or no emotional contact. They might disappear behind a newspaper or into slicing onions when a child is trying to talk to them. Or the disappearance can be into the fog of alcohol or drugs. Subtle rejection is extremely difficult for children to deal with. This lack of connection can cause as much or more psychological damage as verbal abuse. When a parent screams insults at a child it's most certainly hurtful, but at least it is contact. When a parent emotionally "disappears," the connection is severed.

There are a number of reasons why parents are "not there." Frequently it's because of substance abuse, depression, or emotional illness. Maybe they don't know how to be "with" their children because their own parents weren't very good models and rather than try and fail, they simply retreat into silence. Perhaps their own childhood fears of abandonment prompt the distance they create from their children. Fear keeps them from caring too much, investing too much love in the child. What if something happened to the child—like sickness or even death? They may be worrying so much that they are afraid to get close to the child. If something should happen, the loss would be too unbearable. By keeping emotional distance, they avoid these feelings and the possibility of pain. As Judith Viorst writes in *Necessary Losses*, "We cannot lose someone we care for if we don't care."

Children don't understand any of this, they only know they need something from a father or mother who just isn't there. When these children grow up, they are often attracted to people who can't be there for them either. They re-create the same rejection scenario again and again. However, they can change this behavior by identifying its source.

# The Psychological Effects of Abuse

Experts consider rejection messages especially abusive because they have potentially damaging long-term effects. Rejection is the common thread in every type of abuse—psychological, physical, and sexual. Physical and sexual abuse are easier to define because they are observable, concrete, and dramatic. Psychological maltreatment is more difficult to define because it seems so elusive.

It is difficult to determine where one type of abuse ends and another begins. Psychological maltreatment is embedded in all other forms of child maltreatment, and conveys "the message that the child is worthless, flawed, unloved, endangered, or only valuable in meeting someone else's needs."

Psychiatrist John Bowlby describes some detrimental patterns of parenting that he sees as contrary to the process of attachment. They include the following:

- One of both parents being persistently unresponsive to the child's care—eliciting behavior or actively disparaging and rejecting
- Frequent discontinuities of parenting
- Persistent threats by parent not to love the child
- Threats by parent to abandon the family
- Threats by one or both parents to desert or kill the other or to commit suicide
- Inducing a child to feel guilty by claiming that his or her behavior is or will be responsible for the parent's illness or death

Now let's take an in-depth look at what constitutes psychological maltreatment.

Based on the work of Dr. Stuart N. Hart of the Office for the Study of the Psychological Rights of the Child and his task force, of which I was a member, the American Professional Society on the Abuse of Children has categorized psychological maltreatment in the following ways:

- **Spurning** (hostile rejecting/degrading)—includes public humiliation, belittling, ridiculing, shaming, and consistently singling the child out for punishment or criticism
- **Terrorizing**—behavior that threatens to physically hurt, kill, abandon, or place the child or child's loved ones in recognizably dangerous situations
- **Isolating**—consistently denying the child opportunities for interacting inside or outside the home (This includes confining the child or placing unreasonable limitations on the child's freedom of movement)
- **Exploiting/corrupting**—encouraging child to develop self-destructive, antisocial, criminal, deviant, or other maladaptive behaviors (This includes micromanaging the child's life, encouraging developmentally inappropriate drug-related or sexual behavior, or interfering with appropriate autonomy or cognitive development. It also includes using the child as a pawn in divorce proceedings.)

- **Denying emotional responsiveness** (ignoring)—includes ignoring a child's attempts and needs to interact
- **Unwarranted denial of mental health care, medical care, and education** (neglect)—acts that ignore, refuse to allow, or fail to provide necessary treatment for the needs of the child

One or two isolated incidents are generally not considered psychological maltreatment. Rather it is extreme incidents or repeated patterns of psychological maltreatment that usually lead to long-term effects.

You may notice that rejection messages are represented by each category, and cover a vast range, from ignoring and invalidating the child to physical or sexual mistreatment. Teasing, cynicism, and sarcasm often have undertones of anger, and, whether intended or not, are heard as rejecting. Then there is verbal battering such as belittling, shaming, criticizing, or publicly humiliating the child. But rejection does not only spring from harsh words or actions. It is also present in demeaning looks or tones of voice.

---

Rejection messages are embedded in all types of
abuse—physical, sexual, and psychological.

---

Rejection messages are difficult to lasso and define because they are often subtle and can't be seen. For example, if we witness a child being beaten with a belt or spoon, we can imagine the pain the child experiences, maybe we can even see the welts. However, it is not so easy to envision what the child feels when he or she is being beaten with a psychological spoon. Unless, of course, you've been there yourself.

Acts of physical or sexual abuse are more obvious, so children find them easier to explain to themselves. Because emotional hurts are more insidious, it is harder to make sense out of them. It's not the beating or the sexual abuse alone that causes long-term damage. It is the accompanying messages of rejection and betrayal that potentially travel with a child into adulthood. Physical bruises most often will heal; emotional bruises frequently do not.

So, in addition to experiencing physical or sexual abuse, the child also feels rejected, disregarded, and unprotected. Long-term emotional damage results when the child looks to someone for love and protection, and that person hurts and betrays them. As one woman who was sexually abused by her grandfather puts it, "If my own grandfather found me so expendable, won't others? Now I understand why I'm so afraid of relationships: I'd rather be alone than discarded. At work I find myself being ultraresponsible so they can't possibly think I'm expendable."

My own research involved looking at the effects of perceived child-hood rejection on the capacity for adult intimacy. Fifty-two couples reported whether or not they felt accepted or rejected by their primary caretaker between the ages of seven and twelve.

Interestingly, feeling rejected in the family did not necessarily lead to a lower capacity for intimacy. The mediating factor was what the children told themselves about the rejection and whether they developed low self-esteem and self-confidence, dependency, hostility, inability to express feelings, low tolerance for stress, and difficulty trusting the world as a secure and safe place. Some individuals seemed to be more resilient and didn't develop these belief systems or long-term psychological effects. You'll read more about how resiliency affects a child's development in chapter 10.

Recognizing the messages of rejection and their possible consequences is an important first step when you are taking something personally. It allows you to begin to separate the "now" of the moment from the "then" of your early childhood experiences and to gain some objectivity about it. By getting down to the origins, by recognizing your core issues, by immersing yourself in those feelings for a while, you can learn from your experiences and begin to change old patterns. Sometimes we're destined to repeat things until we get them right.

---

**Learning to recognize early rejection messages allows you to separate the "then" from the "now" and to gain some perspective.**

---

Hugh has been upset since the new owners took over at work. Now the rules have changed and there seem to be two sets, spoken and unspoken. It is especially confusing to him because that's how it used to be in his family when he was a child. He had to keep guessing what people wanted from him, always worrying he would make a mistake or make the wrong choice. For example, he'd spend hours trying to figure out which chair to sit in. Just as he thought he had it figured out, his dad decided it was the wrong chair. Hugh's punishment for guessing wrong was a fist to his face. If his dad forgot to take off his ring there would be a big gash next to Hugh's eye.

Hugh recently made a mistake at work that a customer caught. The mistake could have been costly for the company and Hugh was distraught about screwing up. "I went into a complete panic mode. I made a mistake, I wasn't good enough. What if I'm found out? I had a split second to see what the panic was about. There it was staring me in the face: 'I'm alone here. I could be abandoned.' Then I practiced what we talk about in sessions. I knew I had to get some distance from it, had to 'walk alongside it' and not drown in it." In other words, Hugh was able to separate the "then" from the "now," maintaining some objectivity.

Hugh and I explored together what the "then" was like—all the times he felt so overwhelmed as a child. Where did those feelings come from? He remembered, "If I did something my mom and dad didn't like, I was afraid they would leave me; they wouldn't come back home. If I made a mistake it meant I wasn't good enough for them to come home to me."

Hugh's face took on a frightened look as he was remembering being seven years old. It was the fear of a seven year old, not an adult. He remembers how his parents went with his sister to run errands and left him to fend for himself. He was never sure if they planned to return. This memory is an important piece of information for Hugh. Now he can give himself some distance from such enormous feelings. He can "walk along beside himself." He can ask himself, "How old am I feeling right now? What is familiar about this?" There may be just a split second of recognition but that's all it takes to get some clarity and some distance. Observing gets the flow going and opens up space for choices.

Once he had begun to separate the "then" from the "now," Hugh freed himself up from the usual overwhelming feelings. Now he can re-mind himself that he no longer has to feel the seven-year-old's fear. A choice exists for him now, and he can put this childhood memory in perspective so it won't take over with such force. He can be more in control of his feelings, instead of allowing his feelings to be in control of him. Hugh says, "I keep trying to find the magic switch that will turn off these old responses. But now I realize they will always be with me—except now I can be more in control of them."

> Walk alongside yourself. Observing gets the flow going and opens up the space to make choices.

The underlying rejection message that accompanies any abuse is powerful: "You are not valued, you are not respected, you are not loved." Here are some of the all-too-frequent rejection messages heard in child-hood. And these experiences can have considerable long-term effects, as this first example demonstrates.

## "You're Imagining It!" (Spurning)

The young black man on the TV talk show screamed in rage, "Are you trying to tell me I didn't see what I saw or hear what I heard?" His words were directed at Los Angeles police officer Stacy Koons, after the trial in which Koons and three other Los Angeles policemen were acquitted of using excessive force in the infamous beating of Rodney King.

This man's words offer a key to understanding why rioting occurred after this first trial but calm prevailed following the second. The first verdict discounted our perceptions of the beatings. The second jury looked at reality and validated it.

By acquitting the four policemen in the first trial, the jury was, in effect, saying, "You really didn't see the beatings. It didn't happen, you were imagining it."

I began to realize the powerful effect of this invalidation when several of my private psychotherapy clients expressed shock and outrage when they learned of the acquittals. They reacted with the same intensity as the young black man on the TV talk show. This wasn't just anger—this was rage. Remember that anger is related to "now" feelings, but rage usually comes from old feelings—childhood experiences that get triggered in the present.

I began to explore what experiences these economically comfortable clients shared with the rioters in South Central Los Angeles. What I concluded was that the jury's "you're imagining it" message felt like a slap in the face to my clients, reawakening feelings of injustice and betrayal.

The media pointed out how poverty, racism, and lack of opportunity contributed to the South Central rioting. For too long the people who rioted felt neglected, ignored, and forgotten by authorities. But this didn't tell the whole story. What if these feelings reminded them of childhood experiences? Abusive messages from childhood, rekindled by the jury's verdict, may have fueled the rage.

Similar rage was in evidence following the opening of the movie *Boyz N the Hood,* which was filmed in South Central L.A. It sparked disturbances there and other parts of the country. Some speculated that participants were identifying with the social and political conditions depicted on the screen. But there was another explanation: angry reaction to the graphic family scenes of psychological and physical abuse. As people watched the frustration of their lives on the big screen, rage took over and rioting occurred.

What if similar rageful feelings from childhood indignities were rekindled by the verdict of the jury? For my psychotherapy clients, the "not guilty" verdict felt like another betrayal by those in authority. A slap in the face. One more message of invalidation. In South Central Los Angeles the "not guilty" verdict led to rioting. Fifty-three people were killed; thousands of businesses were destroyed.

Parents frequently discount children's feelings, telling them they are imagining something. "It didn't happen." "It wasn't all that bad." This can occur in benign situations when a parent responds to a child feeling upset by saying, "Don't be silly," or to a child's bad dream by declaring,

"You're really not afraid." Such messages are even more of a problem in secretive families.

Secrets are all too common in alcoholic or abusive families. Sometimes children become expendable to protect the family secret. If they try to tell someone, hoping for support, that person might respond, "You're crazy! It really didn't happen like that." Someone might even blame the child: "It's your fault, you could have stopped it."

When children feel no one believes them they get confused. Is their perception real or are they are imagining it?

Many of my clients are still struggling with whether to believe their childhood abuse really happened. They tell themselves they must be imagining it, because that's what someone once told them to believe. Abuse is a betrayal of trust. An abused child feels betrayed both by the abuser and by the parent who fails to provide protection. It's baffling and frustrating when we want to trust the people who are telling us to distrust our own perceptions. This confusion affects the way we view the world and the people in it.

Then we begin to lose the ability to trust. Someone may "beat us up" in some way and then say he or she didn't do it. We reel from the injustice. This is what happened after the acquittals in the first trial. The jury told us our perceptions didn't count. We felt ignored, diminished, dismissed, invalidated. Some of us began to believe we didn't count. Then we got angry, maybe even enraged.

Adults who feel helpless, disappointed, or betrayed may find the abused child within them acting out in a childlike way. When children can't express pain or anger in words, they handle their anxiety in other ways. Some remain silent and withdrawn. Some act out their frustration and rage by calling attention to themselves. Some throw tantrums. Others trash their rooms. Some hurt smaller, weaker children or animals. Others light fires.

It was unsettling for many of us when the jury's verdict questioned our perception of reality. In some, rage ignited and exploded. New feelings of helplessness and betrayal piled on old injustices. The man on the TV talk show screamed out his rage; it was more than he could bear. Maybe it was more than other residents of South Central could bear, as well. The fires and riots may have been their way of saying, "You want real? We'll give you a good dose of reality!"

### Feeling Discounted

Stephanie is tall and statuesque, giving an air of being in command of any situation. It is important to her that people see her this way. She recently confided to fellow students in her masters' program that she was worried about passing a course. They were incredulous—"How can you of all people be worried?" Stephanie's reaction surprised her—she was close to tears. They seemed to be discounting her feelings.

As we talked about it she began to understand how classmates had come to see her as the competent one, the one they could look up to. If Stephanie, "of all people," worried about the exams, where does that leave the classmates? They needed her to be the competent one. That was supposed to be her role in class.

So what were those tears about? Stephanie's role in her family of origin was to be the "little mother." Her own mother felt overwhelmed with five small children to care for. So the family needed Stephanie to be the competent one. There was never any room for her to worry out loud. "I would lie in bed at night and worry secretly and silently about how I would deal with my huge responsibilities."

"When I heard fellow students say, 'How can you of all people be worried,' I wanted to cry. But that's hard for me to do; I was always told, 'Big girls don't cry.' Crying out loud was never permissible for me." When a few tears began to come she kept apologizing for crying in front of me. "No one knows how much effort I put into looking competent. How dare they say that I don't have to worry. I worry all the time."

If our impressions are discounted often, we learn to discount ourselves as well. Sometimes we begin to doubt our own perceptions and stop trusting ourselves. I was recently invited to a fifties party and started reminiscing about a felt circle skirt I had owned in junior high school. Back then I couldn't afford a poodle skirt, so I went to several stores to get ideas. Then I bought an inexpensive, plain felt skirt (pink, of course) and made a wonderful fluffy gray poodle to stitch onto it. I made little individual loops of gray yarn for the ears, chest, and tail. Then I made a rhinestone collar and gold leash. I was really proud of that skirt—it looked as good as the ones in the stores.

I wasn't prepared for what happened next. My aunt asked me where I bought the poodle skirt because she wanted to buy one for my cousin. When I told her I made the poodle, she told me I was lying, that I couldn't possibly have made it. I got really confused. I actually began to doubt if I did indeed make the poodle. After all, she spoke with so much authority when she told me I was lying that I believed her.

Over the years, I'd continue to distrust my impressions of things. There were times I was at a play I didn't especially like, and I'd overhear someone during intermission talk about how terrific the play was. I'd immediately figure I was wrong and they were right.

Do you ever remember when you were little, going up to your mother or father when they looked upset, and asking, "Are you sad?" Did your mother or father quickly tell you, "No, I'm just thinking about something." You're pretty sure you saw a sad look on their face, but they were telling you, "You're imagining it."

I grew up getting confused about things like that. I began not to trust my intuition. I began not to trust my feelings. I began to regard my own senses as unreliable guides. I no longer could trust myself. I didn't know what was real; I hardly dared to ask. If I risked stating how

I felt, my father would respond, "You must be kidding." I perceived the underlying message to be, "Are you crazy?"

Sometimes when I asked questions I was given whatever information was handy at the time, whether it was true or not. I felt I was a bother for being inquisitive. (Years later, I had a supervisor who would give me misinformation when he didn't know the answer to something because he didn't want to ask his superior. I overreacted and blew up at him. Yes, I took it personally.)

When your feelings and perceptions are being discounted in so many ways, it is hard to be true to yourself, so in effect you abandon yourself. Some children not only abandon themselves, but they grow up fearing abandonment as well.

## "I'm Disappointed in You" (Spurning)

*Disappointed* is such a loaded word. When children hear it, they most likely interpret it to mean that they are disappointing to someone. Especially if they have grown up hearing messages like "You're no good," or "You're not good enough."

In chapter 3 you read about expectations and disappointments. Often if we feel disappointed by someone's actions it is because our expectations are too unrealistic. And when we get our feelings hurt because we are disappointed, we often turn around and hurt the other person's feelings by letting them know we're disappointed in them.

When parents are overly critical or push for perfectionism, they frequently get disappointed. How can they not be? Their expectations are so high. So their children come to think of themselves as big disappointments. They do a perfect job at thinking of themselves as imperfect.

What about the dyslexic child or one with attention problems—especially those who went through school without being identified or offered help? Think of the amount of criticism and disdain they had to endure because no one bothered to find out why they were different from the other students. "Pay attention. Stop daydreaming. What's wrong with you?" my teachers would say. The rejection messages were powerful, the damage great.

Some parents hurled words, others hurled objects. But the message was the same: "You're worthless." Name-calling, put-downs, and belittling are all rejecting behaviors. One client was constantly told as a child, "Talking to you is like talking to thin air." In spite of the seemingly nonmenacing quality of this statement, there's a devaluing underlying message here. He recalls, "Being compared to thin air made me feel like I didn't exist. I still don't feel like a very substantial person."

Frequently children are told they are loved on condition they "get good grades," "dress acceptably," "don't show their feelings," "don't rock the boat." Conditional love robs children of who they are. One woman says, "I had to scramble to be what they wanted me to be. I didn't know who I was anymore. I guess I rejected myself in the process."

Another form of spurning is the "why can't you be more like your sister?" (or brother or cousin) complaint. Comparisons like this are invalidating, and the children on the receiving end of these comments grow up expecting to come up short. They feel they don't count. Annie realized how extreme feelings of inadequacy stem from her parents' frequent comparisons of her to a cousin who was a math whiz or to her brother who was always a good little boy. Annie was never appreciated for Annie kinds of things—her poetry, her spunk, her energy. She loses sight of her strengths and continues to see herself as inferior, comparing herself to everyone around her.

Sometimes siblings are not just compared to each other; one child may be more or less disowned when the other comes along. For example, Patty was the firstborn child, but she happened to be born a girl when her father had his heart set on a boy. They spent a lot of time together when she was little. They went fishing, played ball, and he even bought her an electric train. Then a brother was born when she was six years old. Her father began to turn all his attention to the boy. Patty felt ignored. "I was dethroned," she said. My brother became king. She recently rummaged through old snapshots and found many pictures of herself—they were all taken before she was six years old. From then on the camera was pointed in her brother's direction.

## *"If You Don't Behave I'm Going to Leave You in the Store" (Terrorizing)*

This particular threat can be extremely frightening for a child. When you were a kid, did you have visions of roaming the aisles of a department store alone forever and ever, surrounded by rack after rack of clothing, every adult's knees looking more or less the same from where you stood?

Equally terrorizing is threatening to send a child "to live with Aunt Sally," or warning, "I can't stand you anymore, so I'm leaving you home alone." These are common threats but they can lead to fears of abandonment. Harvey's mother threatened to leave him so many times, he began to see himself as "discardable." In fact, he kept a little cardboard suitcase under his bed—packed with his favorite things. When his mother drank too much and threatened to leave the children, Harvey didn't want to get left behind, so he was all packed and ready to go.

My parents used to tell me they'd send me away to stay with my strict aunt if I wasn't good. "She'll teach you some manners," they often said. Then one summer it wasn't just a threat anymore—they did just that. I remember spending what seemed like a month at her house, but my cousins tell me it was more like a week. Well, it was a very *long* week for me. I didn't know when, or if, I would see my parents again. I felt abandoned.

Another form of threatening abandonment is telling a child, "That would kill your mother," or "You'll be the death of me yet." I used to hear these words all the time. Then, as my mother was leaving to go to the airport, I screamed, "I hate you, I wish you were dead." The plane crashed, and I never saw her again. Many other people have had a similar experience of feeling their words or "bad" behavior led to a loved one's death. I used to think I was the only one with that kind of awful power. A child who has had this experience comes to believe he or she is so wrong or so bad as to be able to destroy the very people he or she loves and depends on. Some parents may even threaten to kill themselves. Suicide is the ultimate abandonment, don't you think? How do children explain *that* to themselves?

When children are hospitalized, they often feel abandoned by their parents. Since small children have a different perception of time than adults, their stay in the hospital may seem never ending. Days may seem like weeks and weeks like months. Forty years ago, Ronald went into the hospital for a hernia operation. His parents didn't explain anything about his stay there. The days seemed to go on forever and he only saw his parents a couple of times. It felt as if his parents had left him there, maybe never to return. Fears of abandonment have been with him his whole life. He recently asked his mother for the story about his hospitalization. It turns out he was only there a few days—not the weeks and weeks he remembered. The doctors had advised his parents not to visit very often because he cried so much when they were about to leave. And what did Ronald take home with him? Forty years worth of abandonment fears.

## "Go to Your Room—You Don't Deserve to Eat Dinner with Us" (Isolating, Terrorizing)

Sending children to their rooms for long periods of time as punishment is another form of rejection. This is isolation. The message might be interpreted to mean, "You're not fit to spend time with the rest of the family."

Did you get ever sent to your room? Do you remember how you felt when you sat alone in your room for long periods of time? Do you remember how it felt to not be part of your family?

When children are sent to their rooms, they often go in shame. They said or did something "badly" and feel "badly" about themselves. Their room becomes a place of shameful memories, and this feeling can follow them into their adult years. Punishments can be even more isolating and take on a terrorizing effect when children are sent to bathrooms or to closets for long periods of time. Many of my clients recall the long hours spent shut up in those small spaces.

But some children manage to derive some comfort from these experiences, which follows them into their adult lives. One women was locked for hours at a time in the small upstairs bathroom. She remembers climbing up on the toilet seat, looking out the window, studying the trees, shrubs, plants on the property. Later, she would try to identify them from books. She would wander the neighborhood, making friends with the gardeners. Ever since she was a child, plants have been a source of comfort to her; she even married a landscape architect.

Many children who were confined in closets or other small spaces often develop troublesome fears as adults, fears that limit their daily functioning. In addition, these confinements sometimes meant urinating or defecating on themselves, which added to the shame. But some clients report closet memories that also include small comforts as well—the smell of leather, the feel of fur. Now, as adults, many of these people choose to return to closets when they are upset. But when they do this, they often experience a confusing combination of shame and comfort.

This confusion can lead them to seek out convoluted relationships. They may come to expect that a comforting relationship isn't complete unless it's accompanied by shame. So they choose unsuitable, often abusive partners or friends. They may not trust the intentions of a caring person who provides comfort to them. After all, where's the shame that's supposed to accompany the comfort? Then they might even sabotage the caring and comfort because they're uncomfortable with it and end up tossing away a pretty decent relationship. If enough relationships get tossed away, they might find themselves isolated from other people, perpetuating the familiar feelings of childhood.

Another form of isolating is to prevent a child from having contact with other children or adults outside the home. This frequently happens in alcoholic or abusive homes to protect the family secret. In Ruthie's case her parents were so afraid of what others would think about how they lived, that they cut off all social contacts. Ruthie's only contact with other children was at school. She wasn't allowed to ask friends over, nor was she allowed to go to the homes of schoolmates. She was refused permission to take Saturday art classes or to go swimming at the local pool. Ruthie was a lonely little girl.

## *"Hit a Home Run for Me!"* (Exploiting)

When parents try to live their lives vicariously through their children, it is a form of exploitation. These parents have some confusion about personal boundaries, they don't know where they stop and where someone else begins. (More about boundaries in chapter 11.) Vicariousness is often a form of coercion. Children often feel pushed beyond their comfortable limits, but are afraid to say "no" to a parent.

Vicarious parents encourage their children to meet their own unmet goals—vocationally, religiously, or romantically. Or they urge the children to live out their own unfulfilled dreams by being the "performer" the parents never quite became—in school, on the stage, on the playing field.

These parents see their children's performance in life as a reflection of their own competence. If the children do well, the parents feel like good parents, successful parents. If the children fall below expectations, the parents feel inadequate and shamed. Then the children are often made to feel inadequate and shamed. The children may lose their sense of self, trading "self" for service to the parents.

The children may discover that being in the spotlight is a very lonely place. Bruce recalls how he used to do okay at baseball practice, but he would freeze at bat when his dad showed up at games and yelled out, "Hit a home run for me!" Bruce shudders at remembering the humiliation he felt knowing his dad was up there in the stands, feeling embarrassed that his son would freeze.

What about when parents don't even show up at games or meets? One man recalls, "Dad kept reminding me what an expensive glove he bought for me, but never once came to see me play." One client was a championship high-school swimmer whose parents never came to see her compete. The only adult support she got was from her coach. She was so desperate for his attention that she responded to his sexual attention too.

Jay North, the actor who played Dennis in the TV series, *Dennis the Menace*, described how his aunt behaved when she would accompany him to the set. "She demanded perfection. Everything had to be perfect, and the harder I tried, the more she'd expect of me. It was just such a pressure cooker. Everybody else would congratulate me, and say, 'Good job, good job,' and she'd shout, 'You didn't play the scene right,' and slap me across the face."

I'm familiar with stage moms, too. My mom wanted each of her children to be the star she never became, so she put my brother, Lee, and me in the spotlight from the time we were young. There was always pressure to do poems or skits in front of relatives. My first memory of big-time stardom was when I got a phone call from the *Washington Post* on my fifth or sixth birthday. The caller informed me that I had just won a contest for writing a poem about a new comic strip, "The Saint." You'd think I would have been excited, except for one thing—I didn't write the poem. My mother wrote it without telling me. I wonder how hard it was for her to write like a six year old. I remember night after night having to rehearse that poem because I was going to be lucky enough to get to read it over the radio. It will be committed to my memory forever:

I like to read the *Post* each day
To see what The Saint has to say.
His deeds and actions thrill me most,
That's why I like to read the *Post.*

How could I ever forget those words? They were drilled into my head. Day after day. Some serious drilling took place during the long streetcar ride across town to the radio station. But I did forget them. Unfortunately I was on the air at the time. I got nervous at the radio station surrounded by all the equipment and microphones. There I was, scared to death, pretending I wrote the poem and I messed up of course. My parents were embarrassed. I felt like I'd let them down. This same scenario replayed many times following dance recitals and plays. Each time I'd see that disappointed look on my mother's face. I came to believe that no matter how hard I tried, it would never be good enough. The critical voice would be waiting in the wings, "You made a mistake, you can do better."

I can remember the first time I felt differently about performing. I was on a plane to New York, on my way to tape my first network talk show. I decided during the flight that even though there would be a lot of other TV opportunities, this would be a special experience. Anything that followed would never be quite the same again. I said to myself, "Just enjoy it." And I did. There was no critical voice this time. I think I banished it, expelled it, ousted it. In fact, I *rejected* it!

## "I Know I Can Count on You to be Mama's Little Helper" (Exploiting)

Another form of exploiting is robbing children of their childhood by expecting them to care for younger siblings, take over household tasks, or take care of the parents' needs. These children are *parentified*—there is no room to be children because they are expected to function as adults. Their childhood is invalidated. Their sense of importance hinges on their ability to anticipate the needs of others. This is often the only positive self-concept they develop. Because this is where they get their validation, they continue to take care of others in their adult relationships. "I've always been an over-giver," says one woman. "It feels like caring run amok." You may recognize this behavior as codependency.

Some children get validation by filling specific roles in their families. For example, the role of the "go-between." Sometimes the child acts as an intermediary between the parents and the outside world or between the parents and the other siblings. Sometimes the child runs messages between both of the parents. Mollie was one of these children. Her parents were constantly complaining to each other and using Molly to carry the messages. Recalling the expectations of her role, she used clay in therapy to make a form representing her image of herself as a child. She formed the green clay into a smooth, perfect ball. She recounts, "I felt I was a ball, rolling from one family member to another. There was no room for my own needs to get met. I just got lost." Now she sees how these experiences affect two areas of her life: She has a great fear of losing her sense of self if she lets herself get too involved in a romantic relationship, so she keeps her distance. And she frequently finds herself in trouble with her friends by carrying messages from one to the other. Not only does she feel used and exploited, but later they blame her for the consequences.

A more subtle form of exploitation is making a child feel incompetent so the parent can feel more useful. "My mom seemed to be waiting for me to mess up so she could step in and rescue me," remembers Georgia. "Sometimes she'd ask me to do chores around the house that were too difficult for me. Then she'd step in and show me 'how to do it better." The mother told herself she was being a good role model for Georgia, but in fact, what she was modeling was how to step in and take over. Georgia did the same when she grew up, taking over for her husband, then chiding him for being "helpless."

## "Don't Bother Me, Can't You See I'm Busy?" (Ignoring)

Sometimes parents are emotionally unavailable. They are there but not there. Often the parent is either too busy with work or too involved with their addiction, whatever it might be. For example, there is the alcoholic parent who disappears by pulling down the emotional shade— vanishing behind a bottle or into intoxicated sleep. Children can't figure out where the parent went. They don't understand why the parent doesn't want to be with them. They feel rejected and abandoned. One woman recalls how "the alcohol was more important than me—Dad always chose the bottle. Every night he'd pass out—and abandon me. I wish with all my heart that someone would have reassured me, 'It doesn't mean he doesn't love you.'"

It's hard making sense of the pain that comes from having emotionally unavailable parents. Patsy expresses the anguish she used to feel when her parents "disappeared" after dinner. "My mom would get lost in a novel. My dad evaporated into a bottle of wine. They just weren't available to me when I needed some attention. It was as if I did not exist." As an only child, she was on her own. So she would climb the stairs to her room and close the door. Then she would repeatedly punch herself on the arm. Hard. Why did she do that to herself? Looking back, she says, "Emotional abuse is so slippery. The pain made it seem more real."

## "You're Not Really Sick—
## You Just Want Attention"
## (Neglecting Physical or Mental Health)

When I'm assessing whether or not neglect may have occurred, I ask, "When you were sick, did someone take care of you?" Often the answer is "no." Sometimes taking care of a sick child interferes with parents' other obligations such as work or school. Sometimes, a child needs medical attention or medication and doesn't get it. Sometimes a child needs psychological support and no one pays heed. Sometimes a child needs educational help and no one responds. This is neglect.

## "You Deserve to Get Hit"
## (Spurning, Terrorizing)

Physical abuse is painful, demeaning, and humiliating. But it is not only the physical pain that causes the damage, it is the emotional pain as well. Abuse of any kind is a message of rejection and betrayal. The pain doesn't stop when the welts or bruises heal, it continues into adulthood. There is another aspect to beatings that deserves some attention here: Frequently there is a sexual component to administering a beating, especially if the child has to drop his or her pants or disrobe. And sometimes there may even be sexual pleasure for the person administering the beating.

## "Don't Tell Anyone I Touched You;
## It Has to be Our Secret"
## (Hostile Rejecting/Degrading, Terrorizing,
## Isolating, Exploiting, Corrupting)

There is no question that inappropriate sexual behavior is damaging to a child, but there is also a message of rejection that accompanies it. Forcing a child to perform adult sexual acts or not protecting the child from sexual abuse is exploitation of and emotional disregard of the child. For example, if a little girl is exploited by an adult male, her femaleness is invalidated, her childhood is invalidated, and she is invalidated as a human being on this earth. The long-term emotional scars of this abuse are not only from the sexual acts but from the rejection of the self that occurs as well.

Matters are complicated by another type rejection: betrayal. Lack of protection by the nonabusing adult is confusing for the child. The child doesn't know how to explain such a travesty and asks him or herself, "How could the adult not have known?" "Why didn't he or she protect me?" "If my parents really have 'eyes in the back of their heads' as they always tell me, then why didn't they see this happening?"

The feelings of powerlessness become even more overwhelming because the child feels isolated and alone in the midst of this huge secret that must be kept at any cost. All too often, children believe the cost would be their life if they tell.

# Identify Your Childhood Messages

The bottom line here is that the core messages of any type of abuse are life or death messages. Yes, they really are. Consider for a moment how this can be so. Messages of invalidation are messages of nonexistence. Messages of abandonment call up fears for children that they can't exist without the caretaking of the parent. Messages accompanying physical or sexual abuse can be especially threatening. In a child's eyes, it's often a very scary world out there.

If you want to try to identify old family messages you received (and may still believe) ask yourself questions like these:

In order to survive I had to _____

or _____ would happen.

In order to survive I had to be _____

or _____ would happen.

In order to survive I had to do _____

or _____ would happen.

In order to survive I couldn't _____

or _____ would happen.

You may notice how some of these beliefs have followed you into adulthood. But they often didn't start with you or even with your parents; some of them may go back a hundred years or more. In the next chapter we'll take a look at how messages and beliefs are transmitted from generation to generation, and how the cycle can be stopped.

# 7

# Grandma Passes Down More Than Just Her China

## Cultural and Generational Messages

Grandma passes down much more than china or silver patterns. She passes down many other patterns as well in the form of family traditions, attitudes, beliefs, myths, scripts, roles, rules, expectations, disappointments, and rejection messages. Grandpa also does his share of passing down. In fact, many of these patterns can be traced several generations back.

And let's not forget the influence of the family genes. In *The Highly Sensitive Person,* Elaine Aron describes how having a sensitive nervous system may actually be an inherited trait. Her research points to highly sensitive people as being "a distinct group, separate from the nonsensitive."

One woman told me this story about her oversensitivity to certain sounds. "When I was growing up, everyone in my family was sensitive to the sound of food being chewed—especially crunchy food. It's just like the sound of screeching chalk on a blackboard to me. The other day my husband was trying to make plans with me to celebrate my birthday. But as he was talking to me, he was eating a raw carrot. When he noticed I was inching away from him, he really got upset. I wasn't even aware I was doing it, but clearly his feelings got hurt. I thought he knew how the food sounds upset me, but I guess he didn't remember. He just got focused on how I was moving away from him, and he thought it was something he said. Now he says he's hesitant to make plans with me to celebrate important events. Wow. Look at how my oversensitivity led to misunderstandings and hurt feelings. It's a good thing we could talk about it."

It is not known for sure if sensitivity to *rejection* is one of those inherited genes, but it certainly can be an inherited trait, passed down from generation to generation.

Rejection issues are sort of like recipes. "You know the saying 'the apple doesn't fall far from the tree?'" Fran asked. "Well, in my family it jumps right into the tuna fish salad." Her granddaughter had been amazed to see Fran put grated apples and carrots in tuna salad. "I can't believe you do that—my mother does that too!" And is it any coincidence that Fran's mother and grandmother did the same?

But more than genes, recipes, and family heirlooms are passed down through the generations. Family legacies also determine how we experience our world and how we operate with our own children. For example, have you ever opened your mouth in anger to say something— but wait, where did those terrible, hurtful words come from? They don't seem to belong to you, but you recognize them, don't you? That's right, you used to hear them from your parents. And your parents most likely heard them from their parents.

It's the strangest feeling when you open your mouth and somebody else's words come out—words or a tone of voice you haven't even thought of in years. It's unfortunate but true: messages that most often get repeated through the generations are the messages of rejection.

Parents of young children who are especially sensitive to rejection may perceive the children's behavior as purposeful and take things personally; they may reject the children in turn.

Many of us have experienced times when we wandered off from a parent to explore new territory and got "lost." Most of the time we knew where we were—it was our parents who thought we were lost. And what did they do when we showed up? Did they welcome us and comfort us? Probably not. They often guilt-tripped us or punished us, yelling, "How could you do this to me. You worried me to death!" Wouldn't you say they took it personally?

When babies cry a lot, many parents feel helpless. This triggers some childlike behaviors in the parents, and they may overreact to their babies' behavior. This is especially true for inexperienced, anxious, or frequently stressed parents. For example, babies are known to cry ceaselessly or spit out food or refuse to get dressed or turn away when a parent tries to hug or comfort them. But sometimes parents tell themselves that their baby doesn't like them, thinking of themselves as inadequate or bad parents, even seeing these behaviors as accusatory. They may feel their baby is rejecting them and without realizing it they may begin to reject the baby back.

One young mother I know gave her baby the "cold treatment," affecting a "how can you do this to me" attitude—acting hurt, pouting, ignoring her child. Then the baby began to copy the mother's behavior by turning away as well. Mom then became even more convinced that the baby was doing it just to hurt her.

# The Cyclical (and Reciprocal) Nature of Rejection

Parent-infant expert Selma Fraiberg describes how "in every nursery there are ghosts. They are the visitors from the unremembered past of the parents. . . ." In a study of mothers and young children where there appears to be a lack of attachment, the researchers ask, "Why can't this mother hear her baby's cries? They learn that the young mother was herself rejected and neglected in her own childhood, and they conclude, "When this mother's own cries are heard, she will hear her child's cries." And hopefully, the cycle of rejection in this family will end.

As I mentioned in chapter 6, this reciprocal nature of rejection was studied by Mary Main and her associates. Her initial idea involved researching attachment styles, but an enlightening follow-up study led researchers to look into how rejection messages were passed down from generation to generation. The parents in the original study were given a questionnaire that asked about specific childhood memories of their relationships with their own parents. Examples of the questions were "Choose five adjectives to describe your relationship with both parents; explain what made you choose those adjectives"; "As a child were you held by parents for comfort?"; "Did you ever feel rejected by your parents?"

A fascinating generational pattern of rejection emerged. The mothers who tended to perceive their own mothers as "rejecting" and tried to protect themselves from further emotional hurt were the very same mothers whose infants avoided them following the brief separation. The study concluded that the mothers who felt rejected by their own mothers tended to reject their children who, in turn, avoided them in response to the rejection. By avoiding their mothers these children were in effect rejecting them. And the mothers, ultrasensitive to this rejection, took it personally and rejected their children in return.

Breaking the cycle takes a lot of work. I know this not only from my work with clients, I know it best from my own family experiences.

The cycle of generational messages became clear to me one morning when I got a 7:30 phone call from my daughter, Jocelyn. She was calling from the university, and something was on her mind that clearly couldn't wait. "I figured it out," she told me, "Now I know why I overreacted like I did. It was because I felt ignored." She was recounting a recent argument with her friend Elise. "I was angry and flustered. I couldn't speak clearly, couldn't get across what I was trying to say. And Elise just sat there and didn't say anything. She kept staring at me as I was trying to explain my feelings. She just kept nodding her head, repeating, 'Uh-huh, uh-huh. Yes, I can see that.'"

"I finally managed to blurt out how angry I was. Then she answered slowly and deliberately, 'Yes, Jocelyn, I see that you're angry. I wish you could see yourself right now—the way you're acting.' Her patronizing behavior drove me crazy. I felt like stomping my feet, grabbing her and yelling, 'Listen to me. Please listen to me!'

"Now I realize why I got so angry. It was as if what I had to say wasn't worth listening to—as if it wasn't important enough—as if I wasn't important enough. Mom, this is how I used to feel sometimes when when I was younger and I'd try to talk to you. When I was angry at you about something, I'd try to work up enough nerve to tell you. I'd sit in my bedroom and practice in my head what I wanted to say until it would come out right. I always felt very adultlike for having the maturity to tell you how I was feeling. Wasn't that what you wanted me to be able to do?

"I'd walk down the hall and into your room and try to tell you how I felt. Somehow the words never came out the way they'd sounded in my head when I practiced. You'd listen and nod your head and say 'Uh-huh, uh-huh.' Then you'd say something like, 'That must be really hard for you, Jocelyn. That's a lot to have to worry about.' I felt you were feeling sorry for me when it was you who was the center of my problem. I'd ask, 'Mommy, are you listening to me?' And you'd sort of mumble, 'Yes, Jocelyn. It must be tough dealing with a mom like me.'

"I'd end up going back to my own room and crying. I was frustrated and angry because I felt ignored. I'd practiced so hard what I was going to say to you and I thought I was acting like such a grown-up. Instead I found myself feeling like a two-year-old—wanting to pull out my hair or stomp my feet to get your attention. And here I am, twenty-one years old, still acting the same way because I felt ignored by Elise.

"I wasn't getting enough attention from you and I really felt hurt. I was trying to tell you something important, and you couldn't hear it. I realize something now that I didn't know then. You were most likely trying to protect yourself from your own hurt, and I guess that's what Elise is trying to do now."

It was no easier to hear this from Jocelyn in that phone call than it was ten years ago. And for a moment there, as I was listening to her tell me how hurt and angry she was, I again started to armor myself. It's hard to stay in the present in the face of this kind of honesty, it reminded me of my own childhood hurts—all the times I'd felt ignored or dismissed. My pain was so great I had to armor myself from it back then. That's why I had had so much trouble hearing Jocelyn. This time I could hear her a lot better because I wasn't feeling so overwhelmed by my personal memories. This time I could let her see me as a real person.

## Hand-Me-Down Feelings and Messages

Sometimes the generational legacy of rejection can be cruel. Remember Karen's "barbed-wire" mother from chapter 6? Karen has vivid memories of how her mother would get mad at her and threaten to stick her in the oven as punishment. Karen was at a loss to explain her mother's harsh threats until she recalled her grandmother's basement and the baker's oven in the wall. As we talked about her mother's stories of being locked down there for punishment as a child, Karen finally put it together. "Now I get it. I'll bet my grandmother threatened to stick my mother in that oven—maybe she even did. It probably scared my mother to death, and she began to scare me in the same way." This memory doesn't excuse her mother's threats, but now Karen can understand the origin of her mother's words. She can see how both of them grew up with the same core fears having to do with life and death.

In one woman's family the life and death message that got passed down was "Life's supposed to be a struggle," and she seemed to be the designated struggler for her whole family. "I learned to protect myself by clawing and kicking and biting. Even now I'm always fighting someone—my lover, my supervisor, customers. I guess I'm still carrying on the 'life's a struggle' tradition of my family."

There's no question that fear of abandonment is a prime core fear transmitted between generations. Before I was able to deal with my own issues about abandonment, I didn't realize I was transmitting my fears of abandonment to my young daughter. After my mother and grandmother died, I spent a lot of time worrying that other people important to me might die. As it turns out, something happened that reinforced my fears: my stepmother died of cancer exactly ten years from the date of the plane crash.

Jocelyn used to worry about people dying, too. Whenever her dad or I were a few minutes late picking her up from nursery school or dance lessons, she convinced herself that we had died in an accident. As I outgrew my fears, Jocelyn outgrew hers as well. I first went into therapy when she was seven years old. She remembers being nine years old when her anxieties about death ceased. I don't think it was a coincidence that this was when I began to get a handle on my own abandonment issues.

My abandonment fears also affected Jocelyn in the way I held back from allowing myself to show my love for her. I could love her, but not too much, because in my mind, if I invested too much love in her I might lose her just as I lost my mother and grandmother. So I held back emotionally, at the time not knowing why.

A turning point in overcoming my abandonment fears came in the form of a dream. I rarely remembered my dreams, but this one I was able recall in vivid detail. I was in one of those little amusement park boats going through the tunnel of horrors. On each side of me, behind glass, were all the important people in my life who had died as well as all the people I feared might die. As the boat slowly made it's way down the canal, I was able to speak to each of these people in turn, expressing my feelings of loss and my fears, getting some closure with each of them. It was a powerful dream. From that day on, my fears about death diminished considerably, and so did Jocelyn's. As I no longer feared losing the people I loved, my capacity to show love for Jocelyn increased. There's no question in my mind that as I began clearing the residual fears out of my head, she benefited as well. I wonder if she might have been helping me out all those years by sharing my fears. Sometimes children do that.

Maria's story also shows how rejection messages are handed down. Her dad was called the "Black One" by his family in Mexico because he was darker than his brothers or sisters. As a child, he always felt his brothers and sisters received more favors, including new clothes. In fact, when his father bought shoes for the brothers and sisters, he refused to buy Maria's father some shoes.

Maria has her father's coloring and is somewhat darker than her sisters. As she was growing up she always thought her dad favored his lighter skinned daughters. Maria felt discriminated against when he didn't allow her to have new shoes or clothing. She had no way then of knowing that he was treating her the same way his own dad had treated him. Maria began to see herself as worth less than her sisters. Her self-image soon translated to "worthless," which permeated the way she related to her world.

Now, as an adult, Maria repeatedly finds herself attracted to men who tend to prefer blondes and redheads, then she berates herself for being worth less than the other women. By seeking out these men she continues to compare herself to others and comes out the loser each time. She recreates feelings of rejection and reinforces her concept of herself as unattractive, worthless, bad. She rejects herself.

## Rude Awakenings

Sometimes the problem isn't only messages that get passed down through the generations—it's a lack of them as well. An example would be customs concerning family contact. When Bart comes into the kitchen each morning he never says a word to anyone. Well, to be fair, sometimes he kind of grunts. His partner, Bess can't stand it. She would love to hear a "hello" from him and feels he's ignoring her by not acknowledging her presence. She keeps trying to figure out what she did or said to make him so offish in the morning. In couples therapy, when she finally brought it up, he seemed surprised. He had no idea that he appeared so un-friendly.

Then he remembered how it was growing up. "In my family, no one ever spoke a hello, we just went about our business. In fact, we were so afraid of my dad, whenever he was around we all went into our separate bedrooms so we wouldn't have to talk to him." Bess was amazed at his revelation, "All this time I've been taking it as a personal rejection! In my family we all greeted each other with a big hello, it's what I was used to. I guess I took it for granted it was the same for Bart. I never dreamed it might be so different in someone else's family."

I had a similar experience. When I was sixteen and my father remarried, my brother, Lee, and I acquired a stepmother, stepbrother, and stepsister in the deal. I was stunned the first time I heard my stepmother greet my stepsister with a friendly "Good morning, Sunshine." It was like a whole new world to me. No one had ever made it a point to greet one another in my family. I began to practice this kind of courtesy, but it didn't come easily, and to this day I sometimes forget to bid my daughter a good morning. I still have to work at it.

## The Sponge Effect

Children are great sponges, absorbing their parents' anxieties or depression or anger. Taking in their parent's pain isn't a conscious act—it just seems to happen. Pat Conroy, author of *The Great Santini, Prince of Tides,* and *Beach Music* says, "One of the things I learned in my childhood is that I could take things on myself and hold it all in. I used to try and do that with my mother. If I could take her pain and hold it and hide it, that would make it better. Too bad it doesn't work that way."

When children absorb their parents' intolerable feelings and share in the misery, it spreads the negative energy around and may allow parents to give more attention to themselves and their children. For example, my father used to brag, "Your mother and I never had an argument," but I find it hard to believe they never disagreed or got angry with each other. Where did their angry feelings go? My brother and I used to fight all the time. We were acting out their unspoken anger—chipped teeth and all.

---

Children are like sponges, absorbing their parents feelings.

---

Perhaps because some children get so used to absorbing and acting out their parents' feelings, they do the same with their partners later in life. They may find themselves getting angry for their spouse who "never gets angry," or depressed for the mate who can't acknowledge his or her own depression, or fearful for the lover who shows a brave face to the world. These are examples of projection and projective identification, which will be discussed later in this chapter. And it's a boundary thing, not knowing what feelings belong to whom, not knowing where you stop and where someone else begins. (More about personal boundaries in chapter 11.)

Parents who have experienced anxious attachment in their own childhood are inclined to seek care from their children, according to the attachment and loss studies of John Bowlby. Children who become caretakers for their parents often become anxious, guilty, or phobic. Some children even stay home from school to keep an eye on the parent. This anxiety is called "school phobia." It's not a fear of school as many people believe, it's a fear about the catastrophes that might befall a parent while the child is away from home. So the clever child tries to avoid the anxiety of worrying all day about the parent and devises excuses to stay home from school in order to protect the parent.

## Good Kid/Bad Kid

Let's take a look at the concept of "good" and "bad" within families. In some families one child appears to be designated as the "good" one, while another child is thought of as "bad." It's as if a script has been written and the children play out their respective roles. But unlike a play, this is for real, and there's no room for the children to rewrite their lines.

These good and bad roles often span several generations. For example, Danny is named after his mother's brother, Dan, who is the black sheep of the family. He looks like Uncle Dan, too, even down to coal black hair and blue eyes. He grew up hearing the litany of poor ole Uncle Dan's badness—"He's just no good. He gets into fights and loses one job after another because of the booze. He's been married four times." And Danny? It's no surprise that he was called incorrigible in junior high school and was often kicked out of classes. When it was time for high school, he was sent to the school for "bad boys." He married early and it lasted a year. He's been married twice more for short periods. Danny came to think of himself as a bad boy, a failure. He began to believe his parents were right all those years when they used to tell him, "You're just like your Uncle Dan."

Keith's experience of growing up was very different. "I was expected to be the one who accomplished everything my parents couldn't. I had to make top grades; there was no room to be less than perfect because all the hopes and expectations for the future of my parents rested on my shoulders. It was up to me to perform 'like a good little boy' in order to meet my parents' needs for a better life." It wasn't until Keith did a genogram, a family diagram with descriptive details about each famly member, in my office with me, that he realized how his dad had been expected by his own father to succeed, but couldn't do it well enough. So the mantle got passed down and now it was Keith's turn. "The trouble is," he now realizes, "I lost my identity by trying so hard to be the 'good son' they wanted me to be. I manufactured a "good boy" veneer with nothing underneath but sawdust."

The notion of "good and bad" was another source of confusion for me in my childhood. I never knew from one day to the next whether I was supposed to be good or bad. You see, I had a "good girl" mom and a "bad boy" dad, and each seemed to have an expectation that I'd follow in their respective footsteps. Sometimes I was bad when my mother was counting on me to be good like her, and sometimes I was good when my father was expecting me to be bad like him. I guess I couldn't always read their minds correctly. I guessed wrong a lot.

To make matters more confusing, my parents used to recite this nursery rhyme to me: "There once was a girl who had a little curl, right in the middle of her forehead. When she was good she was very, very good, and when she was bad she was horrid." I was positive that rhyme was written about me. After all, I did have really curly hair, with at least one curl in the middle of my forehead. I was the same little girl who was banished from nursery school on the first day for throwing tantrums and being "uncontrollable." And the same little girl who was asked to leave Sunday school a year or two later for being "disruptive." And the very same high school student who was frequently booted out of study hall for disturbing every one by talking—they called me "obstinate." By the time I was in college I didn't want to be that "horrid" little girl with the curl any longer, and I not only started straightening my hair, but I started to clean up my act. Yet, to be honest, being "bad" was so much a part of my identity when I was growing up that a part of me still wants to hold on to it—my eyes glow at the thought.

## Will the Real You Please Stand Up?

Often, we are unable to acknowledge certain aspects of ourselves. Parts of our personalities stay hidden from us because they are not acceptable to us. This is what Carl Jung called *the shadow*—the dark part, the part we don't want to know about ourselves, and wish wasn't there. This comes about in childhood as we can begin to notice we bring on someone's displeasure by displaying certain emotions or behaviors. In other words, these emotions or actions were "bad," they were unacceptable to others so we submerged them.

These cultural demands appear to affect boys at an earlier age than girls. Even before the age of five, boys are encouraged to "be real men," to push down their feelings—especially soft, vulnerable ones. But for girls, societal influences make their strongest impact during preadolescence, according to studies by Carol Gilligan and the American Association of University Women. Girls, who until then have been confident and straightforward, begin to lose their ability to speak up for themselves. In order not to lose the love and approval of important people in their lives, they develop a "Perfect Girl" facade—compliant, nice, self-sacrificing. As they lose their voice and self-esteem, they reject their authentic selves. The case studies in Peggy Orenstein's *School Girls,* Emily Hancock's *The Girl Within,* and Mary Pipher's *Reviving Ophelia* offer poignant portraits of such girls.

So, rather than take a chance on feeling humiliated or rejected, both boys and girls learn to hide "unacceptable" behavior in order to get approval. The suppressed behavior might involve showing anger, sadness, independence, sensuality, curiosity, or talent. Robert Johnson, in *Owning Your Own Shadow,* says some of these hidden characteristics are "pure gold"—but we end up rejecting these parts of ourselves because they were unwelcome to family or society.

Johnson reminds us that these "refused and unacceptable characteristics do not go away; they only collect in the dark corners of our personality." In fact, they begin to seep out, most frequently when we judge or criticize others. We often cannot tolerate in others the very same traits we can't stand about ourselves. Through a process of distortion called *projection,* we mistakenly imagine those traits exist in the other person when we cannot acknowledge them in ourselves because they are emotionally unacceptable. As one woman said, "If we can't own our own stuff, we try to give it away to someone else. In a way, projection protects us from ourselves by spreading the garbage around."

It really gets confusing when the other person accepts the projection and acts in accordance with it. This is called *projective identification*—a trading of feelings, needs, or thoughts. Maggie Scarf describes projective identification as "a psychological barter which occurs at an unconscious level." It is a "displacement of what is inside the self to what is outside the self . . . seeing in the other what cannot be tolerated in the self." This dynamic occurs not only between members of a couple, but between parents and children and in the workplace as well. For example, one person finds a feeling too "hot" to deal with; to acknowledge having it would cause the person extreme anxiety. So what happens? The person tosses it to the other person who takes it on, finds it's too "hot" to hold, then throws it back. Because the first person disavows the feeling, the only way he or she can deal with it is via the emotions of the other person, who reciprocates by identifying with the projection.

For example, a woman who grows up in a family where there is an overt (or even covert) rule against expressing anger, may find her own angry feelings unacceptable. She may say to herself and whoever will listen, "I never get angry." Because she disavows her own feelings, she may project them onto her partner (or child or co-worker) cueing, or even provoking, that person to act aggressively. While she's calmly berating the other person for his or her anger, she doesn't have to experience her own, because the other person is expressing her anger for her. The anger that she can't deal with in herself is "out there" courtesy of her partner, and she can deal with it vicariously.

In a similar way the person who learned to "never be sad" sees his or her depressed moods only in the partner—who unconsciously conforms to the projection and carries the sadness and despair for them both. Scarf notes that the relationship begins to look different when one of the partners "has had the experience of *taking back a projection*—accepting that, for example, the craziness, hostility, incompetence, depression, anxiety, etc., that is being perceived in the partner may be emanating from the self." Once the partner "has *refused to accept a projection*—to behave crazily, angrily, become depressed or the like, in order to accept the spouse's suppressed and dissociated feelings—changes have to start occurring in the relationship." Scarf goes on to say that "each member of the couple must reown and take responsibility for those aspects of his or her internal world which are being put onto the partner. This means *learning to experience ambivalence*—the good and bad within the other and the good and bad within the self, . . . seeing both one's goodness and one's badness, one's craziness and one's saneness, one's adequacy and inadequacy, one's depression and one's happy feelings, etc., as aspects of internal experience rather than *splitting off* one side of any of these dichotomies and being able to perceive it only as it exists in the mate."

Recognizing the disavowed parts, the dark side, leaves less room for critical judgment of others and of ourselves as well. Owning our shadow side as well as our more desirable features is an important part of the road to self-acceptance—to wholeness. There's a lot of room in there for all the parts to coexist. Why not encourage them to befriend each other? Each part could teach the others quite a few things. They all have information to share, but you'll find some of them are more talkative than others. Try getting to know them.

In *The Missing Piece—Solving the Puzzle of Self*, Drs. Claudia Black and Leslie Drozd suggest nine useful tools for embracing all aspects of yourself, and I've paraphrased them here:

- Motivation
- Commitment
- Strengths
- Healthy defenses
- Firm (not rigid) boundaries
- Ability to create a safe place
- Ability to be present, grounded, and balanced
- Ability to gain distance and perspective
- Ability to be

## High Hopes

The legacy of high hopes for the next generation is poignantly portrayed in Amy Tan's *The Joy Luck Club*, which follows the fears and hopes of four Chinese families through three generations. The mothers' fears compel them to desperately try to arrange better lives for their daughters. The daughters see their mothers' behavior as emotional or physical abandonment. The mothers' hopes for their daughters are so high and their expectations so unrealistic that the daughters experience it as rejection.

In order to fulfill their own dreams, the mothers constantly prod their daughters to do better. Instead of supporting and encouraging them, the mothers criticize and nag them, creating intergenerational experiences of "raised hopes and failed expectations" by hoping for "something so large that failure is inevitable." As Jing Mei tells her mother, "People rise to other people's expectations. And when you criticize, it just means you're expecting failure." Her mother replies, "That's just the trouble, you never rise. Lazy to get up. Lazy to rise to expectations."

Jing Mei's friend, Waverly, a child chess whiz, complains to her mother, "Why do you have to use me to show off. If you want to show off, then why don't you learn to play chess?" But her mother's response is chilling, and Waverly remembers, "My mother's eyes turned into dangerous black slits. She had no words for me, just sharp silence."

Some children seem to know what their parents expect from them, but others get confused. I was one of those confused children and it hadn't improved much when I reached adulthood. After my mother died, her sister would occasionally try to fill in as a long-distance substitute mother. She'd remember my birthday, send me "care packages" of clothes, keep in touch, and be supportive of my endeavors. When I was about thirty years old, she was hospitalized for surgery, and I called her and sent a get well card. Ten years later she told me how disappointed she was that I didn't think to fly to her bedside when she was in the hospital. Of course I translated that to mean she was disappointed in me. I felt confused (and guilty) that it hadn't crossed my mind to fly there.

A distant cousin explained the family "rule" to me. She said that my aunt may have seen me as a kind of "quasidaughter," and in my maternal family, the daughters were expected to take care of their mothers. After all, hadn't my own mother died while accompanying my ill grandmother to the Mayo Clinic?

## The Messages Resonate

The influence of our families has an impact on us throughout our lives and in all of our relationships—friends, lovers, and colleagues. Let's take a look at ways that early family patterns interfere. First of all, in any interaction between two people, there's also a roomful of family members—both dead and alive—present. Let's take a look at how many influences might be there. First of all, the messages of the mother and the father of each person are hovering around, so already we've got four other people in the room. If stepparents are involved, the number increases. Adding the influence of all the grandparents makes eight more people. It it any wonder an angry interchange can be so powerful and overwhelming? Look at how crowded the room is, how many old messages might be flung back and forth, and how many people could be taking something personally at any given time. Is it any wonder confusion reigns?

During couples therapy you can imagine how intense my office can get with all this generational family energy around. Sometimes I want to put up folding chairs to accommodate everyone who is trying to get a word in. Criticisms and judgments of the brothers and sisters or mother or father or grandmother or grandfather get imported into the relationship. And the room fills up with so many thoughts, beliefs, or messages that don't actually belong to the couple.

In order to make space for the couple to love each other, it's important to keep these negative thoughts out. One way to do this is for the couple to have a "bad thoughts" jar—sort of like a chore jar that some families use for particularly nasty chores. The chore jar works like this: The chores no one wants to do are written on slips of paper and put into the jar. Whichever chore you draw is the one you do—no complaining allowed. But with the "bad thought" jar the thoughts go in, but don't come out.

The couple's task with the "bad thoughts" jar is to write down and toss into a jar or box whatever particularly nasty thoughts they may have. The jar functions as a container for whatever bad-mouthing, criticism, and general mean-spiritedness may have been passed down through the generations. Hopefully, when either one of the couple opens his or her mouth to speak to the other, his or her own words will come out, instead of the words of a mother or father or grandmother or grandfather. Maybe this will allow space for their words to be respectful, loving, and accepting. This is a way to keep the parents out and make space for the couple.

Work situations can get pretty overwhelming, too, when there is a disagreement between co-workers. Each individual's family floats around the office, and the room can get crowded by all the thoughts and beliefs, each family member wanting to put in his or her two cents' worth to liven up the negotiations. Again, all those old messages and influences need to be booted out to make room for the thoughts and words of the two people involved.

Situations at your job may replicate your very own growing up experiences. You might have a boss who ignores you, or insults you, or is heavy-handed. So you may find similar issues coming up at work that you experienced growing up—things such as loyalties and betrayals, secrets, alliances and coalitions, and communication deviances—and you may react the way your family has "taught" you to react.

Where exactly do these intergenerational messages come from? How can you learn to recognize them, especially the subtle ones? I often do a genogram with many of my clients to look for family patterns. In this

> In any interaction between two people there's also a roomful of family members present exerting generational messages and occasionally creating chaos.

family diagram it's helpful to go back three generations, even if names and details aren't known. This isn't a diagram of history like a family tree where you look for dates and historical facts; it's a diagram of the broad context and repetitive patterns and family messages that get passed down from generation to generation.

Because of my interest in how fear of rejection affects personal and work relationships, I tend to look for patterns of acceptance or rejection messages that get passed down. This includes unavailability of parents due to drug, alcohol, or work addictions and family "scripts" such as good/bad, success/failure. Other messages passed down are personal safety issues, trust issues, guilt feelings and anger—often due to historical prejudice, or uprootings, or even mass tortures or deaths that have affected some religious, racial, or cultural group. And then there are the various patterns of abandonment, such as chronic illness or early deaths or sudden moves from place to place, or parents who leave because of separations or divorce. One man discovered a pattern of disownings that took different forms throughout the generations. He'd had no idea such occurrences happened in his family.

I do genograms with individual clients, but it's fascinating when working with couples, to have each partner draw their family genogram during a couples session. Then we can compare their family patterns to understand how exquisitely the couple "fits together."

Here is Vanessa's story; it shows how old family messages affect her fears that important people will not stay in her life. From the genogram she discovered how impermanence was a multigenerational refrain in her family. Her genogram on page 134; however, I've streamlined it here so that it contains only the information pertinent to Vanessa's fear of rejection and abandonment.

The firstborn child in Vanessa's family was Van, who died at the age of two. Vanessa was conceived a few months after his death. So the name Van became Vanessa, and Vanessa  became a replacement child for Van. "As I grew older I realized I was living in Van's shadow, and every day was a struggle to be my own person," recalls Vanessa. "I could never be that little boy they had pinned so many hopes on." In addition, her parent's fears that something might happen to her, too, were constantly hovering over her head. They tried to have another baby but were unsuccessful.

To complicate matters, Vanessa's family moved from town to town every two or three years adding to her confusion about identity and security. She found herself leaving friends, schoolmates, and surroundings. And why did they move? "My mom always said that my father would get restless if we stayed too long in one place," she said.

So what did we learn from Vanessa's genogram? We saw that patterns of impermanence began to emerge as far back as four generations. On the paternal side, Vanessa's great-grandmother died suddenly of an infection at age fifty-eight. Vanessa's grandmother lost a child at six months of age, and when Vanessa's father was seventeen years old, his forty-year-old father died in a boating accident. In addition, her "restless" father left them on and off several times during the first twelve years of her life.

And what about her mother's side? When Vanessa's great-great grandfather was a young boy, the family left their country and friends in Ireland to come to the United States during the Potato Famine. When Vanessa's mother was sixteen years old, her own mother died suddenly from pneumonia at age thirty-eight. Vanessa's mother married a few years after, choosing a man who also had a family history of loss and abandonment. Any fears that either of them may have carried came to be realized when Van died.

And how has this generational pattern of uprootings and loss and death affected Vanessa? Well, she has had one short-lived marriage, one not-very-long-term relationship, and currently has a very rocky romance where each of them keeps threatening to leave the other. All of her relationships have been with men who have their own family histories of sudden leavings and deaths. And, no, she does not have children. "Nothing's permanent," says Vanessa.

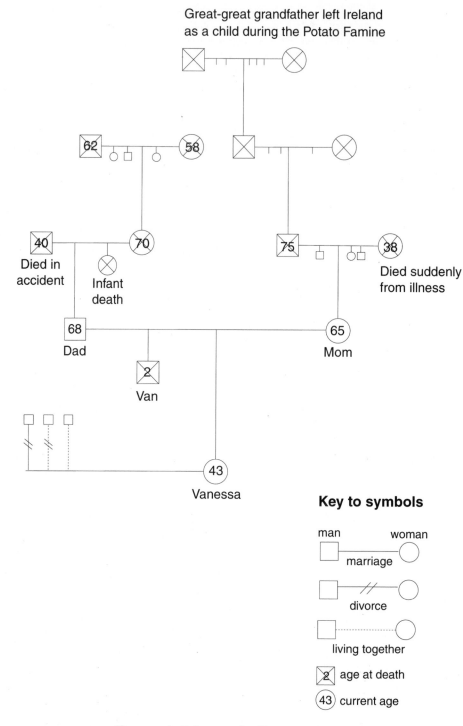

Figure 4: Vanessa's Genogram

# 8

# Eating the Leftovers

## *The Power of Mealtime Messages*

Family mealtimes serve up an array of experiences in taking things personally. Mealtimes in some families are like being at the Mad Hatter's tea party, where interactions are surreal, confusing, and full of put-downs.

> The table was a large one, but the three were all crowded together at one corner of it: "No room! No room!" they cried out when they saw Alice coming.
>
> "There's *plenty* of room," said Alice indignantly, and she sat down in a large armchair at one end of the table.
>
> "Have some wine," the March Hare said in an encouraging tone.
>
> Alice looked all around the table but there was nothing on it but tea. "I don't see any wine," she remarked.
>
> "There isn't any," said the March Hare.
>
> ... "Your hair wants cutting," said the Hatter ..."
>
> "You should learn not to make personal remarks," Alice said with some severity: "it's very rude."
>
> "The Hatter opened his eyes very wide on hearing this: but all he *said* was, "Why is a raven like a writing desk?"

Mealtimes are a microcosm of family interactions, similar to describing the details of one slice of a pie and generalizing to the rest. Recalling family dinner-table happenings can offer you a vivid picture of what it was like growing up. I often ask clients and workshop participants to draw a sketch of their family at the dinner table. Then I ask specific questions such as, "Who was there? Who talked to who? What were the rules?" It takes only a few minutes of doing the exercise to get the flavor of what the mealtime experience was like. This leads to a taste of what life was like growing up in that family. If you want to try your own drawing, you'll find more information about it at the end of this chapter.

Because the messages we take on about ourselves at the dinner table have such a powerful effect on our lives and relationships, the mealtime sketch is a fascinating activity for couples to do together in a therapy session. Discussing their individual childhood dinner table experiences, provides an important key to clearing up confusion and misunderstandings in their relationship.

When I suggested the drawings to William and Betsy, William looked confused. "We didn't have a table," he said. "We were too poor. We just grabbed some food from the pot on the stove and sat around on the floor or wherever. We hardly ever ate at the same time or in the same room. We fended for ourselves. I usually read a book while I ate."

Betsy stared at him in amazement. She'd known William seven years, but she'd just learned something new about his childhood. Only a few minutes ago she was complaining how chaotic their mealtimes were, how William was always reading a book or getting up from the table every few minutes. Sometimes he didn't show up for dinner at all. Now, as he related his childhood mealtime experiences, she began to understand how difficult it was for him to just sit still and eat.

"Sit still and eat" was an unbreakable rule when Betsy was growing up. Her father made rigid rules for behavior at the table. One rule was that everyone must show up to family dinners—no one was allowed to make other plans. So Betsy always assumed that people who live together eat meals together. Was it any wonder she got so upset when William brought a book to the table to read? She wanted to talk to him during dinner and felt rejected when he seemed to prefer the book to her. She needed William to be present at the table, and he wasn't able to do that because he had never learned how to sit at a dinner table.

I know a woman who also grew up with a lot of dinnertime rules, and they were constantly recited to her at the table. In her family the daily message from her mother was, "Sit up straight and eat." From her father the message was, "Shut up and eat." Her brother, taking them at their word to "Eat everything on your plate," would eat the gristle, then noisily spit it out on his plate. Everyone ignored him. These days she prefers to eat alone, reading a book in peace and quiet. Is it any wonder?

# Pass the Rejection, Please

From early childhood, Tess developed her own style in clothing, favoring bright colors and mix-and-match patterns. But her father would try to squelch her idiosyncratic fashion statements by bellowing, "Don't you dare come to the table dressed like that." Tess remembers sadly, "He'd try to shame me into compliance. I couldn't be who I really was."

One man would get up from the table with an upset stomach and have to spit up in the bathroom. His wife would tell herself that the meal she cooked wasn't good enough—an old childhood message to be sure. Even when his problem was diagnosed as an ulcer, she still took it personally, believing that it was her fault. In couples therapy, he recalled how the mealtimes of his childhood were nerve-racking. He lived in fear that his critical and often mean-spirited father would drink too much again and humiliate him and that his mother wouldn't protect him from these abuses. The dinner table was not a safe place for him and the knot of fear in the pit of his stomach followed him into his marriage.

In some families there was a demand by the adults for total respect from the children at mealtimes, yet these children didn't have the opportunity to develop respect and trust for themselves. How can you trust yourself if your father leans over and salts your food until you're sixteen years old? Or if your mother cuts up your food when you can do it yourself or heaps your plate with second helpings without asking you first—then gets on your case if you don't eat it all? Or if one of your parents orders food for you in a restaurant without honoring your preferences? Or if you're repeatedly tricked by your mother at the ice cream parlor? What if your mother asked, "What flavor do you want?" If you hesitated she'd belittle you for not being able to make up your mind. When you finally stammered "Strawberry," she'd say, "No, you don't. I'm buying you vanilla."

How can children who experience these kinds of invalidations learn to trust or respect themselves? One woman's mother takes over in the kitchen whenever she is invited to the daughter's house for dinner. And her daughter's feelings get hurt every time. The mother even brings her own salad dressing, because she doesn't like the one her daughter makes.

"I hated to go to restaurants with my parents because I didn't get to order what I wanted from the menu," remembers one man. "My mother wanted to sample everyone's food and taste three different menu items so she insisted my father and I each order something different from what she ordered. It didn't make any difference if I wanted to order the same thing she did. I felt like my own wants didn't count at all, that I was always getting someone's tablescraps."

To this day, he doesn't order his own plate of food in restaurants. He samples from the plates of his wife and children. You could say he eats the "leftovers." And in other areas of his life, he re-creates those childhood mealtime experiences by "tasting around the plate." So it's not too surprising that he had four different majors in college, or that he starts up new business enterprises one after another. "I like to have a finger in every pie," he says.

## Eating Away at the Pain

One woman recalls, "My mother was a schoolteacher and would make lunch for herself every morning and rush off to work. But she hardly ever made lunches for me or my sister to take to school. So I'd "borrow" bits and pieces of lunches from the other children. She'd tell herself she couldn't be worth much because Mommy didn't care enough to make her a sandwich. And as she grew into adulthood, she continued to tell herself, "I'm not worth much," as she stuffed herself with bits and pieces of food. Food has come to symbolize love, and overeating is her way of comforting herself.

Phillip's mother was usually zonked on prescription drugs. She rarely cooked dinner, so he had to fend for himself. Over the years he fixed himself a lot of peanut butter sandwiches for dinner. Once in a while the family ate meals in the same room, but never at the same time. He began to use food to transport himself to a more secure world. He still uses eating as an escape, the same way he uses TV or reading.

Angela and her mother and sisters were forced to sit at the table quietly while the father ranted and raved about how inadequate each of them was. He would go around the table and tell each of them in turn how fat and unattractive they were. While he spoke, they'd lower their heads, avert their eyes, and keep on eating, stuffing themselves with food in an attempt to cushion the verbal blows.

Eating as an escape, eating as a way to comfort ourselves, eating as a way to pad and protect ourselves, eating as a way to manage feelings—all of these behaviors came out of the messages we received about food and mealtimes when we were young. Some of these messages translated into how we came to see our emotional selves and caused low self-esteem. Other messages translated into how we see our physical selves and caused body-image distortions. When an adolescent girl looks in the mirror and sees her whole body as overweight because her thighs are large or her calves are a little thick, or her upper arms are muscular, the distortion isn't in the glass, it's in the eye of the beholder.

Often we see ourselves as fat, large, or ungainly because someone else saw us that way. When messages about weight are thrown at children who don't seem to have a weight problem, it's a safe guess that one or both of the parents are concerned about their own weight, can't acknowledge the degree of their anxiety, and project their fears onto one or more of their children. Examples of this dynamic are seen in mealtime messages such as, "Don't eat so fast, you're eating like a pig and you'll turn into one," or "If you take another helping you'll get fat." Then they put that pie or cake right in the middle of the table. It looks so tempting, and it's okay for everyone else to dive right in—except of course for the child who might "get too fat." It can be very confusing when parents send mixed messages like these.

Sometimes parents' anxiety about their own weight is transferred to their children in other ways as well. Maryann's mother was always dieting "to lose five or ten pounds" and complaining often about how fat she was. She used to tell Maryann, "It wouldn't hurt for you to lose a few pounds as well."

Whenever they went shopping for school clothes together, Maryann's mother bought her everything in a size too small as an inducement to lose weight. For years Maryann has dieted in an attempt to take off a few pounds, but seems to gain the weight back all too quickly. She doesn't believe her friends when they tell her she looks fine, and was shocked when an aunt told her recently that she was never a fat child, in fact, she was "pretty normal."

Although I'm barely touching on food issues and body image here, it seems a chapter on mealtime messages warrants this small side trip to explore how these issues affect taking things personally. But there's a lot more to say about these issues. For further information on food, weight, and body image, see the notes for this chapter.

## Mealtime Sketches

Although Lyle was comfortable enough at restaurants or large parties, he couldn't understand why he was so miserable at small dinner parties (whether they were at the homes of friends or in his own home). He'd clam up and find himself thinking, "There's something wrong with me, I'm not doing it right." "Right" meant the way his dad would do it. Lyle, of course, was comparing himself to his father, who was the perfect host, a sparkling conversationalist. "He was so entertaining, the focus of everyone's attention—I just can't be like that, as hard as I try."

When we drew Lyle's dinner table he didn't draw one table, he drew two. First, he drew the kitchen table where the family usually ate dinner. "It was a round table where Dad was the boss but not the star. At that table there was more equality and I knew where my place was." Next, Lyle drew the rectangular dining-room table where the family sat with relatives or other guests. "This is where my dad would shine. He'd sit at the head of the table and hold court. And from the time I turned thirteen, my place was across from Dad—I was expected to be the 'other head' of the table. It was awful. I felt I was in a glass container, wanting to participate but not knowing how. It was like being there and not being there at the same time. I knew I was expected to speak up but I was afraid to say anything for fear of embarrassing Mom and Dad. Once I managed to work up the courage to make a funny comment. I was proud of myself because I thought I was doing what was expected of me, but Mom considered it off-color and slapped me in front of my cousins. I was so shocked and humiliated, I can still feel my skin burning where her hand struck my face.

"I never knew what to do, it was all so confusing, so I just gave up and clammed up." At that moment Lyle made the connection between then and now: "That's exactly what I do now at small dinner parties," he said. "I clam up." Lyle's challenge, now that he recognized the source of his problem, is to make a comfortable place for himself at the table. He's been experimenting.

Kaye also drew two dinner tables. But hers were of the "before Dad" and "after Dad" variety. "I drew one dinner table for before my alcoholic father left home, and one for after. Mealtimes were so different once he left because I no longer had to hold my breath." Kaye's mealtime anxiety had stayed with her through the years until she was able to locate the source of her distress. Now she can remind herself that her father is no longer in the picture, she can relax.

When I was growing up, dinnertimes were so awful," remembers one man. "We all waited for my father to explode. What would set him off this time? Even if he made a sudden move to reach for the salt, we'd all duck. My mom might just as well have been serving tension for dinner—it was so thick, you could cut it with a knife. I knew if I tried hard enough, something I'd say or do would set him off, so I'd clown around and sure enough, he'd rage at me. Then we could all breathe a sigh of relief and go on with our meal in peace. Mealtimes continue to create tension for me. Even talking about it makes me feel sick to my stomach."

Mealtime messages affect many of us at a visceral level. Perhaps it's because with each bite of food we also ingested toxic messages. If your childhood mealtime experiences are still leaving knots in your stomach, acid in your esophagus, or a burn in your heart, here are some ways to deal with these residual effects:

- Identify the body sensation. Is it a tightening? A pressure? Knotting? Heaviness? Where is it located in your body? What else do you know about this feeling? Can you give it a shape, texture, temperature, color?

- Establish the original context. What was the atmosphere? What was said? Who said it? How old were you? Did you feel exposed or did someone try to protect you? Did you try to protect someone else?

- Sympathize with the child who had those upsetting experiences, but remind yourself that you're an adult now, and the person who said or did those things can no longer hurt you.

- Find a way to rewrite your earlier experience. The mealtime drawing exercise is one way of doing this.

If you want to try your hand at drawing your dinner table, it's fine to use stick figures. Place your family around the table, and include yourself as well. Draw a large enough table to accommodate everybody. Now take a moment to visualize what it was like to be at that table. Do you remember where you sat? Who sat next to you? Did people talk to each other? What did they talk about? Who talked to whom? Who did you talk to? Who talked to you? Is there anything you'd like to say now to anyone there? Ask yourself what the mealtime rules were. Who made those rules? Who followed the rules and who didn't? Who pretended to follow the rules? Who got caught? What were the consequences?

Now return to the image of what it was like to be at that table. Give yourself plenty of time to reexperience the full range of feelings that may arise. As you think about being there, what do you feel in your body? Where do you feel it? Notice your breathing. What is it like?

Now ask yourself if there is anything you'd like to say to anyone there. To whom? What might that be? Can you say it now to the figure in your drawing?

If you could add leaves to the table to make it bigger, is there anybody you'd like to add to the table? Who? Why? If you could remove place settings, who would you like to take away? Why? Can you imagine the person or people gone? Now that they are absent from the table, does your body feel any differently? Are you breathing any differently? What else would it take to make a comfortable place for yourself at the table?

## Mealtime Revisited

What happens if you've moved away from your family and you're expected to go home again for a family visit or reunion? You might find yourself sitting at the same table with the people who made you feel uncomfortable as a child. Contemplating a trip home is a high-anxiety time for many people. Going home again can awaken long-submerged feelings. No matter what your age now, or how long you've been away, all it takes is a few minutes with your family to trigger childhood feelings, apprehensions, and misgivings. Putting words to these fears is a good first step. Then there are ways to be creative about planning the trip, keeping your boundaries clean and clear (see chapter 11), and staying in control of the situation. Here are some suggestions:

- Plan to go for just a few days even though everyone else may be staying longer.

- Try not to depend on your family. If possible, stay with an old friend, a sibling you get along with, or even consider renting a motel room.

- If you do stay with your family, consider renting your own car for at least part of the visit.

- Plan to a take a breather and get away. Take long walks, go on a day trip, or visit old friends.

- If you've been involved in any kind of twelve-step program, find a meeting in your hometown. It will be familiar to you and will help you to feel more centered.

- Even if you've never been in therapy, consider going for a few sessions before your trip to identify both your fears of and your goals for the visit.

- Don't even *think* of confronting any family members about old issues without having a clear idea of "cake" and "icing" (remember this concept from chapter 4?). A therapy session is a great place to practice what you want to say.

- Most importantly, find a way to physically leave if you're too uncomfortable to stay. As a child, you felt you couldn't leave. You were stuck at that table, or in that house. As an adult, know that you can leave and give yourself permission to utilize that option.

You know you've turned a corner when you can recognize options. Read on to see more possible sources of rejection messages and how to get beyond them to a place loaded with options.

# 9

# Friends Today, Gone Tomorrow

## Peer Rejection Messages

Peer culture is powerful. It can provide positive experiences in areas of social, moral, and sexual development that are a springboard to healthy adult interactions. It can provide opportunities for sharing feelings, for modeling, and for checks and balances. Peer interactions can be nurturing and restorative, but they can also be malignant and destructive, with friends placing a psychological blight on each other.

We've all felt rejected by our peers—friends, schoolmates, cousins, or siblings—at one time or another when we were growing up. Peer rejection takes many forms: ignoring, shunning, teasing, name-calling, harassing, betrayals, and rumor-spreading. It can be found in the classroom, on the playground, in competitive activities, between friends, and most certainly between enemies. It amazed me how many long-forgotten memories turned up when I was anticipating writing this chapter. Most of them were painful memories.

It doesn't take much for feelings to get hurt. A lot of times it starts in the sandbox, when one child flicks sand at another. The picked-on child feels hurt and confused. "Why me? What did I do? Do I just sit here and take it? Do I try to ignore it and pretend nothing happened? Or do I up the ante and flick sand back?"

Even one ugly action or name-calling incident can lead to a negative self-image that sometimes lasts through adulthood. One day some friends and I were sitting around discussing how these kinds of experiences stood out. Kathleen recalled, "A boy at school called me the worst possible name. He said, 'Kathleen, you're a cootie.' I was crushed, and I've never forgotten that incident." Our friend Martin speculated, "I'll bet you were a really cute little girl. Maybe that boy actually said, 'Kathleen, you're a cutie'."

Kathleen's eyes widened, her face softened, "Do you think that might be true? Do you suppose if I hadn't been so ashamed and told my father what happened, he'd have reassured me and said the same thing? You mean I didn't have to believe all these years that someone thought I was a cootie?"

I remember a similar one-time experience from kindergarten that had a long-lasting effect. One day as I walked into school, onto the playground, the cutest boy in class came bounding up to me. He asked if he could walk me across the playground. (*Me?*) I was so excited—all the girls would see me walking with him. Then as we walked together, he asked if he could hold my hand. (Hold *my* hand?) He chose *me* to walk with, he chose *me* to talk to, he chose *me* to hold hands with. I was in heaven. Then suddenly I felt a terrible sharp pain in my thumb, and he ran off. I looked down at my thumbnail. It was bloody. He'd dug his fingernail into my cuticle. It only took a split second for me to go from feeling special to feeling humiliated. And besides that, it really hurt.

It's said that we develop an image of who we are by the way we're treated by others. If others treat us with respect, we feel cherished and come to think of ourselves as loveable. If we're treated with scorn, we feel reviled, and come to think of ourselves as unlovable. When peer relationships are destructive, scars form—that are not easily healed. As you may have guessed, the memory of the playground incident didn't just evaporate. It affected my ability to trust others for many years to come. For the longest time I kept wondering why that boy didn't like me, what I might have done to cause him to do that to me. I'll bet that boy had no idea he'd have such a profound influence on my future social development. I was telling this story to Kathleen and Martin, and they both thought that boy actually liked me and was just trying to show off—you know, like pulling pigtails.

# Discrimination Has Lots of Faces

Since grade school I've experienced many rejection messages in the form of discrimination from peers. I remember when the Campfire Girls at my school used to ask me to participate in some of their activities, hoping I'd join their group. One Saturday I went with them to a circus performance and one of the mother's asked me, "By the way, what church do you go to?" "I don't go to church," I answered. "I'm Jewish." I'll never forget the stunned look on her face. All the girls ignored me the rest of the day. They acted as if I'd tricked them or something. And my confusion and hurt were even greater when they wouldn't have anything to do with me back at school.

Prejudice is hard to explain to yourself when you're a child. We lived in a row house, and I used to play with the girl next door. It was hard for me to understand why members of her family would periodically spit on our porch. It was even harder to understand how she could spit on my porch one day and want to play with me the next, as if nothing had happened. I wondered what I did wrong.

Even normal grade-school classroom activities can be hurtful, too. One woman remembered, "The teacher let one of the girls pass out birthday-party invitations in class. I kept waiting for her to walk over and hand one to me, but she didn't. I just stared in disbelief. I couldn't believe I wasn't invited to her party."

Another recalled, "St. Valentine's Day in grade school could be just awful sometimes. I always dreamed of being the one to get the most valentines, but I never did. In fact, sometimes I hardly got any. I think the authorities should ban exchanging valentines in grade school. It only leads to hurt feelings. And now, twenty years later, when I'm in between relationships I get especially sad on Valentine's Day. I bet it's because of my miserable memories."

Another source of hurt feelings are sports experiences that never seem to go the way we fantasize they will. Kevin was the smallest kid on the block. He was always chosen last for the neighborhood softball games. "I was a pretty decent hitter, but that didn't seem to matter to the team captains—nobody seemed to want me. Because I was chosen last, I always had to bat last. Whenever I'd come up to bat I'd hear the other kids whisper, 'He's an easy out.'" As he looks back now he recalls, "The position I played was 'left out.' I can joke about it now, but back then there was nothing funny about my hurt feelings. It just didn't seem fair. How could I prove myself if no one gave me a chance?" Kevin still has a need to prove himself. He pushes himself hard and arranges to be the one to do any choosing that needs to get done. This way he makes sure he won't be treated unfairly again.

## Middle-School Madness

And then there's middle school—surely a breeding ground for cruel and unusual punishment. Feeling left out and singled out goes with the territory. In these early teen years just about everyone is highly sensitive to rejection. It flies through the air so fast, if you don't duck, you'll get splattered with it. All sorts of betrayals abound—teasing, shunning, ostracizing, friends turning on friends—all of which can be hurtful and leave long-standing scars. Young people can be so incredibly cruel to each other. This time in a child's life can be like a roller coaster, totally unpredictable from day to day—someone will be oh-so-friendly one day and totally ignore you the next. The name-calling and teasing are unmerciful. Jealousies abound, and some of the interactions seem mean-spirited.

Do you remember Shirley Ellis' 1965 hit record, "The Name Game"? The song makes fun of a variety of names by concocting all sorts of rhymes. But it isn't funny when someone happens to be capping on *your* name, especially if it's a peer. "I was unlucky enough to have my grandfather's name," shuddered Branford Smith. "But the taunts got worse when the kids discovered my initials were B. S. They never let me live that down." Perfectly fine names like Mark Franklin, Paul Preston, and Penny Upton became a nightmare for their owners when the significance of their initials was discovered by their peers.

"The worst are the freeze-outs. Some days I show up at school and no one talks to me," complained fifteen-year-old Sarah. "It really stinks. All of a sudden none of my friends will have anything to do with me. I'm alone all day. Sometimes I get so desperate for someone to talk to, that I'll hang around with kids I hardly even know."

A woman I know also remembered what it was like to be desperate for companionship: "One Saturday my mother nagged me to find a friend to do something with. She must have wanted me out of the house. I called and called, but no one was home. I ended up phoning a girl from school I hardly knew and asked her to go to the movies with me. Of course all my friends were at the movies when we walked in."

## Teasing Causes Tears

Girls don't express anger directly and resort to teasing and cattiness because "they are not permitted to fight physically with their enemies according to Mary Pipher in *Reviving Ophelia*. They punish by calling a girl on the phone to say there's a party and she's not invited. They punish by walking up to girls with insults about their clothes or bodies. They punish by nicknames and derogatory labels, they punish by picking a certain girl, usually one who is relatively happy, and making her life miserable."

Boys like to tease girls, too. They want so badly to talk to the girls, to sound clever and witty, but they don't know what to say or how to say it. So they tease the girls. Well, it certainly does fill those awkward silences, but the possible long-term effects are staggering. "Teasing about my body in junior high has stayed with me all these years," recalled one twenty-eight-year-old woman. "The boys used to call me 'pinhead,' and to this day I'm self-conscious about my large shoulders and small head. I think about it every time I try on clothes. And it's the same with my friends, too. Whatever body part got negative attention from the boys back then is the focus of their self-consciousness all these years later."

"I was so mortified when the boys would call me 'zit-face,'" shuddered one young woman. "I got so self-conscious about my face that sometimes I'd stay in my house all weekend. And you know, even today if I have a pimple, I'll often stay home because I think everyone is looking at my face."

Another memory comes up for me. When I was in high school the boys used to call me "chicken legs" because I was so skinny. I couldn't shed the name. It was so disheartening when I moved across country and the new crop of boys thought they were being so clever and original to think up that name for me. Right before I went off to college, one guy advised, "If you want to have a boyfriend, you'd better fatten up your legs." To this day, I tend to disbelieve any compliments about my legs, I guess I'll probably always think of them as "chicken legs."

"I just hated gym class," recalled one man. "I was still a skinny kid when the other boys were beginning to look like men. It was mortifying to have to change clothes in the locker room in front of the other guys because it never failed that someone would tease me, calling me 'runt,' or 'pee-wee.' Even to this day, I'm self-conscious at my health club. If I see some guys talking quietly, I assume they're whispering about me, even though I have muscles now. I can't help it."

A woman I know grew up feeling like she was the butt of everyone's jokes—her older sisters', her cousins', her friends'. The teasing made her feel vulnerable all the time. "I quickly learned," she told me, "that if I could put myself down before anyone else could, they'd be laughing with me and not at me. Except I wasn't really laughing. I felt that it was my job to be teased. I still do. That must be where my self-deprecating attitude comes from."

You want so badly to blend in at this age. Being average is the most important thing. It's not good to be too tall or too short, too flat or too bosomy, too thin or too fat. Being different means you'll get teased or ostracized. Some of the names I remember kids calling each other are freckle-face, four-eyes, ski nose, Dumbo, thunder thighs, string bean, and that favorite taunt—fatty, fatty, two by four.

> **Being average is the most important thing at this age.**
> **You want so badly to blend in.**

## Cliques

The developmental task for adolescents is to develop a sense of self and become autonomous. So they (appropriately) begin to pull away from their parents and for a window in time, their friends become their whole life. Parents often take it personally—they feel rejected by their teenagers and threatened by the power of peers.

Peers derive much of their power from cliques. These tight little groups can be cruel and intimidating. Local standards are set by one clique or another, and when adolescents are not "playing the game" of conforming to these standards, they're frequently scapegoated. According to Mary Pipher, "scapegoating functions as the ultimate form of social control for [those] not sufficiently attentive to social pressures." It's almost as if cliques are bound together by some sort of common enemy. The "enemy for the day," so to speak.

I have painful memories of when my best friend in junior high school suddenly quit talking to me. I had no idea why. One day she was my friend and the next she started hanging out with my arch enemy! They'd whisper together, eat lunch together, and I'll never forget how miserable and alone I felt walking behind them as I watched them walk home together. It seemed like a nightmare, something surreal. I remember thinking, "How could something like that be happening to me?" That experience brought with it a huge gouge in my sense of well-being. My ability to trust was demolished. For many years I attributed my lack of self-confidence to that experience. Now, of course, I realize that my difficulties in life are due to more complex reasons than that one incident, but it sure took a huge toll on me.

## Troublesome Threesomes

Let's look at the threesome situation. Children often find a friendship with one other person to be too intense, so they bring in a third person for balance. However, threesomes are hard to sustain and there is usually some pairing off. The makeup of the pairs may be constantly shifting, but one thing is for sure: Someone is going to feel left out.

One woman remembered how she always felt left out when her two friends created a secret language. "Only the other two little girls knew what it meant. And what was the language that made me feel upset and out of the loop? 'A-B-C, 1-2-3.' That was the code. Pretty simple stuff to be causing me so much misery."

Who among us hasn't felt left out around secret languages? When I finally figured out Pig Latin, the other kids would start talking Poodle Talk—right in front of me. I just hated it—and I hated them for making me feel so stupid. Even when I would finally learn the language, I had such a hard time speaking or understanding it. I wonder if my present inability to learn languages could be connected to this old aversion.

Have you ever felt left out in a threesome? As one woman recalled, "I felt like a third wheel with my friends when they had especially high energy together. I'd pull back and walk behind them. I'd find myself walking two steps behind them, then three, sometimes even five, all the while feeling sorry for myself. With each drop back, I seemed to be creating an even more intensified sense of being on the outside. I'd find myself becoming more and more invisible, thinking, 'They're so involved in conversation, they don't even know I'm not walking with them. I could be talking to myself out loud and they wouldn't even notice.'

"Sometimes," she noted, "All these years later, I still find myself dropping back when I'm walking with two other people—and feeling sorry for myself just as I did in the old days." Then she adds, "sometimes I even concoct a whole scenario about two people bad-mouthing me to each other, and plotting ways to leave me out of their plans. Thank goodness, that doesn't happen very often."

## On the Outside Looking In

"I just hate it when someone I know has a sleep-over and her mom limits the guests to eight girls. There isn't room for me unless someone else cancels," laments a fifteen-year-old I know. "Then I get a last-minute invitation. I usually drop everything and go, too, because it's important to me to be part of the crowd."

Jon, a sophomore in high school, has a similar complaint. "It happens all the time when a bunch of us want to drive from one place to another and there's only one car. Somehow I find myself the sixth person trying to get into a five-passenger car, and I seem to be the one to get left behind. I wish people would find a way to make room for me once in a while."

I, too, remember feeling on the periphery of the crowd in junior high and high school. It seemed as if I was always on the outside looking in—never totally excluded, yet never really a part of the group either. Recently, at a high-school reunion, a bunch of us were sitting around reminiscing, and I heard one of the most popular guys say how he never felt part of the crowd. Can you believe that? I was shocked. I always saw him as being the very center of everything, but it seems he didn't feel that way. And here I thought it was just me who was so sensitive.

Moving from one community to another can be a setup for rejection—especially if the move is to another part of the country where the customs might be different. Attitudes towards and behavior involving drinking, smoking, drugs, can be different from community to community. Moving from a place of one regional accent to another can be a wretched experience—you might be branded as "different" for speaking differently. One women recalled how she moved from California to a very small New England town where everybody knew everybody else and the families had all come over on the Mayflower. And she, poor thing, was Catholic! It wasn't okay to be different.

When Callie was thirty-two, she went back to school to learn to be an electrician. She was excited about being accepted into an apprenticeship program and was enthusiastic about getting the training she needed to do the work she wanted to do. "But I didn't bank on the attitude of the men I was working with," she said. "No one would talk to me unless it was absolutely necessary. They gave me the cold shoulder. And then a strange thing happened. Although I'm pretty gregarious, I began to clam up, both in social situations and at home. In fact, I became so quiet that my cat would startle if I said something." Why did Callie react so strongly? It seems that the silent treatment from her peers at work sparked memories of long-ago silent treatments—of the junior-high and high-school variety.

# When the Tables Turn:
# From Bully to Victim

"I was sort of the neighborhood bully," remembers Donald. I was pretty little, but I acted tough. I was an angry kid and got into trouble a lot, taking out my frustrations on the other kids on the block. Now I realize I was probably mimicking behavior I saw at home. My parents not only fought with each other, they fought with the neighbors, too. I remember when I was about eight years old, my parents forbade me to see to my best friend because they got into a fight with his parents.

"About that time something happened that changed my experience of life. I shot a kid with a homemade bow and arrow—it narrowly missed hitting him in the eye. The whole block was in an uproar after that happened, and the other boys joined forces and ganged up on me. I remember the day they threw me down on the ground, and I was afraid to get up, afraid I might not survive the attack. Something happened in those moments. I was no longer the bully, I was the victim. From that day on, they picked on me unmercifully. There was no one I could tell. My older brother had just gone off to college, and there was no way I could tell my parents about my humiliation. I was all alone for the next three or four years. That's a long time to be lonely.

"This experience affected my relationships with men for many years. I was always slightly distrustful, afraid of being teased or picked on. But I fought back in the business world, I had to prove my manhood so I did it in a highly competitive business. And I was very successful.

"I finally quit the corporate rat race and started to work for myself. Then, through therapy I began to find new ways to express my fear and anger. Now I watch as they come up and accept them as part of me. I've learned something important: I don't have to be aggressive in business anymore to feel like a man."

# Sibling Skirmishes

"I blame it on my older sisters excluding me when we were children," laments one woman. "I just idolized them and wanted so badly for them to include me. No matter how hard I tried I was always the little sister and they were always together, sharing activities that I was too young to take part in.

"Some of these old feelings still haunt me. I assume others are superior to me and wiser. I do fine in one-to-one contacts, but whenever I'm with two other people I expect to feel left out."

By talking about it, she began to notice how she contributed to her own "left out" feelings. She would clam up during conversations and withdraw, then wonder why the other two people were talking more to each other than to her.

Now she could remind herself she was no longer the five-year-old wanting to do "big-girl" things with her older sisters. She realized she could change her behavior when she noticed the times she was beginning to feel left out. She recognized that she could choose whether or not to make an effort to stay connected and involved with the conversation.

Caitlin did get to do 'big-girl things.' In fact, she was a companion to her older sister. "I was born when my sister was ten years old," remembers Caitlin. "She helped raise me because my mother wasn't around much. She'd dress me up and comb my hair and take me out and show me off. Finally I began to realize how she used me to get attention for herself. After a while I began to get uncomfortable and object to this. When I reached my teens, I insisted that I wanted to choose my own clothes and comb my own hair. She gave me lots of arguments but once she realized I meant business, she couldn't stand my push toward independence, and she pretty much stopped giving me attention. I felt she just dropped me overnight. I'm still hurt—and angry, too."

Dean remembered, "I always thought my parents were playing favorites—I was the bad child and my sister was the good child. I was younger than her by three years, but even though I really looked up to her, I just hated that 'know-it-all' attitude of hers. She was so good at everything she tried, and I was always competing with her, and failing miserably. And she was so mean to me—teasing me and calling me 'Blubber Lips.' She always said, 'I get to be mean because I'm your older sister.' All these years later I find myself trying to get back at her for how she used to treat me. I try to make her feel bad every chance I get. Sometimes I can even make her cry."

So what about physical fighting between siblings? "When I remember how my twin brother and I used to fight when we were kids, I'm surprised we don't have anger toward each other now," said another man I know. "We both still have scars from those early arguments." Parents are often alarmed by it and don't know what to do, but according to Stephen Bank and Michael Kahn in *The Sibling Bond*, this fighting has

Fighting between siblings can have positive aspects: it allows for human contact and is reassuringly predictable.

some positive aspects. "The contact that is basic for human survival is immediately available in a near-at-hand and ready-to-fight sibling. Sibling aggression has a reassuringly predictable quality: if one punches or pinches or insults a sibling in a particular way, the retort, though painful, is familiar and expected."

But what if the fighting gets out of hand and one sibling terrorizes another? Sometimes the children are reenacting what they witness in the household, especially the hostilities of the parents. In other instances, anger is unacknowledged and stifled between the parents but played out by the children. Intense anger between siblings is frequently related to favoritism shown by the parents, especially when there is too little affection to go around to begin with. The arrival of a new baby can set off fears and anxiety in an older child that get acted out against the infant.

# A Beacon of Light

Is it any wonder how depressed teenagers can get? They are so overcome by intense feelings of despair. They are steeped in the feelings of the moment, going from extreme to extreme. Occurrences like these can seem overwhelming, because the teens haven't yet accumulated the life experience that teaches them things do get better, that it's not the end of the world. The best thing about adolescence is that it's time limited. How I wish these teens could believe that.

What would happen if young boys and girls could learn early on that they are not the "only one" feeling left out? What if they could have the opportunity to share their stories and their feelings, and discover creative solutions? A fifth-grade teacher I know had her class write anonymous answers on slips of paper to the question: "Describe a time you felt left out." She collected their comments in a canister and read them each out loud, inviting comments from the whole class. "Has anyone else ever felt the same?" she asked. "How did he or she handle it?" Most of the children were surprised to learn that they were not alone in the big world of rejection. The exercise sparked many other discussions in class. Some were about general issues, such as how body language contributes to inclusion or exclusion, and others were more specific, such as whether or not the children would rather ask to sit with a group at lunch or whether they would prefer to be invited to sit down. "Invited" won handily, and from that day on, cordialness improved.

Something else came out of the discussion as well. One little girl, Hannah, was friendly with her classmates in school, but was never asked to come to their homes on the weekends. Because Hannah's parents were divorced and she lived in the suburbs with her father on weekends, the other girls told themselves it was too far away for Hannah to travel back to the city to play with them. So they never asked her. Then on Mondays they'd talk about their parties and outings in front of her. She was interested and would ask a lot of questions in an attempt to join in their experience.

The casual observer wouldn't know Hannah was feeling left out. But the teacher knew, and with Hannah's permission, she commented to the girls, "You never invite Hannah to your parties. It's true that she lives far away and might not always be able to attend, but you've never given her the chance to say 'no.' What do you think she is telling herself?" Tears came to their eyes as they realized she'd been feeling left out all this time.

What a gift this teacher gave her students with this "left out" exercise. They were amazed that other students had similar fears and experiences. They realized they were not alone in the world. Best of all, they got to try on someone else's feelings for a while.

Writing this chapter was an interesting process, both for me and the people I interviewed. As each of us recalled our childhood or adolescent experiences, a new clarity emerged. Even though the experiences may have been tucked away out of memory, the messages and negative beliefs that came from them have for many years colored how we think of ourselves.

Calling a memory up again and looking at it from the perspective of an adult is a magical experience for many people. Doing it in a group of adult peers is even more fascinating because we have to benefit of their insights as well.

I encourage you to examine your early friendships and sibling experiences to see how they've affected your patterns of behavior and your work and personal relationships.

By looking back at a childhood experience through adult eyes, you can put it in its proper context. Identifying the youth and inexperience of the children who hurt your feelings may help break the myths that were formed based on that experience.

# Part Three

# Making Changes, Moving On

# 10

# One Foot In and
# One Foot Out

## *Learning to Depersonalize*

Ever since I was a child, tangled things have frustrated me—especially jammed hangers, knotted necklaces, and my too-curly hair. Hangers still make me want to scream. Fragile necklaces can be dealt with using mineral oil and wax paper, and a good detangler works wonders for hair. When we find a way to detangle the meanings of other people's words or actions, we can step back and depersonalize messages. By combing through the words, tones of voice, and perceived attitudes of others, we can better know which information to take seriously and which not to take personally.

## Resilience

Children grow up with different detangling abilities. Some children learn to cope with stress as a challenge rather than a defeat. These children, like the branches of a tree during a storm, seem to be able to bend without breaking. They are often called the "resilient ones," the "survivors," "the transcenders."

They find strengths deep within themselves that enable them to stay intact as they move through the difficulties of life. Most people have been able to develop small pieces of strengths here and there. The challenge has been to recognize the strengths and weave them together—reinforcing them. Yes, it's true that sometimes it seems we don't have much to work with, but that's where counseling can help out—by identifying and solidifying strengths and moving on.

When I researched perceived childhood rejection and adult intimacy, I found that experiences of rejection alone did not necessarily lower a person's capacity for intimacy. The mediating factor appears to be whether negative belief systems, behaviors, or personality dispositions developed because of the individual's experiences of rejection by parents. Why were some children able to grow into adulthood without developing these negative patterns? Most likely it's because of their resilience.

Why do some children seem to have this buoyancy, this natural knack for coping with the trauma in their lives more successfully than other children? What makes them different than those who are more damaged by the winds of life's experiences? Somehow they've learned a kind of emotional martial arts—they know when to bend and spar and fend off blows. Experts speculate that resilient children have a different view of the world than other children, and therefore, they have different responses to life situations. They operate out of empowerment rather than impotence. They develop self-regard rather than self-degradation. Their approach to life is reflective rather than impulsive. They can step back from a situation, be objective, and keep their perspective. When positive experiences are lacking inside the family, they have been able to reach outside the family for what they need. These children have most likely been inspired by at least one person in their life, such as a relative, teacher, or neighbor, who provided the modeling, nurturing, and unconditional acceptance the child might not have otherwise received.

Margie will vouch for the importance of such a person. Margie was a lonely little girl. She had absentee parents—a workaholic dad who was physically missing and an alcoholic mom who was emotionally vacant. But Margie used to spend a lot of time next door, at Betty Palmer's house. They'd bake cookies together and eat and chat over a glass of milk or a cup of tea. In Betty Palmer's kitchen, Margie came to think of herself as important and learned someone could and did take an interest in her. When parents aren't available, it's important for children to have a "cookie lady" (or man) in their lives. Lucky for Margie, Betty Palmer was her "cookie lady."

Lillian Rubin author of *The Transcendent Child*, refers to children like Margie as "adoptable"—trusting and open enough to recognize opportunities and accept a hand when it is offered. These children found an "interest or activity—books, music, art, sports—that took them out of the family and into another world. . . ." They had "the ability to attract others who . . . become the mentors and surrogates who light the way and fill the gaps left by the past . . . who can help fill the empty spaces inside." These transcendent children lived at the periphery of family life, either because they were abused or because they didn't fit. As one person said, "I felt like a dog in a cat family." They were able to distance themselves, *dis*identify, and "grasp alternatives when they came into view." They were able to stop knocking on a door that was closed to them, to recognize that members of their family were not able to give them what they needed. Resiliency is also addressed in chapter 10.

Another researcher has found that a primary factor in how well children survive traumatic childhoods is whether or not they take things personally. Ronald Rohner, in his studies of worldwide rejection, found that three important characteristics contribute to resiliency in children: development of a sense of self, self-determination, and the capacity to depersonalize."

Let's take a look at each characteristic. A *sense of self* means children have an awareness of themselves as individuals, have clear boundaries, and respect themselves as unique and separate from other family members. Once children have this awareness of self, they can develop a sense of *self-determination* in which they feel some sort of personal control over their environment and important life events. This is also called an *internal locus of control*. Then the third ability can follow—stepping back and taking perspective, which Dr. Rohner calls *depersonalizing*. It includes the capacity to distinguish which actions are directed toward them and which actions are not directed toward them. In other words, these children don't take things so personally.

For example, read the following stories to see how two different children handle similar situations with their parents: Hank's dad unexpectedly cancelled their plans to go to the park together because he had a bad headache. Hank had been looking forward to this special time with his busy dad, and he was disappointed for sure, but he was able to understand that his dad's headache had nothing to do with him. In other words, he was able to depersonalize the situation. But what if Hank had blamed himself and told himself that *he* is the headache, that his dad was really canceling because Hank did something wrong, or wasn't good enough? Then Hank would have been taking it personally, faulting himself, and making his dad's problem his own problem.

Sandra, on the other hand, was a sensitive child and tended to overreact in many mother-daughter interactions. One day her mom, nervous about cutbacks at work, arrived home stressed out and snapped at Sandra when she wanted some attention. Sandra immediately assumed her mom was angry at *her*, that she was somehow at fault. So she pulled out that old familiar mental checklist and did a rundown in her mind of all the mistakes she might have made that day, the things she might not have done well enough. Yes, Sandra was taking it personally. If, however, she had been able to depersonalize the situation, she might have reminded herself that her mom was upset about something that happened at work and probably not angry at *her* after all. She would have been able to separate her mother's feelings and experiences from her own, and distance herself enough from the situation to not react so emotionally.

Sometimes people need a little help in learning how to depersonalize. It seems to me that antidepressants can function as "detanglers." They offer the space to take a step backward from words or behaviors of others, so we're not so quick to overreact—not so quick to take things personally. But the medications only allow the space to step back, they don't teach *how* to to do it. Wouldn't it be great to be able to learn what you're doing differently so you can carry this knowledge with you after you stop the meds? Psychotherapy can help with this process. I always think of it as teamwork: the client, me (the psychotherapist), the psychiatrist who does the prescribing, and the medication. We all work together.

## All about Me

Because I always took things so personally, when I'd walk into a room I'd often think people had been talking about me. As I've grown more comfortable with myself, I've outgrown this reaction—well, most of the time. However, recently I walked smack into this old dynamic when I entered the dressing room of my exercise studio. Two woman I knew were sitting there talking, but the minute I walked in, they stopped. For an instant I thought they had been talking about me, just as I would have a few years ago. It only lasted a moment, until I realized that I must have walked in on a private conversation that most likely had nothing to do with me. It was a great marker for me. It had been a long time since I'd reacted that way.

A woman I know described how she'd overreacted after she made a comment to her office mate about a work procedure. His only response was, "Give me a break." She seethed for days, but with some coaxing and coaching she decided to check out what he meant. It turns out he hadn't even heard her statement. He was listening to his Walkman and was commenting that the radio station had played the same song three times in an hour. His comment had absolutely nothing to do with her, although she'd presumed it did.

As we saw in chapter 1, very young children see themselves as the center of their worlds, where everything revolves around them. This is developmentally appropriate, and we wouldn't expect it to be any other way. But as an adult, being the center like that presents a special kind of problem. In that center position all eyes are on you and it's no wonder you might feel like a the bull's-eye in a target—just waiting for the dart's sting.

It's easy for children to personalize the actions of others because they're not yet able to see things from the other person's perspective. As they grow up, they learn to step out of that center space, and look around them, and they begin to develop the ability to put themselves in other

> If you see yourself as the center of your world,
> it's hard not to think of yourself as a target,
> just waiting for the dart's sting.

people's shoes. At the same time they're gaining some awareness of their feelings and experiences. They can begin to gain some perspective regarding the actions of others and can see things as others see them. In other words, they can begin to *de*personalize.

Some of us develop this ability, but some of us have some trouble moving out of that place of specialness where it seems like the spotlight is always on us. We have trouble distinguishing between events that are directed toward us and those that have nothing to do with us. We see examples of this all the time in news stories: Someone gets jostled in a fast-food restaurant or a bar and thinks the other person pushed him on purpose; a fight breaks out, maybe a knife or gun gets pulled; maybe someone gets hurt or killed. It's a good bet that somebody took something personally.

The trouble is, we get caught in a Me, Me, Me way of thinking about our world. If we can outgrow the idea that the world revolves around us, then we can begin to realize someone else's thoughts and feelings are not necessarily the same as ours. Once we can develop the ability to see things from others' perspectives, we can begin to step away and depersonalize their words and actions. We can understand that in most instances their behavior is not necessarily intentionally directed at us, not meant to hurt us, not meant to shame or embarrass us, not meant to reject us. Most of all, we can begin to get past the notion that their behavior is meant to be a personal affront. Other people are frequently wrapped up in their own worlds, with their own histories and experiences and anxieties that usually have nothing to do with us. Nothing.

If it seems someone is pointing a finger at you, remind yourself that in fact, the finger pointer is often talking about his or her own fears or anxieties. Remember the discussion of projection from chapter 7. The traits we cannot tolerate in others are often our own unacceptable characteristics—things we cannot stand about ourselves. Try to remind yourself that no matter what someone says to you, no matter how terrible it may be, turn it around. That person is most likely talking about him or herself.

In situations like these, you could use the steps first presented in chapter 3 for checking things out. Here are those steps again:

**Step One:** Describe the problem in observable, nonblaming terms.

**Step Two:** Describe how you felt about the problem.

**Step Three:** Describe how you explained the problem to yourself.

**Step Four:** Describe how you would like the interaction to go next time.

Don't be afraid to use your own experiences to hypothesize about what that person might be thinking or feeling. Sometimes it's the only way to put yourself into someone else's shoes. But remember that your feelings and experiences are not necessarily shared by the other person, so don't presume they are. Unless you check it out with the other person you won't know for sure. But it does give you some insight into what might be going on. Perhaps then you can even respect the person's opinion although you might not agree with it.

> **Once we can see things from other people's perspectives, we can begin to depersonalize their words and actions.**

As we saw in chapter 3, empathy is the ability to move out of your own world and into the shoes of someone else. But what if somehow you never learned to empathize? Is it too late to learn? There's no question it's harder for some people than for others, but I believe it's often doable. Where should you start? Here are some questions to ask yourself to find out if you have difficulties empathizing:

- Do people tell me I'm totally caught up in my own world or that I think mostly of myself?

- Can I hypothesize about how other people might be feeling? Can I remind myself that I can't presume how they feel because their experience and feelings may be quite different from mine?

- What was going on for me in situations where I've been snappish or curt? What was I so upset about that I took it out on other people? Was I scared, anxious, embarrassed, angry, vulnerable? Could the same kind of thing be going on for the other person now?

Just as being able to empathize can help you to depersonalize, so can learning to create distance when you find yourself in overwhelming situations. By finding a way to avoid the flood of emotions that may be swirling around you, you can begin to think more clearly.

I've learned five effective ways to help stop the flooding process. Some of these have been discussed in previous chapters but this is a good time to recap.

The easiest approach is the old standby: Count to ten slowly. It really works to pull yourself out of the situation and give yourself just enough distance to regain your balance. The second approach is to say to yourself, "I'm only feeling embarrassment here, not shame. Just because I'm embarrassed doesn't meant I'm ashamed." Shame and embarrassment are not the same feeling. Learn to recognize the difference and try to keep them separate. As soon as I feel any kind of embarrassment coming on, I use the third approach: I laugh at myself before anyone else can.

I've developed a kind of giggle that pops out automatically when I start to feel embarrassed. It puts me back in control of the situation and side-steps potentially embarrassing moments from moving into the realm of shame.

> ## Remind yourself, "I'm only feeling embarrassment here—not shame."

Before I developed the giggle, I used to take myself so seriously I wondered if I might even be humor impaired. As a child I used to think people were laughing at me all the time, so it wasn't easy to learn to direct humor at myself. As I practiced, I discovered I wasn't really laughing at myself. It was more like I was laughing *with* myself. Once I began to lighten up everything changed—I found I wasn't taking things so personally.

> ## Don't be humor impaired, learn to laugh *with* yourself.

A fourth technique is to say to yourself, "I don't have to deal with this input now. I'll put it on 'tape delay' and play it back later. A variation would be to jot down the other person's words if pen and paper are handy and tell yourself you'll deal with them later.

Each of these proactive methods will help you get some distance from feelings so you don't overreact. What other techniques can you create?

Another way to protect yourself from emotional overload is to visualize a plastic bubble around yourself where nothing can hurt you. You have the ability to install or remove the bubble at will. Nobody can get to you while the bubble is in place. And nobody knows it is there but you. Imagining a plastic shield in front of you works also.

When I worked in Child Protective Services in San Francisco, I taught myself a technique I've been practicing ever since. I'd like to share it with you. When I find myself having to deal with a difficult person, someone whom I have a hard time respecting, I try to find something to like. Maybe it's their smile, intelligence, sense of humor, or sense of style. When I focus in on that characteristic, the person senses my respect for him or her, even though I might be "respecting" the color of his or her shirt.

All of these suggestions have two things in common—they allow you to have some control over the situation and to gain some objectivity. "When you're feeling overwhelmed and disoriented try to find a way to reorient yourself. The best way to turn down the pressure from "flooding" is to get some distance from it. Be creative in developing what works for you. One man likes to ground himself by pressing the thumb of one hand into the palm of the other hand. He applies enough pressure to bring him back to consciousness, to himself, to his feelings. It's a way of soothing himself.

Self-soothing is an absolutely wonderful practice. Many of us may already find ourselves occasionally touching or stroking our own hand, arm, shoulder, hair, chin. You may have written off this repetitive touching as a nervous habit, when in fact, it might be a creative way of calming yourself. The next time you become aware of stroking yourself, just notice how you are taking care of yourself. Try noticing its positive effects.

And there are other ways of calming yourself through repetition. Remember how the muscician I told you about in the introduction would calm himself by chanting, "Don't take it personally, don't take it personally, don't take it personally . . ." When you're feeling rejected or out of control, a soothing touch or a rhythmic chant can be calming in a hypnotic kind of way. The important thing is to gain enough distance to depersonalize the actions of someone else. You need to give yourself some distance in order to gain some perspective.

When both feet are planted in a situation, you may find yourself standing in quicksand, losing your balance, and feeling trapped. So the trick is to have one foot in and one foot out as a way of staying connected but at the same time maintaining some objectivity.

When you're able to grab some objectivity, remind yourself, "This is not necessarily a rejection of me or a personal attack." Ask yourself, "How much of this belongs to me and how much to the other person?" Which feelings are theirs and which are mine?" If you can disentangle your feelings and experiences from theirs, keeping boundaries clear, you'll be better able to depersonalize the situation. Keeping boundaries clean and clear isn't easy, however. Chapter 11 will show you how.

# 11

# Just Who Do You Think You Are?

## Keeping Boundaries Clean and Clear

When my professors would talk about "boundaries" in graduate psychology classes, I couldn't, for the life of me, understand what the concept meant. I strained to get the point in lectures, but it eluded me. I found myself rereading the same paragraphs again and again, but the words made no sense. Finally it dawned on me—I didn't have a clue regarding personal boundaries because boundaries hardly existed in my family when I was growing up.

For years I struggled to understand boundaries and limits. Each person comes to develop his or her own conception of the meaning of personal boundaries. "I have a right to have the integrity of skin around me," one woman declared in the process of our work together. Another client realized, "I know I have boundaries when I notice that the other person's boundaries are mushy." A man I know recognized how a sense of depression sometimes fills the room when he's with his partner, "For the first time I knew this feeling was not mine."

## Boundary Rules

Boundaries between family members are determined by generational roles and rules. Role appropriateness means clear separation between the marital unit and the children, as well as caretaking by the parents rather than by the children (more about this later in the chapter). Rules pertain to who participates in transactions and in what way. However, rules are not always verbal, and the unspoken ones can be the most confusing. Especially if you were supposed to guess them or if they contradicted the spoken rules—trying to decipher rules sometimes meant ambiguity and even chaos. There may have been times you felt you were losing your mind from all that confusion, but most likely what you were losing was your boundaries. Roles and rules should be clearly defined so there does not have to be guessing and mind reading. When there is a clear pattern of roles and rules in families, then there are clear boundaries.

## Personal Boundaries

Psychologists John and Linda Friel offer seven categories of personal boundaries. I've used their descriptions as a foundation and added some of my own impressions.

**Physical boundaries** means other people respect your physical space. These boundaries are violated when someone goes into your room, uses your stuff without asking, or reads your diary. They're also violated when someone touches, or tickles you when you don't want him or her to, or hits you.

**Intellectual boundaries** means others respect your ideas or thoughts. These boundaries are violated when someone tries to discount your thoughts, saying things like, "You're imagining it" or "You don't really think that, do you?"

**Emotional boundaries** involve respect for your feelings. These boundaries are violated when someone tries to invalidate or ignore your feelings, takes you for granted, or psychologically abuses you by criticizing, belittling, or shaming.

**Social boundaries** means a respect for your choices of social contact. They're violated when someone criticizes where you go or who you choose to be with, for example, "Why on earth would you want to go out with *her*?" or "Why would you want to see *that* movie?"

**Sexual boundaries** are about the right to privacy and choosing who can touch you, where, and how they can touch you. In other words, no one can touch you without your permission. Some sexual boundary transgressions such as stranger or acquaintance rape are obvious, but others, such as tickling, staring, and leering can be confusing because they are not so obvious.

**Money boundaries** involve how you earn it, spend it, save it, and how much you need to feel a sense of security. There's no question that different attitudes about money can cause relationship problems, especially if you don't respect the other person's style.

**Time boundaries** means having respect for your own and others' ways of getting things done. Some of us are on time or even early for meetings or getting projects done. Others of us are "under the wire" people and thrive on the excitement of deadlines.

Poor personal boundaries are often mistaken for personal affronts. For example, I used to have poor time boundaries—I was chronically late. The people who were waiting on me would usually get offended, and who could blame them? The obvious reason was that I didn't plan very well, and I'd try to squeeze in too many tasks or errands before meeting someone. However, I finally figured out the not-so-obvious reason—I was choosing to be later than the person I was supposed to meet. Why? Because waiting for someone made me too anxious. I would worry that they forgot, or stood me up, or some other form of rejection. Better they should wait for me, even though it meant they might get annoyed at my lateness.

---

**Out-of-bounds behavior equals poor boundaries.**

---

## Boundary Confusion

Having boundaries is like having a fence around your house. Pia Mellody asserts that these symbolic fences serve three purposes:

- To keep people from coming into our spaces
- To keep us from going into the spaces of others
- To give us a sense of wholeness

A low fence at the property line allows for a flow of energy and ideas between neighbors, yet both know where their rights begin and end. However, if one or the other builds a high wall, a barrier is created and the energy ceases to flow freely. People who build walls instead of boundaries are looking for extra protection, extra security. If only they knew how to set clear limits, perhaps they wouldn't feel the need to build walls.

---

**Too often we build walls instead of boundaries.**

---

If you grew up in a family with little or no boundaries, you might better understand what they are by first looking at what they are not. Feelings, needs, and thoughts are contagious in families with poor boundaries. Family members slip in and out of each other's physical and emotional space by speaking for each other, feeling for each other, and thinking for each other. They have trouble separating their own feelings, needs, and ideas from those of others. These families are often referred to as enmeshed but a better description might be *enmashed*. In these overly close and entangled families, people are often inappropriate with each other and engage in out-of-bounds behavior.

Family therapists sometimes use stories like the following one to describe boundary confusion in an enmeshed family: A waiter brings the wrong vegetable to the table, and one family member turns to another and says, "I forget which of us doesn't like peas." Or sometimes they tell the story describing how every time the brother gets yelled at, the sister cries—she doesn't know what feelings belong to who. Oh, yes, there's the saying about how one person gets cut and the other bleeds.

These descriptions may sound like exaggerations but they're not. My brother, Lee, told me how, when he's walking along and sees someone slip and fall on a snow-packed Baltimore Street, *his* body hurts with the pain he imagines the other person is feeling. And if a family member gets a cut, he's in real trouble. I, too, have had problems around cuts since the time I was little. If I cut myself or saw someone get cut, I'd faint. Once I was rehearsing for a school play and someone whispered that one of the actors was carving initials in his arm. Unfortunately I glanced toward him, imagined the pain, and fainted dead away.

I used to confuse emotional pain, too. I remember when my daughter, Jocelyn, was in the fifth grade and one Saturday she phoned several friends to play. No one was home. It seemed they were all at another little girl's birthday party, and Jocelyn wasn't invited. I was a wreck all day, imagining how upset she must be that she was left out. I felt so bad for her. Finally I couldn't stand it any longer and said something to her. It turns out she wasn't at all upset about not being invited—but she complained a lot about being bored because she had no one to play with all day. "Why would I care about not being invited to Lora's party?" she told me. "I don't like her and her mother only invited my friends because she wants Lora to be invited to *their* parties." Oops. These were my very own "left out" issues—not Jocelyn's.

Similarly, what about parents who become a little too anxious each year when school starts for their children? One mom made a flurry of phone calls and left several messages at the school before classes even started. When the calls were not returned, she got hold of the teacher's home phone number and called there late one night. "I just wanted to touch base before school started," she said, "because my daughter's a little nervous about school starting." The teacher was surprised by the call and irritated by the intrusiveness. Then she realized how anxious the parent must have been to make those calls. What were Septembers like for this mother when she was a child? Might she be reexperiencing back-to-school apprehension from her own childhood? Was her own mother a nervous wreck at the beginning of each school year, too?

Feeling pain, distress, or anxiety in these overpowering ways can be an indication of boundary confusion—not knowing where you stop and someone else begins. Maybe your sense of self is not as well defined as you would like; you may find yourself spilling over into the space of others and letting them spill over into yours. As a result, you may sometimes struggle to figure out which feelings belong to you and which belong to someone else. And you don't always know what is intrusive or inappropriate.

---

> **Poor boundaries can mean spilling over into the physical and emotional space of others—and letting them spill over into yours.**

---

Perhaps the confusion came from never learning to respect the personal space of others, nor to expect others to respect yours. Especially if you grew up in a family where people entered bedrooms or bathrooms without knocking or they borrowed something without asking or they shared personal information with others without first seeking permission.

I remember when my daughter was in second or third grade she wrote a charming essay called "Problems." I was so proud of her ability to write about her feelings that I xeroxed her paper and passed it around to my friends. I was dumbfounded when one friend wondered, "Did you ask permission to share Jocelyn's personal thoughts? After all, she wrote it for her teacher, not for your friends."

Quite frankly, it had never occurred to me to ask permission from Jocelyn to share her work. When I was growing up, each set of parents in the extended family tried to out-brag the others about their children's talents. No one ever dreamed of asking their children for permission to show their work around. My family didn't really have a firm grasp on good boundaries. And you may be wondering if I asked Jocelyn for her permission to share this and other stories with you. I sure did.

Respect for individuality goes along with respect for personal space. Sometimes we grow up with an overwhelming feeling of "we-ness" in our families. We're unable to learn respect for who we are as individuals, distinct from the rest of our family. Perhaps, as chapter 6 described, parents can be living vicariously through their children, seeing their children as extensions of themselves and often trying to live their own unfulfilled dreams though them. Sometimes parents don't see their children at all— and the children become invisible. It's as if the children are nonpeople with nonnegotiable needs. Their likes and dislikes don't even matter. A classic story is about the young mother who insisted there was no way her young daughter would like oatmeal. Why? Because she, herself, couldn't stand it.

Here are some examples of what it's like growing up in boundary-less families:

Carl remembers feeling like a pawn in his parents' chess game, "My mind was a battleground for other people and there was no consideration for my feelings, my needs, my wants. I wasn't allowed to exist for myself—there was no me. I felt jerked around, powerless, and frustrated. I wanted to scream at them, 'You have no idea who I really am. I'm a person, I'm not your toy!'"

One man remembers being told by his mother, "You're not thinking clearly." From his mother's point of view he wasn't thinking clearly because he wasn't thinking like her. The message he took away was "It's not okay to think for yourself."

Chris recalls "giving up my self, my soul for my family—to be what they needed me to be. But it was never good enough. To this day, they don't want me to be myself and they try to make me feel bad about the person that I am. I guess it's because I'm not enough like them. You know, I really don't want to be like them but I feel guilty and disloyal if I'm not."

One woman can see now how growing up in an overly close family has contributed to her problems at work. She keeps trying to create an extended family for herself in her business, but gets too close to her employees, trying to be friends with them and confusing employer/employee boundaries. Then she takes it personally if they disappoint her.

Sonia, recently divorced, overheard her mother telling the saga of the divorce to other relatives. But as she listened, she realized the details were about the mother's own divorce, not Sonia's. When Sonia asked her mother to please check her facts, the mother replied, "Why should I, I know exactly what happened to you."

In the same vein, a woman who wrote an article about her childhood received a call from her estranged mother who said, "Your facts are all wrong. I'm calling to tell you what your childhood was really like."

One man told me, "My mother didn't have any idea *what* she needed, but she expected me to fulfill it anyway! I was only seven years old and I used to try hard to read her mind, but I couldn't. As an adult I was almost always confused about which feelings or needs were actually mine and which belonged to other people. Then one day I was finally able to say to myself, 'This feeling is not mine.' For the first time in my life I knew where I began and where I ended. I could trust my own perceptions. I think I'm beginning to understand what boundaries are!"

Another man talked about the facade he developed as a child. "I couldn't be myself in my family, and now as an adult, it's okay if people reject my facade, but not what's underneath." After a long pause he adds sadly, "You know, I hardly know what's underneath anymore."

Let's take a closer look at facades for moment. If your family taught you to present a false front to the world, you probably developed a "false self" as well. You might put huge amounts of energy into appearing strong (when you really feel like a puddle inside), wise (when you're afraid you're really stupid), confident (when you're really scared to death), in control (when you're actually feeling out of control). It gets to the point that you don't even know what's inside anymore. As one client realized, "I've discarded who I really am. Instead it seems that I'm standing behind a cardboard cutout, like the stand-up cutouts of movie stars at the theaters." If she could peel away the facade, what would she find underneath? Well, she didn't know—that was the work to do in therapy.

Sometimes we need to peel away the layers of negative messages we've developed about ourselves in order to get to the good stuff underneath. But that can be scary, too. As one man said, "If I'm not all these terrible things, then who am I?" How do we bridge the gap between what we've come to believe about ourselves and what we might find deep inside? No wonder it's such hard work to explore who we are. No wonder so many of us have confusion about boundaries and who we are in relationship to other people.

Boundary confusion in families can lead to inappropriate and intrusive behavior. This is especially true if roles get confused. For instance, when a child is expected to take on the role or responsibility of an adult, a major boundary-crossing takes place. This lack of appropriate boundaries can lead to the ultimate invasion of someone's personal space: abusive behavior. Whether the abuse is psychological, physical, or sexual there is an invasion of the child's space. Where there is sexual abuse, the child is expected to take on an inappropriate adult sexual role as well. This crosses the parent-child boundary as well as crossing the boundaries of propriety.

### Crossing the Generational Gap

Depending on a child to function as an adult is a crossing of generational boundaries. Examples of this include the "parentified" child who takes care of the parent when the parent should be taking care of the child; the child who is expected to take major responsibility for a younger sibling; the child who is expected to be a "go-between" for the parents; the child who tries to stop the fights of the parents.

Janie remembers being six years old, and her parents would be screaming at each other. "I'd jump on the coffee table, pull myself to my full three-foot height, and read at the top of my lungs from my favorite book. I called it the 'Happy Family' book." She's been intervening in fights ever since. Recently she describes being so proud of herself when she didn't let her co-workers pull her into their noisy dispute. "At least," she says, "this time I didn't hop up on the desk and recite the 'Happy Family' to them!"

When Nick was a little boy he, too, figured out a way to handle his parents' fights. Although he could barely read, he'd grab the Yellow Pages and start to phone divorce attorneys until his parents stopped yelling at each other.

Both of these young children were acting like the adults when their parents were out of control. As we saw in chapter 6, sometimes the grown-ups aren't doing their jobs and the children have to take charge. In order to survive, these children cross generational boundaries by learning to take care of themselves and the adults as well. These same children grow up being confused about their relationships to other people, not knowing where they stop and someone else begins.

This confusion often leads to what has been popularly termed *codependent* behavior. Codependency has been variously defined as when one's sense of self is contingent upon someone else's approval. According to John and Linda Friel, the codependent person tends to "[overreact] to outside forces and underreact to inside forces." But I see codependency as being primarily about boundaries. It's a blurring of who you are and who the other person is, what your feelings are and what someone else's feelings may be. Boundary confusion can also become codependency when one person tries to protect someone else's feelings without finding out what they really are.

For example, Dolly became very upset when she found out from a distant cousin that her uncle had suddenly died two days before. Not one immediate family member had bothered to call her and she took it personally. She told herself that they had forgotten her, that they didn't care enough to call. In fact, her aunt's explanation was quite different. She didn't want to tell Dolly until it would be too late to book a plane flight for the funeral. The aunt felt Dolly couldn't afford to take the time off from work to fly across the country. The aunt presumed to know how Dolly would feel and made the decision for her in a misguided effort to protect her niece.

## Boundary Skills

Good boundaries involve knowing where you stop and the other person begins. A man I know who grew up in a family with very few boundaries has learned to experiment with boundaries. As he tries out new interactions, he says to himself, "This boundary seems to feel good in certain situations. I'll make this boundary mine."

A good place to begin work on boundaries is to frequently remind yourself that you do indeed exist separately and distinctly from other people. You do not have to think their thoughts or feel their pain. Your experience of life can be uniquely your own. Your needs can be different than their needs. Yet, you can be empathic to their needs or experience, you can put yourself in their shoes for the moment, but you don't have to stay there. Having good boundaries means you can choose to move in or out at will.

---

**Good boundaries involve knowing where you stop and the other person begins.**

---

The previous chapter on depersonalizing is called "Keeping One Foot In and One Foot Out." This, too, is about setting personal boundaries. Keeping one foot in and one foot out can work for you in intimate or work relationships. These are the same basic tools we talked about in the previous chapter—counting to ten or taking a time-out by stating you want to leave the room for a few minutes but you'll be back shortly. The trick is to disentangle your feelings from others' so you can be close enough to feel connected, yet distant enough to be objective and more effective.

Psychotherapists, too, can avoid tripping over their own feet during a session, by keeping one foot in and one foot out. A family therapy instructor once reminded me that when we see individuals, couples, or families, it's easy to lose ourselves in the dynamics of the clients. Finding a balance, however, isn't always easy. If a psychotherapist keeps both feet out, he or she may not be engaging enough with the client(s). But jumping in with both feet, the therapist runs the risk of becoming entangled in the issues of the client(s).

If therapists start to lose a sense of which feelings belong to them and which to the client, they can do either or both of these two things: Comment that they sense a certain feeling exists for them and that they want to check out with the client whether it might be something the client is experiencing. If need be, therapists can excuse themselves from the room and take a short breather to get grounded and maintain their own boundaries.

---

**Establishing good boundaries means being close enough to feel connected, yet distant enough to be objective and more effective.**

## Yes and No

Learning to say "yes" and "no" defines who you are in the moment—and what you stand for. In fact, these words are great boundary setters. The trouble is many of us did not have very good modeling of boundaries in childhood. We had no idea how to define what we stood for or what we needed. In fact, in many families, defining things was discouraged, or even forbidden. Instead, things had to be vague, cloudy, amorphous. Family members played guessing games with each other because being specific was simply not okay. And what could be more specific then learning to say "yes" and "no" loudly and clearly? Too often we learned to say "yes" when we really meant "no" and we learned to say "no" when we wanted to say "yes."

When Ginny, a college student, asked her therapist if she could interview him for a class assignment regarding his specialty, he said, "No, I am not able to do that because of my limited time." Then he added, "My having to say 'no' has nothing to do with you, it is only about my time limitations." Because he was sensitive to Ginny's issues with rejection, she did not take his "no" personally. She understood that "no" is not a rejection, it's only a limitation. In fact, it's one of the best ways to define boundaries.

---

### "No" is not a rejection, it's only a limitation.

---

Some people have a hard time saying "no" because they are afraid they won't be liked and are afraid of being rejected. In fact, they're easy to get along with because they say "yes" a lot. Other people have difficulty saying "no" because they have a hard time hearing it from others. If someone says "no" to them, they hear it as a rejection and take it personally. They're afraid of hurting the feelings of others the same way they're afraid their own feelings might be hurt. So instead, they become indecisive, wishy-washy. Psychoanalyst Alice Miller in *Thou Shalt Not Be Aware*, states that "someone who cannot say no at the decisive moments . . . of life, . . . loses . . . authenticity." She's talking about our friend from chapter 4, "Don Juan, the Seducer." Remember how "Don's" mother needed him to be dependent on her and rewarded him for his dependence? It wasn't okay to be himself because she might be upset with him. He wasn't able to say to her, "I am your child, but you have no right to my whole being and my whole life." "Don" still has trouble saying no as an adult, and it gets him into a lot of trouble in his relationships.

In spite of how you grew up, you can learn to say "no" to someone clearly and definitively. You no longer have to pretend to go along with

> "... someone who cannot say no at the
> decisive moments of ... life, loses ... authenticity."
> —Alice Miller

an idea or plan for fear of hurting someone's feelings, possibly hurting the relationship, or losing the love of that person. A woman I know needs a constant reminder that it's okay to say "no," so she hand-lettered a sign for her office:

NO. is a complete sentence.

One of the best ways to set clear boundaries is to learn to clearly say "yes" and "no." It seems to me that when someone asks you to do something, you can answer in one of four ways:

- "Yes, I can do that."
- "No, I can't do that."
- "I'll think about it and get back to you."
- "I can't do that, but this is what I can do."

In the same vein, a friend of mine is fond of paraphrasing David Viscott's reflections on important things to be able to say to people:

- "Yes, I want to. ..."
- "No, I don't want to. ..."
- "Ouch, that hurts!"

With some practice, you will soon be able to learn to assess a situation without feeling rushed into a "yes" or "no." You will also, with practice, learn to give the appropriate response.

Claudia Black, in *Repeat After Me*, has some excellent exercises for practicing saying "yes" and "no." She suggests asking yourself some of the following questions:

- What do I hear when someone says "no" to me?
- What do I feel when someone says "no" to me?
- How did my mom say "no" to me?
- How did my dad say "no" to me?
- Have any "nos" in my life made me angry?
- When I say "no," I feel _____ .
- Now try asking yourself these same questions about saying "yes."

If you want to practice saying "yes" or "no," practice with another person. Maintain a comfortable distance from the other person, look the person in the eye, and loudly and clearly say "yes" or "no." Now try it a little louder.

By the way, "no" can take other forms as well. A young woman I know has found a phrase that works for her: "Stop. This is uncomfortable for me."

## Boundaries and Sex

Boundaries play a big role in sexual experiences. It is often said that making love is a temporary blending of boundaries, a merging of two people, two spirits, two energy forces. For many it is scary to merge like that and they find themselves holding back. For others, when they do let go, they find themselves struggling to return to their own space, sometimes even having to abruptly disconnect from the other person in order to reconstitute. So they roll over and fall asleep, often to their partner's chagrin.

One of the best ways to bridge this temporary loss of self during passion and return to yourself is to have a few moments of prolonged contact with your partner after making love. You can hold or touch each other—the spoon position is great for this, or even holding hands. The time needed varies, but it's often just five or so minutes. Then, after this transition time, when you're back to yourself again, move to your own comfortable space and sleeping position and drift off.

For some people, sex interacts with boundaries in another way—it provides a container for anxiety. For example, Amelia realized one day why she jumps into sex so early in new relationships. "I get so anxious trying to figure out the relationship, and sex defines the relationship right away for me. Sex is known, so I initiate it because the unknown is so unsettling to me. Trouble is, when I define a relationship right away through sex, I have a hard time seeing it in any other way."

Sexual boundaries are easier to maintain when you practice sticking to them. In *Breaking Free*, Pia Mellody suggests reminding yourself, "I have the right to determine with whom, where, when, and how I will be sexual and who will be sexual with me."

## Boundary Boosters

There are several techniques that can help maintain personal boundaries. Mellody suggests visualizing an energy field, perhaps a gelatinous mass around yourself. A translucent bubble is another option, one you can expand and contract at will. Either of these would serve as a protective layer that allows you enough distance and objectivity to filter out intrusive or hurtful messages.

Mellody also describes visualizing an internal boundary as well, such as a metal plate over your chest, perhaps with little doors that open to the inside. Only you can control when they open.

I like her suggestion to hold your earlobe with your thumb and forefinger while inclining your head slightly toward the person to whom you're talking. This is a reminder that your job is to listen, not to defend yourself.

There's no doubt that learning to have healthy boundaries as adults is hard work but it is doable. Keeping these points in mind will help you navigate through boundary confusion:

- Figure out where you stop and the other person begins.

- Know that you exist separately and distinctly from other people, with different feelings and different needs.

- Reminding yourself that another person's words or actions are often about that person and that person's history and not about you.

- Learn to say "yes" and "no" loudly and clearly.

When you have good boundaries, you begin to have a more defined sense of who you are and can work on communicating your needs clearly.

# 12

# Emptiness Is Just Space, It Need Not Be Painful

## Needs versus Neediness

Needs are a fact of life, whether we acknowledge them or not. The truth is, we all have them—and it really is okay. The trouble is, many of us grew up not knowing this, and if we tried to express a want or need, we might have been told something like, "You're selfish" or "You're more trouble than you're worth." When I heard things like that, I'd tell myself I was too worthless to have any needs. Not only did my needs not count, but I managed to discount myself as well.

You may have been too busy during childhood taking care of everybody else, and there was no time for your own needs. Maybe you were the parentified child, the responsible one. You may have felt needed by others but often didn't get what you needed from them. Perhaps you got the message that there was no space in your family to have needs. Maybe you were made to feel ashamed if you had needs, and now you're afraid you'll be ridiculed for having them. Somehow having needs was labeled bad or shameful and got relegated to existing in an underground manner, with ploys and manipulations. If you couldn't put words to the need there could be little clarity about it, creating a kind of desperateness about getting it met.

There was a big hole there that just wasn't getting filled. You felt needy, and that wasn't a good feeling, so you began to confuse having needs with neediness. How could you find words for something you weren't even supposed to have? How could you even begin to define your needs? And if you didn't have words for them, how could you ask for what you needed? You probably never learned how. "I don't remember anyone ever hugging me when I was a little girl," one woman recalls. "Sometimes I really want a hug from my boyfriend, but I don't know how to ask."

If you can't be direct, how do you go about trying to get what you need? You might go underground, trying one ploy after another, hoping something strikes gold. Because this approach is indirect, it appears manipulative. Remember in chapter 2 how Jane wasn't aware of what she needed from Larry, but tried to maneuver him into offering to drive her where she needed to go? She desperately wanted him to read her mind—to her this meant he cared about her.

If you're not able to define your needs, to give them form or color or texture, then you don't have anything tangible to hold on to. It's as if there's nothing there—a space, a void—a hole that wants to be filled but doesn't know what it needs to fill it. You may not be very comfortable with spaces—they make a lot of people anxious—so you struggle to fill them up. Yet musicians will tell you that it's the spaces, the silences between notes, that make music. You may not know how long the silence will last, but you do know another note will come.

---

> **If you can't be direct, how do you get what you need?**

---

## Empty Spaces: To Fill or Not to Fill

We try hard to fill that space inside ourselves—that hole that feels like neediness. Gena recalls, "I didn't get emotionally fed enough in childhood, and I'm hungry all the time." She goes on to describe a "gnawing pain," a huge, empty space inside of her. "I look to other people to fill it up. I pick a man to try to extract what I need. But I wish I could take it from inside myself."

We did some visual imagery about this empty space. Gena visualized a big brass wine goblet, with a wide base and substantial rim. But as the wine flowed in, she could only see the bottom filling. "I want the cup to fill up faster and faster," she explained, "but then I do something to stop it before it gets half full. There seems to be a membrane on top of the wine, a barrier. I think it means that other people have to fight to get past my barrier."

Gena came into the next session all excited and told me, "I decided to visualize pouring the wine from the metal goblet into a smaller, delicate crystal wine glass. It's much easier to fill. The same amount of wine appears to be more because the glass is smaller. Now the glass is over half full." We realized that in fact, wine is usually poured half full, leaving room for it to breathe. Gena brightened. "Yes, of course. If the cup were all the way filled with wine, I couldn't breathe! Yes, indeed. It needs air and light to intensify its potential. There's more than just the wine, there's the light and the bouquet. Yes, I think I could learn to appreciate the unfilled parts of me. After all, emptiness is just space, it doesn't have to be painful."

Of course it would be nice if that ole hole would disappear forever, but there are times it reappears, and it may feel especially big and drafty. One woman, wanting to find a good way to deal with that space, visualized creating a patchwork quilt around the hole. She imagined herself adding on different sizes of patches representing the love of the people around her—her mom, her dad, her roommate, her favorite teacher. Then she designed some patches to symbolize how she was learning to think of herself. "Being more sure of myself, more comfortable with myself fills up the empty space." As the patchwork piece took shape and became defined, that hole seemed smaller and more manageable. I guess you could say she stitched a layer of *whole*ness around the hole.

You may want to try your own visualization sometime to see what images may arise for you. You just might catch a tiny wisp of something that will be useful to you. Find a quiet place and sit where you'll be undisturbed for fifteen or twenty minutes. Close your eyes if you'd like, and as you sit quietly let the sound of your breath escort you into an internal realm of discovery. What can you learn about that place of need inside of you. What does the space look like? Is it large or small? Does it stay the same or does it change size? Can you discern details or is it opaque? What is the shape? Color? Temperature?

Do you want to alter this space? What would you like to do to make it more manageable? Give yourself permission to let possible ideas come to you during the next few days. And you can always make some time again to sit quietly and see what images come to you. Sometimes nothing comes up, or the images are illusive. That's okay. You might try again later or even have someone trained in guided imagery lead you through this process.

## Confusing Needs with Neediness

What about the times when that hole feels huge? These are the times you might confuse having needs with feeling needy. Perhaps you try to hide your needs from others to appear strong, like Stephanie, who had to be the "big girl" in her family. She is still afraid to identify her needs to others because the floodgates might open and she'll become vulnerable and needy in other people's eyes. So she has stopped identifying her needs—even to herself. If I'd ask, "What do you need, Stephanie?" she'd lower her eyes and answer in a barely audible voice, "I don't know."

If our needs weren't met very well when we were children, we tend to become afraid of them as adults. We fear we'll overwhelm people with this gnawing hunger, this bottomless pit, this gigantic cavity. We either pretend to be self-sufficient and/or we fear our neediness will gush uncontrollably all over everybody and everything! We may come to believe it's an either/or situation with no in-between choices. But there are choices.

Having needs isn't the same thing as being needy. It's okay to have needs, to try to identify what they are, and to find ways to ask up front for what you decide is important to you. It's okay to need something from someone. And no matter what the big people told you when you when you were little, it really is okay to consider yourself and your needs.

The studies mentioned in part two about preadolescent girls describe how they become influenced by cultural demands and lose their sense of self and sense of direction. The resulting confusion follows them into adulthood and they often don't know what they're sensing, feeling, or thinking. Nor do they know what they need. When asked, they're quick to say, "I don't know."

> ## Having needs doesn't mean you're needy.

There's no question that there is a fine line between too much self and too little self. Let's take a look at some of the self words. "Don't be so self-centered," someone might say. We were taught it wasn't okay to be selfish, self-serving, self-indulgent or to have self-interests or a sense of self-importance. These words infer too much concentration on the self without concern for the interests of others. But do these terms have to be mutually exclusive? Holding oneself in esteem and with love does not have to be at the expense of others. By loving and honoring ourselves we can love and honor others. Interestingly, two words that are defined as unselfish are *self-effacing* and *selfless*—both connoting an invalidation of the self. What about the term *self-centered*? Why couldn't self-centered mean being centered within yourself—being in touch with what you need and what you want, with your feelings and your thoughts. In fact, as Elaine Aron writes: "[Highly sensitive people] are less likely to mention being aware of the world around us, and more likely to mention our inner reflections and musings ... thinking about our own thoughts is not self-centeredness. . . ."

"Taking care of myself doesn't mean I'm selfish!" enthused one woman. "Now I'm able to ask for what I need." This has been a struggle for her from the time she was a child. She saw having needs as asking for help. "My family was poor and often without food. My mother would send me over to the neighbors to ask for sugar or milk or eggs—and sometimes money. So, to me, 'asking for help' means begging." It's no wonder that as an adult, she crosses her fingers and hopes someone catches her hints.

If you can find ways to be direct, you don't have to be manipulative. If you can find the words to express your needs, you don't have to hope someone will read your mind. Then you don't have to be disappointed or feel rejected. A clear request most likely will get a clear answer such as "Yes," "No," or "I can't do that for you, but this is what I *can* do," or "I have to say no this time, but try me again." Even the "nos" don't feel so rejecting if the request has been straight forward

The idea of interdependence, or mutuality, in relationships is an important one. This means finding a comfortable place between independence, dependence, and codependence—a place of interconnectedness, where each person is able to ask the other for what he or she needs. You can be you, yet at the same time be connected to the people and things in your world.

## "Go Away a Little Closer"

Another area of frequent misunderstanding has to do with needs for space versus needs for contact. Frequently one person feels the need for contact and wants to share space, while the other person feels the needs his or her own space. This can certainly cause problems for couples. For example, Eddie wants to touch Deena when they sleep, in fact, he wants to sleep with his arms around her. But she feels stifled and complains that she can't breathe freely. Clearly Deena needs some space, but how much space does it take to reduce her anxiety? How much touching does Eddie actually need to feel he's making contact with her? What would it take to reassure himself that Deena is close by his side? Deena suggested touching with their feet only, and it worked. This turned out to be enough contact for Eddie to feel secure, yet it gave Deena the space she needed. By paying attention to what each of their bottom line needs for closeness were, they were better able to communicate these needs to each other and work something out.

Sometimes couples have different ideas of the type of closeness each wants. One may want more physical closeness while the other wants more emotional closeness. Often neither gets what he or she wants or needs and each may feel hurt and misunderstood and take it personally. Have you experienced these kinds of feelings of rejection?

Let's move on to emotional closeness—no doubt much more complicated to deal with than physical contact, but let's give it a try. What's the bottom line for trusting that you're both making an attempt toward emotional closeness?

Jill has trouble communicating her needs to her partner. She often can't put words to something she wants or needs. Without form or shape, the needs become overwhelming to her. This is when she goes into a childlike demanding place where she wants what she wants when she wants it. "It seems like I'm four years old again with a child's perception of time. When Ronnie says 'I'll be downstairs in a few minutes and we'll leave for the movies,' the minutes seem like hours." When Ronnie practiced being specific about time, for example saying, "I'll be available at 6:30 and we can go out then," there were fewer misunderstandings and incidences of taking things personally.

One woman expressed how left out and rejected she feels when her husband wants to read or space out in front of the TV. She wants contact with him; she wants to touch and talk. In couples sessions we speculated about what it would be like sharing space but not time. In other words, I asked if they could be with each other and still stay connected but not request or expect the other person's direct attention. What are the bottom line needs that would enable her to feel secure in the relationship? For example, could she be with him in the same room while he reads and work on a project or read a book of her own?

Les and Frannie have worked out a way to do this. Les has an open invitation to check with Frannie about whether it's okay to join her in her home office while she's working at the computer—not to talk, but to read or write or whatever—to share space but not time. Of course Frannie has permission to say "no" when she feels Les's presence will interfere with her concentration. Once in a while Les might take her "no" personally, but usually this has been a good arrangement. They wonder why they never thought about this option during the first five years of their relationship—it would have prevented so many fights and hurt feelings.

Remember Jane and Larry from chapter 3? She felt left out whenever Larry retreated to his study for hours at a time when he needed to be alone. What are Larry's bottom line needs for a breather? What if he took space for himself for thirty to forty minutes instead of two hours? Is that enough time for him? Could Jane tolerate this time alone without feeling left out and rejected by Larry?

How do you find some common ground with your partner? You've made a good beginning by realizing that you both want different forms of the same thing—contact. Try putting words to the kind of physical or emotional closeness you really want. By assessing and defining individual needs, a workable deal can usually be negotiated. Maybe you could even get some of those needs met, but you'd have to know what they are first. What do you want from the other person? What do you really have in mind? What do you want him or her to do or say?

So if you're one of the people who tends to say "I don't know" if someone asks you what you might need, what can you do about it? It's true that sometimes it is hard to be specific. You may only have a vague idea of what will make you feel better—perhaps some kind of psychological chicken soup. But the more undefined the hole is, the harder it is to fill. It's pretty hard to let someone else in on your needs if you don't know them yourself. How could you know when the need is filled if you don't know what you're filling?

> "When you know what you want,
> you'll know when you've found it."
>
> —Steve Bhaerman and
> Don McMillan

I give my clients the following questions to ask themselves each day upon awakening. For many, this is very difficult at first:

- "What would make me feel good today?"

- "What do I want? What do I need?"

- "From whom?" (Yourself? Someone else?)

- "In what way? What form would it take?"

You might also ask yourself how you would know your want or need is met. Defining these needs, putting words to them, may be a brand new experience for you because no one gave you permission to do it before. Don't be surprised if you struggle with it at first. Try to have patience and keep practicing. Doing this exercise regularly could change your perspective on life. Practice checking in with yourself throughout the day about how you feel and what would make you feel better. You will develop a more defined sense of yourself—and new respect for both yourself and your needs.

Now that you are beginning to recognize your own wants and needs, how do you go about communicating them to another person? Here are some possible ways to phrase your request:

- Sometimes I find myself hinting around about something I want or need from you. I'd like to just tell you directly. I need for you to _____ .

- I have a request to make of you. It's important to me that you

_____ .

Hearing yourself speak your needs out loud works wonders. Be aware that it's often much easier to say what you don't want from someone than what you do want. Negatives always seem to be on the tips of our tongues, don't they? For example, it's easier to say, "I don't want you to keep reading the paper when I'm talking about a problem." Instead, emphasize what you *do* want: "I would really like to make eye contact with you when we talk. Could you please put the paper down while we're speaking?"

You can practice doing this by standing in front of a mirror, making eye contact with yourself, and saying the words out loud. Start out with small, inconsequential requests; they can be real or hypothetical. Just listen to the sound of those words coming out of your mouth. You can practice with a therapist. If you can corral a friend or partner for a practice session it's even better. By practicing with someone else, you get the added bonus of hearing a "yes" or "no." You can take turns, too. Have the other person ask, and you can practice accepting or declining.

How many times have you cringed when somebody said to you, "Go ahead and take a chance. What have you got to lose?" And you say to yourself, "Take a chance on what? Possible rejection? Embarrassing myself? Feeling stupid for asking at a bad time?" All those old fears start bubbling up, don't they?

So what to do about it? To tell the truth, learning to ask for what I want or need has been a bumpy ride for me. I've plugged away for years on this challenge—gaining ground to be sure, but all too slowly. I must have been ready to turn the proverbial corner the day I heard motivational speaker and author Patricia Fripp point out, "The answer will always be 'no' if you don't ask." Wow. I got it. And what a difference that motto has made to me. Asking for something takes on a whole new coloration now. I made a choice to no longer set up a situation where the answer would always be 'no'. I could see I was cutting off all my options by not asking. Now it's as if an internal dialogue takes place, and the feisty part of myself counters with, "I'll show you that I won't take 'no' for an answer without asking first."

> "The answer will always be no if you don't ask."
> —Patricia Fripp

Identifying needs and asking for what you need are only part of the picture. What if your attempts at asking are successful and someone actually offers you warm, loving, comforting gestures—can you *accept* them? Can you take them in? Can you trust they are real? Or do you tell yourself that in spite of getting up your courage and asking for what you want or need, that if the truth be known, you "don't deserve it," or "they must have an ulterior motive," or "they'll only take it away again."

Suppose however, you could let yourself just say, "Thank you." I'm talking about the same "thank you" I suggested earlier in the book when someone gives you a compliment. You may find with a little practice at accepting yourself, you can choose to take in compliments and caring gestures. The key is letting yourself make that choice.

# 13

# You Mean I Really Have a Choice Here?

## *Learning about Options*

In stressful adult situations, we are often frozen in our childhood experiences of fear, shame, or anger. We become paralyzed—dazed, shocked, stunned, stupified. Karen calls it "going into freeze-frame." She once told me, "It's like time and space are suspended, I can't move, I can't think straight." In moments like this Karen isn't able to make a choice. It's as if there are no options available to her. Have you ever experienced this feeling?

Because Karen used to joke, "I wouldn't know an option if I stumbled over it," during therapy sessions we'd look for options in all sorts of places. It was like a treasure hunt. Often we'd find them hiding out in some unlikely places. Frequently we'd have to use a magnifying glass and a little ingenuity to recognize them.

As a child, Karen didn't know she had choices, especially where her personal safety was concerned. She grew up with the fear that comes from frequent verbal abuse abuse—and she felt trapped. So we walked through some of her old childhood experiences. I asked her, "What if the adult Karen could stand beside the "child" Karen and coach her about possible choices. What might these be? If the child had those options available at the time, what would she have said? What would she have done? How would she have felt?"

One day Karen came into a session grinning and said, "I guess I'm finally learning about choices. I just saw the movie *Platoon*. At the end, when he's desperately running, I found myself thinking, 'If I were him, what would I do here?' I realized I was thinking about choices for the first time that I can remember!"

The realization that choices were available was a turning point for Karen. From that point on, in many tough situations, she was able to ask herself what her options were. She still finds herself in some overwhelming situations, but they aren't nearly as bad as they were before.

You may have grown up not knowing you had options or could make choices. This is especially true if verbal, physical, or sexual abuse was a part of your life. Children often think there are no choices, no way out. They think their only option is to stay and take it.

It's not only in abusive families that children don't learn about choices. Choices also don't seem possible in authoritarian, rigid families, where the children have to toe the line. Choices are restricted in families where the parents are overprotective, and children don't have the opportunity to think or do for themselves. Children feel especially helpless and confused if they grow up in a double-bind family where there are two conflicting messages given (often one is verbal and one is covert). They are expected to obey both messages at the same time and often get very confused. They have no way to comment on the confusion or to leave the scene (except perhaps by spacing out). It seems they have no options; they feel bound up, trapped. It's a no-win, damned-if-you-do-and-damned-if-you-don't situation.

## Choose and Lose

Struggling to make choices in no-win situations in childhood can lead to overwhelming anxiety that may resurface in adulthood. An especially painful double bind for a child is when a parent overtly or covertly asks a child to choose between mother and father. In this instance making a choice seems impossible. There's no way to win.

I was always called by my nickname; the trouble was my mother and father each spelled it differently. My mother spelled it *Laney*. My dad's version was *Lainey*. I never knew which spelling to use—whenever I chose one over the other, I would feel disloyal to one of my parents. I was so afraid of hurting someone's feelings that I would alternate the spelling of my name! Can you imagine what that did to my sense of identity? After my mother died, I changed the spelling to *Layni*. Finally, I owned my own name.

Years later, when I was interviewing for a counseling position this loyalty issue resurfaced. I had taken training with each of the codirectors in the past. During the interview, the male codirector turned to me and said, "If you get this position, which one of us would you choose to supervise you?" I translated this to mean "Who do you like best? Choose one of us." I just stared at him, the words reverberating in my head. Choose one. Choose one. Choose one. How could I possibly choose one? I couldn't proceed with the rest of the interview. Later I realized that I froze in the interview because I was in a doublebind, there was no way

I could have answered correctly. And as much as I'd have liked to, I couldn't run out of the room. In this particular situation, trying to make a choice would only result in a wrong choice—it was a no-win situation for me. If only my head had cleared a little bit, I might have replied, "That's a really difficult choice because it puts me in a no-win situation."

But at the time, I was feeling overwhelmed with old emotions, and wasn't able to identify that I was feeling caught in the middle of a childhood loyalty issue. This kind of flooding is debilitating, and it's difficult to identify options and nearly impossible to make and act on choices.

When this kind of paralysis sets in it's most likely a reaction to past rejection experiences: judgments and criticisms, communication breakdowns, misguided expectations and disappointments, self-flagellations, efforts to avoid the pain of another rejection, cultural and generational hand-me-downs, and confusion about personal boundaries and needs.

Emotional overload tends to cloud choices. When you are confused it is hard to choose. Sorting through your emotions would be a good place to begin as you travel the path of choice making. Can you walk alongside yourself, take notice of your emotions, listen to them, and let them guide you to some possible choices? For some of us, identifying our feelings is not easy. For others, it's just about impossible. When I was first in therapy, the therapist taught me that if I was clenching my jaw or my fist, there was a good chance I might be angry, even though I wasn't aware of it. But first I had to learn to notice when I was clenching.

In addition to identifying those feelings, also try expressing your thoughts about how stuck you are. Hearing yourself think out loud allows the space you need to recognize possible options. It can be a "Wow! I never saw it like that before," experience. Writing about it in a journal works well, and making an audiotape of your thoughts is also effective. What works best for you depends on whether you're visual or auditory. Since overwhelm tends to be amorphous, putting it into words gives it definition, and this allows choices to emerge.

It's not easy to struggle with simultaneously conflicting feelings or wishes. That's why ambivalence can be such a confusing concept. For many people, ambivalence means love and hate or good and bad. But there are many ambivalent feelings and thoughts—some are so subtle it's easy to miss them. And missing them can lead to big trouble as you'll soon see.

You know you're ambivalent when you experience uncomfortable inner conflict. You know you're ambivalent when you can't make a decision. You feel stuck, like you're straddling a fence. You may find yourself in ambivalent work and personal situations far too often, such as

- Wanting a promotion, yet dreading the added work hours it would require

- Wanting to spend time with a child or partner, and at the same time wanting time for yourself

- Wanting connectedness but needing separateness
- Wanting a romantic relationship, yet not being quite ready to make a commitment
- Wanting a loving, nurturing relationship but choosing someone who's not able to provide what you need

When two internal voices are at odds with each other, this conflict causes anxiety.

So what can you do about this? The most important thing is to give both voices a chance to be heard. Let them carry on a dialogue with each other. In other words, give voice to both sides of the ambivalence. Try making two lists: a What I Have to Gain list and a What I Have to Lose list. It also helps to have someone to talk to—especially someone skilled in guiding your discovery of the various messages. What happens, you may ask, if you're only able to hear one voice? You may end up projecting the other part onto someone else—your partner, boss, friend, child or parent. Getting past the ambivalence leaves room for choices.

Having options means allowing the flexibility to change the way you think about something. So why not choose to change how you think about rejection? Why not sculpt it into a somewhat different form—reframing the meaning. For example, if you ask someone to do something for you, and they must say "no," you can choose to see this as a "decline" rather than a rejection.

An actor I know, disheartened after so many auditions where she wasn't "the right type," posts this reminder on her wall: *Selection, not rejection.* Framing rejection in a more positive way tends to soften the blow, removing some of the old emotional charge behind it.

## Take a Breather: The Balloon Exercise

This breathing exercise is a good basic tool for creating space for yourself in the midst of swirling debris. It can be used as an all-around routine stress-buster, for circumventing anxiety takeovers, and for getting to sleep. You can take it with you wherever you go. It can be done in private or in a roomful of people. It helps to practice this exercise once a day to get comfortable with it, so when you want to use it you don't have to think, "Oh, yeah, that breathing exercise. Let's see now, how does it go?"

Sit comfortably in a chair, legs and arms uncrossed to let the energy flow. Close your eyes if you wish. Breathe in through your nose, filling your stomach as if it were a balloon. Shift the breath up to your lungs and out through your mouth as if it were the mouth of the balloon. As you slowly expel the air make a sound. Again, take in air through your nose, shift it up to the neck of the balloon and slowly expel it through your mouth with a sound. Repeat this four or five more times—or more. You'll find this to be calming and centering.

You can easily alter the sound to match wherever you are. In private, loud sighs feel pretty good. But in a roomful of people you might want to imagine making a full-blown sound, but make a barely audible one instead.

## Choose to Change

It's difficult for many adults to comprehend the existence of choices because it feels unnatural. New ideas seem scary. New behavior seems risky. So things get put off—sometimes indefinitely. People sometimes call this procrastination.

> In childhood it seemed there were no choices.
> Now when we're presented with choices
> it feels unnatural. New behavior seems risky.

Procrastination impedes action, making choices difficult or impossible. Procrastination is a good example of how fear of rejection can lead to self-rejection, which then leads to more fear of rejection. Let's say there's a phone call, letter, school assignment, work project, or creative endeavor that you've been meaning to check off your to-do list. But if you're afraid of what might be waiting for you from the receiving end, you might be tempted to procrastinate. Rejection might be waiting, right? After all, someone might criticize your project or find your idea lacking in some way, or say "no" to your request. You may say to yourself, "Why take the risk of putting myself out there, only to get disappointed?" This fear may lead you to keep procrastinating. It's another way of avoiding the pain of a possible rejection.

But it's hard to avoid getting down on yourself for procrastinating. This self-rejection can take the form of negative self-talk, a bucket full of shoulds, calling yourself names, denying yourself privileges. And the next thing you know, you're even more timid about choosing to take that next risk. It's like the old days of feeling there are no choices. And when you feel as if you don't have choices, it's pretty hard to make them.

People who have trouble making choices begin to think of themselves as procrastinators. They feel overwhelmed with everything they have to do. Chores, errands, assignments don't seem to get done. The more they worry about what they have to do, the more they seem to get immobilized by it all. There's only so much energy available at any one time, but if all the energy goes into worrying, there's not much left for doing. By procrastinating they are making a choice: they're choosing to worry and to not complete their tasks. Instead, wouldn't it be nice to choose to take action?

While I was researching and writing my dissertation, I learned a lot about procrastination, and I found a new way to think about it. I used to believe I was procrastinating whenever I'd start an unrelated project. I knew I was supposed to be sitting at my computer—writing. I would do all kinds of tasks, from polishing furniture to cleaning out the fireplace to sweeping the walkway. But I soon realized that each task served a useful purpose. They actually energized me to eventually sit down and write. Doing laundry was the most helpful task of all because once I was downstairs there was a good chance I'd gravitate toward the adjacent computer room.

That dissertation process taught me another terrific trick for turning inaction into action. I learned how to keep from getting overwhelmed by the enormity of a large, even huge, task. A complicated project is always made up of smaller sections. Why not concentrate on those sections, isolating each as a separate, doable task. And with the completion of each task comes a feeling of accomplishment. In other words, go chapter by chapter, sketch by sketch, report by report, or spreadsheet by spreadsheet.

Remember the Rubik's Cube? It wasn't possible of course to get everything into place immediately, was it? The way to do it was row by row, one side, then the next, then the third and fourth . . .

Another form of action is prioritizing. This is one way of making choices. One woman I know used to feel so overwhelmed by the number of things that had to be done, it was absolutely crippling. She'd wake up with a start in the morning, anxious about all the tasks she had to take care of. But wait a minute. On reflection, she realized they didn't all have to get done that day. Or even that week. She began to make lists in her head of the most important, and the least important. Her anxiety began to subside as she reminded herself that some things really can wait. As she learned to sort these things out in psychotherapy she discovered the possibilities of making choices.

It's important to use the ideas presented in chapters 10, 11, and 12 in order to gain some distance from a situation and walk alongside yourself. Observing gets the flow going and opens up the space to make choices.

Once you discover you can create options for yourself, your perception of the world will change. Opting to make choices creates a new

Prioritizing is another word for making choices.

> Observing yourself opens up the space to make choices.

sense of balance for you. You can weigh and measure possibilities. You won't think of yourself as so helpless, as such a victim of circumstances. If you tend to think of people and things out there affecting you, then you give away your power to "out there." By making choices, you are shifting the locus of control back to yourself. You are making it internal, rather than external. You are depending on yourself and not others.

Thinking of yourself as a victim of circumstances is disempowering. You can begin to change this way of thinking about yourself by practicing making small choices and learning from each misstep you might take. The next time perhaps you'll do it differently. Learning from mistakes widens our field of choices.

This growth process is told so well in Portia Nelson's "Autobiography in Five Short Chapters":

### I
I walk, down the street.
>There is a deep hole in the sidewalk.
>I fall in
>I am lost ... I am helpless
>>It isn't my fault.
It takes forever to find a way out.


### II
I walk down the same street.
>There is a deep hole in the sidewalk.
>I pretend I don't see it.
>I fall in again.
I can't believe I am in the same place.
>>but, it isn't my fault.
It still takes a long time to get out.


### III
I walk down the same street.
>There is a deep hole in the sidewalk.
>I see it is there.
>I still fall in ... it's a habit.
>>my eyes are open.
>>I know where I am.
>It is my fault.
>I get out immediately.

**IV**

I walk down the same street.
    There is a deep hole in the sidewalk.
    I walk around it.

**V**

I walk down another street.

Have you ever tumbled into the same hole more than once? How long did it take for you to climb out? Have you noticed if the discovery time and the extricating time keeps reducing? Have you experienced the realization yet that there is indeed a fork in the road and you can choose another path on your journey?

Making choices is being proactive, rather than passive. It can be a powerful, exhilarating feeling—and so freeing. A man came into a session one day saying, "I choose to be my own source of power instead of looking 'out there.' It isn't fair for me to expect things from other people that I can't give to myself. So I decided to trust my instincts, my heart, and my mind."

You, too, can determine your choices. The best way to practice is to ask yourself frequently, "Do I have a choice here? What might it be?" All you need is one more possibility besides the one you already have. That gives you a choice of two. Don't worry too much about making a wrong choice. As Susan Jeffers declares in *Feel the Fear and Do It Anyway*, "It really doesn't matter which choice you make. Each choice produces a different experience." She reminds us that "security is not having things, it's handling things." By telling yourself, "I can handle it," you can move past fears that arise. In his work on self-actualization, Abraham Maslow summed it up pretty well by encouraging people to make "the growth choice rather than the fear choice."

### Break Free of Either/Or

If you find your thinking is polarized into either/or possibilities, you might want to try to find a third option by visualizing a continuum, similar to the one in chapter 4: where one choice is at one end and the other choice is at the other end. Visualize a place along the continuum that might contain a third choice. Any place will do; just visualize a mark somewhere along the continuum line. Now call it something—anything you want—just to give it a name.

> "Make the growth choice rather than the fear choice."
> —Abraham Maslow

For example, sometimes it seems the only choice is to sit on angry feelings or explode in anger. So, imagine a continuum with explosive anger at one end and swallowed anger at the other. Can you picture making a mark somewhere along the continuum? It can be towards either end or towards the middle. Anywhere you want to put it.

If you came from a family where there was either explosive anger or nothing at all, it may take some work to identify another place on the continuum where you can be angry. But take your time and give it a try. When you can visualize the mark, give it a name. Call it "taking a risk and saying something," or "confronting the situation," or "making my feelings known." All it takes is one mark to create an option for yourself. One man who is a housepainter describes this process as "choosing a new tint on the color wheel, like a warm white. In fact," he continues, "once I realize I have options, I no longer feel so trapped or stuck. And when I'm not so frustrated, there's no need for anger any longer."

---

Imagine a continuum with one behavior choice
at one end and a second choice at the other end.

Now imagine a third choice along the continuum,
anywhere you want to put it.

---

## Accept Yourself

Remember too, that although you couldn't choose your family, you can choose to bring people into your life who can tolerate feelings, who can allow you, even encourage you, to feel your own feelings. Yes, you really can. You're allowed to because you're not six years old anymore.

You can make choices about yourself, too. Remember, you can choose to spend more time with the parts of yourself you really like instead of parts you'd rather not be with. As one woman says, "I know that certain traits will always be a part of me. Maybe I can inflate some features and deflate others. Then I can choose where I want to put my energy." This includes making a choice not to change certain aspects of your behavior, but instead, accepting these as a part of who you are.

---

You can choose to spend more time with
the parts of yourself you really like instead of
the parts you'd rather not be with.

Another important choice you can make has to do with the beliefs you've held about yourself based on your childhood experiences and the messages you perceived from others. For example, if you've come to believe you're "no good," "lazy," "weird," or "stupid," or any of the other labels someone might have put on you as you were growing up, it might be time to make the choice to change how you think of yourself.

Yes, it is possible, and no, it doesn't take years to accomplish. There are so many new and effective tools out there, psychotherapy can be a big help, especially if you find the right person to work with in an individual, couples, or group setting. Try to find someone who can join with you in teamwork to create a safe place where you can learn that you indeed do have options. If that person is interactive and can give you honest, caring feedback, it's a plus. If he or she can help you find ways to reframe old experiences and messages, it's a gift.

Relabeling is an option you can create for yourself—it's a fresh way of looking at experiences you have previously viewed through a negative lens. "I used to think of myself as a control freak," recalls one man. "Now I see how good I am at making order out of chaos." A woman I know is learning to think of herself as "inquisitive" rather than continuing to accept the "devious and troublesome" label her parents gave her. Another woman now sees herself as "feisty" rather than a "troublemaker" as her teachers labeled her. She used to tell herself that they didn't like her, but now she can see how her teachers' attempts at modifying her behavior was most likely out of caring.

Malcolm began to tell me about how as a young boy he felt ignored and invalidated by his father. His father, a carpenter, would take him out to job sites for the day but never bothered to teach him any carpentry skills. His dad just told him to entertain himself and stay out of his way while he worked. On the other hand, when the father took Malcolm's younger brother with him, he taught him carpentry basics. Malcolm explained it by saying, "My brother was a lot like my father, while I was the 'heady one.' It's no surprise that my brother grew up to be a contractor and I became a teacher and writer."

Malcolm's early feelings of disinterest and rejection by his father affected his later view of himself, yet there seemed to be a more positive way of looking at this. Could it be that Malcolm's father's disinclination to involve him in the carpentry was actually a sign of respect, an acknowledgment of his son's preference for working with his head rather than his hands? Perhaps it was an acceptance of who Malcolm was rather than a rejection of who he was not. As we talked, Malcolm seemed to sit a little straighter and taller, "I never thought of it that way before. Maybe I was really okay in my father's eyes."

Choosing to relabel negative labels with a positive spin can be a creative and productive exercise. It's even more effective when you approach it as a process over time, rather than looking for instant answers.

The following suggestions are meant to be a starting point leading to an ongoing process of discovery:

1. First, choose a label that someone stuck on you when you were young. For example, I'll use the label "lazy."

2. What was the context for that label? Who said it? What was the situation? (As you may remember from the introduction, I thought I overheard my aunt saying that about me when I was a young child.)

3. From your present adult vantage point, can you see the situation differently from how you saw it when you were a child? (In my case, I asked my aunt about it and she had no memory of ever thinking or saying it.)

4. Can you choose not to label? (In my case, my aunt is saying the label really didn't exist.) Or can you choose a new label? Do this by asking yourself what positive aspects this old label contains. (For example, I asked myself what the positive connotations of "lazy" might be. "Laid back" is one. "Relaxed" is another.) A good thesaurus is helpful here. And the hardware store sells excellent products for scrubbing off sticky label residue.

## Piecing Together the Pieces

There are lots of techniques for working toward making peace with old childhood hurts. Just about every self-help book or therapist has a suggestion or two, so here are two of my favorites: the first involves inviting the participation of siblings or other extended family members, and the second offers a different approach to the old "write a letter you'll never mail" exercise.

Consider asking a brother or sister (or cousin or other relative) to be a "family historian." Invite your historian to lunch—or better yet, into a therapy session with you. Oh, I know you are probably saying, "There's no way they would ever agree to join me in a therapy session." Well, if you ask, you might be surprised—the role of historian could be appealing. This teamwork approach is great for picking up threads of sketchy memory, comparing notes, and piecing things together. But do remember that when there is an age difference of a few years between siblings, each may have grown up in a slightly "different" family. Situations often change in the space of three or four years—the family finances, the pressures and stresses, the physical or emotional health climate, or even the amount of alcohol a parent consumes each evening. Even though perceptions may vary, having input from another family member can give you valuable information. How does your historian see your old role in the family? Your relationship to other family members? Your interactions with your friends?

There may be times when you would like to express feelings to a family member or some person in your past or present but it is not always possible or prudent. What if that person is not available? What if the person is dead? What if feelings are so intense that you don't trust yourself to talk directly to that person? How can you deal with these yucky feelings? Why not consider Sheldon Kopp's suggestion in *If You Meet the Buddha on the Road, Kill Him!* He proposes writing not just one, but a series of three letters.

The first letter is a never-to-be-mailed declaration of your feelings and needs. This is the letter you have written in your head many times. Now, knowing you will never mail it you can consider putting some or all of your thoughts and feelings on paper.

The second letter is a hypothetical reply from the person you wrote the first letter to. In this letter you get to capture the essence of his or her personality and write down all the denials, rationalizations, put-downs, sarcasm, or defensiveness that you used to get and still expect to get from that person.

Now for the third letter. This letter will contain all the things you have always wanted to hear from that person but never did. And because you asked for what you need in the first letter, this one could contain acknowledgment of mistakes, statements of love and caring, possibly even a little icing—an apology. This is about what *you* need from that person, and because you are writing it, you can choose to write anything you want to hear.

If possible, read these three letters aloud—to a therapist or to a friend. At the very least, read them out loud to yourself. The words you've chosen to include in these three letters can be very liberating.

Either of these exercises can be another step toward respecting your own courage and resilience.

Along with choosing to respect who you are, you can also choose to appreciate the ways you learned to adapt to your childhood experiences. You can choose to honor the coping skills you learned in childhood, even if they weren't always learned under the best of circumstances. These are strengths that can be refined until they become assets.

# 14

# I'm Gonna Hone My
# Imperfections!

## Turning Stumbling Blocks into
## Building Blocks

The Chinese character for *crisis* is made up of two parts: *danger* and *opportunity*. Crisis tends to light a fire that can initiate positive action. Crisis allows people to dip deeply within, to open doors that have heretofore been closed, to breathe energy into new directions, to be creative out of necessity. If you experienced crises and trauma in childhood, you developed lifesaving strategies to help you get through those difficult years. You acquired special skills that may have been labeled as "bad," or "useless." However, the expertise you developed as a child can help you take better care of yourself as an adult and can be helpful in your work or personal relationships. These qualities may have come from existing in a crisis mode, but now you can offer yourself an opportunity to transform them into highly functional skills.

For instance, you know how easy it is to take things personally. Why not capitalize on this sensitivity? By being attentive and trusting the intuition you developed as a child, you can become exquisitely sensitive to people and situations around you. After all, the one skill most of us learned exceptionally well was putting out our antennae and "tuning in." Observing, noticing, paying attention—these were our strengths.

Was this as true of you as it was of me? Did you, too, have highly developed eyes and ears? Were even the pores of your skin ultrasensitive to incoming signals? Think back for a moment to how much energy you put into noticing cues around you. Reading your parents' moods—the way your mom sighed or the way your dad walked through the front door—was one way you learned to get through the day. Did you find your own way to take care of yourself in your family? What skills did you learn growing up? How did you come to learn them?

You may have discovered different ways to maneuver through some difficult times. Did you learn to play a specific caretaking role, such as the mediator, the placater, the scapegoat, the go-between, or the joker? These roles were important to the functioning of your family, and you had a job to do—fill that role. This provided you with an identity—you were needed. In fact, you may continue to see yourself this way, repeating the same function in your adult relationships. For example, one woman identified her role as "the garbage bag for the family. Being a scapegoat has been my job description for thirty-two years. I don't want this job any more."

In addition to your assigned role, perhaps along the way you developed certain adaptation strategies to protect yourself. If something threatened your well-being or your peace of mind, or if something felt like a life-or-death situation, you did whatever you had to do to survive as best you could. The trouble is, sometimes you did not just adapt to your situation, you may have overadapted. By the time you reach adulthood, these overadjustments aren't always serving you so well.

> You discovered ways to maneuver yourself
> through the difficult years of childhood.
> You developed certain strategies to protect yourself.

Maybe you put up barriers, building walls around yourself. I remember my wall very well; it was brick with turrets on top; no light got through. As an adult, as I learned to feel safer, sunlight began filtering through, and the wall began to come down, brick by brick. Did you build a wall, too? Do you remember what it was made of? Is it still with you at times? When does it come back?

Maybe you learned to space out—to emotionally "leave." It's as if in that moment you were not a part of time. In *Unchained Memories*, Lenore Terr describes this altered state of consciousness as "unlocking the gears and coasting a while on neutral." When you were young and the physical or emotional pain became too great to bear, you probably didn't think you had the option to leave the room, so you did the next best thing: you found a way to emotionally disconnect from the pain. There is a word for this—it's called *dissociating*. You could watch from a safe place where you could protect yourself.

Maybe you would bring in an imaginary friend to discuss things, someone to confide in, someone who could protect you if you needed it. You might even still find yourself talking to that imaginary friend once in a while. Sometimes someone overhears you. Have you ever been standing in line and the person in front of you asks, "Did you just say something?" Of course you answer, "Who me?"

Unfortunately, other people didn't seem to appreciate the usefulness of these skills you acquired. They didn't understand why you would put yourself in the middle of family discussions, or why you joked around to deflect family arguments, or why you spaced out. Because these protective devices were seen by others as weaknesses rather than strengths, they took on negative connotations. Now, here you are an adult with a treasure chest of useful attributes, but you're unable to gain access to them. In fact, you may see them the same way other people taught you to see them—as quirks, shortcomings, defects, weaknesses. How can you turn these stumbling blocks into building blocks? How can you re-package these undervalued traits into valuable assets?

---

Unfortunately, other people viewed these skills as weaknesses, and you probably did, too. How can you repackage these undervalued traits into valuable assets?

---

## Transforming Self-Rejection into Self-Acceptance

Sometimes it's hard to see past your own flaws. You may have missed out on the essential building blocks of childhood—things like self-esteem, self-assurance, or social skills. You may be saying, "I only have stumbling blocks. I don't have any building blocks." One way to try to rediscover some forgotten childhood tools is to visualize your real-life childhood building blocks. Were they wooden alphabet blocks? An erector set? Legos? Or Lincoln Logs?

Visualize taking them down from the shelf and spreading them around you on a table or the floor. Can you imagine what they felt like in your hands? How did you put them together? What was your step-by-step process of building? How did you select which pieces to use? What did you build? Did you make windows or doors? If so, how did you frame them? Did you cover your structure with a roof or did you leave it open to the air? Did you save the finished structure or put the parts away for another time?

What can you learn from recalling your building process? Can you transfer these skills over to how you approach tasks and problems today? Instead of undermining, you can practice bolstering, reinforcing, fortifying, buttressing, bracing, or shoring up your resources. In fact, you can be your own personal foundation architect.

## Repackage Those Usable Skills

Jessica calls it, "honing my imperfections." For years she believed she was a "freak" because she had been told she was "different" from other children, and her parents seemed embarrassed by her. Indeed she was different, because she was an old soul in a child's body. "I thought my parents didn't love me when I was extraordinary so I tried hard to be ordinary. I muffled my questions and comments, I stifled my creativity, and before long I seemed to lose my voice. Since it wasn't okay to shine when I was a child, I became a lump of coal.

"It took years before I realized that a flaw or two need not keep a diamond from shining. I don't think I'm weird anymore. There really is a certain charm to the way I do things, a sparkle. Pardon the pun, but I guess you could say I'm learning to respect all facets of myself."

Another woman's face lit up during a session. "I just realized I actually have skills from being an abused child that I can use in my real estate business. I can read people and their moods really well. I can size up people and situations. I'm flexible. I can get along with people. I sure learned a lot about looking and listening when I was a kid. I'm an expert!"

A client recalls how adept he was as a child at emotionally "leaving the scene." "At the blink of an eye I was gone." Now, when he finds himself getting immobilized in uncomfortable situations, he reminds himself that he has good skills in emotionally leaving and uses them to explore another option—physically leaving the scene. He's able to tell himself, "I have a choice here. I know I can leave. I can excuse myself to get some fresh air, go to the rest room, or make a phone call. Then I can regain my composure, return to the situation, and be more objective."

You may have grown up in a family where people didn't communicate clearly; they talked in circles and expected you to "read between the lines." What a lot of energy that skill took! But this know-how is very useful for hypothesizing; I'm sure you can find a way to use it creatively. Just remind yourself to not slip into old habits of presuming what other people might mean. Check it out instead.

It is useful to be able to selectively hold on to a few of those old ways of doing things. Just because you overdosed on it when you were younger, you don't have to toss it all away. Some of it might be usable, in fact, quite functional. For example, one man grew up with parents that demanded perfection, and there was no way he could be perfect because nothing was ever good enough. He became overly critical, mostly of himself, but of others as well. Now he is transforming his natural ability at being exacting into a job he loves and is good at—he's a senior editor with a big-time newspaper. He found a way to substitute the high price he paid as a child for a high-paying, satisfying profession.

I've benefited from childhood skills that I'd previously thought were absolutely useless to me. When I was a child and the emotional pain became too great, I'd "leave." I got skilled at imagining I was somewhere else, usually the place where the walls and ceiling met. I became quite accomplished at this. Recently I had the opportunity to experiment with this skill in two very different situations—in a doctor's office and on a TV talk show.

When the dermatologist had to cut my cheek, I just knew I would either faint dead away or bolt off the table. I asked myself, "What would I suggest to a client in this situation?" The answer was easy: "Do some deep breathing." So I did. As I began to feel in control of my breathing, I also began to feel in control of the situation. But because I used to faint around blood, I really did not want to be in the same room with that person cutting my face. So I let part of me stay there and be present and I allowed part of me to "leave." Then I didn't have to worry about the blood or feeling faint or any of it. The next day, the doctor called to ask me what I had done to be so calm on the table—he joked that he wanted to "bottle it" to sell to other patients.

Again, my childhood skills for leaving came to the rescue when I was taping my first network talk show in front of an audience. I was really nervous and wanted to bolt right out of there. So I kept one part of myself present, able to answer questions and be involved in the discussion, but I let the rest of me leave. Most people watching the show would never have guessed how nervous I was. They had no idea I was transforming an old, obsolete skill into something useful to me in the moment.

My choice of professions, social worker-turned-psychotherapist, was most certainly an outgrowth of my early caretaking experiences. The same is most likely true about other helping professions. Most of us got fabulous on-the-job training as children.

A woman I know refers to it as "trading on the adaptive skills of growing up." As a child, she was the go-between, the link between members of her family. She also became very skilled as the family translator. This was no easy task in her family because the messages were so murky. She adapted by making sense of things for the others. By taking on this important role, she had an identity in her family—it gave her a sense of worth. She told me, "I was the 'lightning rod' for the family. But being in the middle like that was a huge responsibility. As far back as I can remember, I'd lie in bed at night worrying, trying to make sense of things, trying to figure things out. Sometimes I'd get frantic from worrying that if I didn't do my job right, my family would fall apart. I guess you could say I was working overtime."

As an adult her work reflected her childhood experience. She became so good at figuring things out that years later she figured out something that would benefit lots of people: She developed a program that translated highly technical language to the general public.

Edward also used to be the go-between in his family. He was the one who mediated the all too frequent family fights. He was the wise one, the one who could reason and help everyone see possible solutions. And what did Edward grow up to be? A top union negotiator. He's recognized as one of the best mediators in his area. He's calm, wise, careful, able to watch for cues from each person. He is a super problem solver. But he isn't always able to solve his own problems. Recently, because of the stresses of his time-consuming job, his personal life began to overwhelm him. He felt insecure about dealing with day-to-day personal problems. He was becoming immobilized and withdrawing from family and friends. He finally realized he couldn't solve his problems by himself and turned to therapy for some help.

Together we looked at how he could find ways to transfer his negotiating skills from one part of himself to another—from his "work compartment" into his "personal challenge compartment." By learning to identify all the qualities that make him a good mediator, he could learn to "negotiate" with the various parts of himself. Now he checks in with each of the parts, getting their opinions, making sure he fully understands each position, and making sure each part feels respected by the others. He makes sure there is a kind of unionizing of all sides involved. He doesn't feel so stuck anymore. Edward learned to borrow skills from one compartment of his functioning and transfer them to another. When he recently found himself in conflict over whether or not to accept a time-consuming work project, he wasn't able to make a decision. In fact, he was immobilized by the ambivalence he was experiencing. So he checked in with both sides of the ambivalence, putting it all out there on the table. Then he could move forward.

"I always had to keep a pulse on what what was going on in my family, just like I keep a pulse on my relationships now," said Debbie. "I guess that's the nurse in me." And Joyce, had a similar experience. "If I stop managing, things would collapse—just like in my family of origin."

One man learned at an early age to manipulate people in order to get what he wanted, because in his family it wasn't okay to ask for something directly. He became skillful at handling his parents and good at strategizing; he would plan out how to take subtle, almost unnoticeable actions in order to get the results he desired. You might not be too surprised to learn that he's a chiropractor now and gets paid to do manipulations five days a week.

One woman grew up in a family where "everyone was allowed to get away with murder, and I just stood helplessly by. I lost my voice; I couldn't speak up." Now she's become an expert on capital punishment and makes speeches about prisoners' rights.

Another man began to realize how his childhood experiences affected his present response to building his business. He grew up in an unpredictable household; the chaos and violence threw him off balance. As a result, taking the risks necessary for building up his business was nerve-racking for him. Together we looked at how how much he knew about handling unpredictability—how much he learned as a child about keeping his balance and taking charge in the face of crisis—and how skillful he has become at going from crisis to crisis. Why not use this know-how in making a success of his catering business? And he did.

Sally also grew up in a chaotic, unpredictable family. She watched her mom and dads violent fights all the time. Several times she almost got hit by flying dishes. So at an early age she learned to be watchful, keeping her eyes and ears open so she and her little sister could get out of the way. She learned to anticipate these fights and plan ahead; it was a matter of personal safety.

Now Sally uses this ability in her work. She is one of those fabulous waiters who miraculously appears out of nowhere the minute you even begin to think you might want something. In addition, she supervises the rest of the staff easily because she is so adept at anticipating problems in the busy and popular restaurant.

Sally's early experience of learning to anticipate her mother's moods is more than helpful in her current relationship. It's no surprise, of course, that her partner is pretty moody. Fortunately, that early practice adds to her ability to notice when her partner needs some personal space. And Sally "stays clear"—not out of fear as in her childhood, but out of respect.

Allison also developed a keen eye. She noticed everything going on, but because the family was so secretive and presented a facade of perfection to the world, she wasn't allowed to comment. "In fact," she says, "if I noticed things, it blew their cover, and they'd say I was imagining it. If I tried to ask questions they'd silence me by calling me stupid. That's how they negated what I noticed about them. My keen eye got me into trouble back then but now it's like reclaiming the defect." It is this very same ability to observe fine detail that makes her a talented photographer.

There are times, however, when Allison's focus on detail causes problems in her relationship. "It's the old 'forest for the trees' cliché," she says. "Sometimes I get so caught up in the specifics I can't make connections to the bigger picture." Because her partner sees things from a global perspective, they seem to be on different wavelengths, missing each other's point of view. When she told me how she sometimes creates collages from her photos, we were able to form a plan. She agreed that collage-making is a skill that involves creating an integrated large picture from a lot of smaller photos. How does she do it? She selects the photos she wants to use, experiments with their placement, all the while keeping her keen eye on the overall effect she wants to create. Why not borrow from this skill, creating a new perspective in negotiating with her partner?

Perhaps, like Sally and Allison, you too learned to be watchful as a child and were good at noticing cues around you. Paying close attention to your parents' moods was a way you could try to protect yourself. Sometimes it may even have seemed like a matter of life or death to you. Just as in the examples above, you were probably great at things like watching, anticipating, planning, strategizing, or mediating.

Since you're already good with your eyes, why not practice another form of watchfulness? Try substituting the old "watch and fear" with "watch and learn." For example, what about going to a park or café or some other public place and observing the interactions of people around you, sort of like the way you might watch other people at a formal dinner table when you don't know which piece of silverware to use. You might learn new behaviors—how people show openness to talking to each other, how people show interest in each other by smiling, how people nonverbally make a statement that they want to be alone.

---

Substitute the old "watch and fear" with "watch and learn."

---

## Watch Yourself

Okay, so here's the deal: By transforming these talents you learned as a child, you can learn to take better care of yourself as an adult. You already have impressive training for noticing cues. Now, instead of watching everyone else for cues, why don't you practice watching yourself? Practice giving yourself this kind of attention and intention. When you have your own attention, see how much you can learn about your strengths.

Imagine taking a step or two away and walking alongside yourself. What do you notice? How are you moving? Do you have energy? Are you tense or are you relaxed? What is your breathing like? Are you really breathing? Are you smiling? Could you be happy? Are you clenching your jaw or your fists? Does this mean you are angry? Practice tuning in to yourself. Practice using your skills at noticing. You might be surprised at how many cues you take in. Noticing yourself and your actions is the first step to changing behavior. How can you even begin to change something if you are not aware of it?

By walking alongside yourself, you can be more objective about yourself. You can begin to notice small changes and learn from them. One of the most important questions you can ask yourself is, "What is different this time?" or "How did I do it differently?"

> Noticing your actions is the first step to changing behavior. How can you change something you're not even aware of?

## Survey the Past

Taking it a step further, a good way to transform crisis into opportunity is to survey the past and ask yourself, "What can I learn from this that I can use in the present and perhaps carry into the future with me?" This attitude allows you to develop a new approach to life in which you see things from a different perspective and make new choices.

A client and I were working together to see what skills he had carried over from childhood that could be put to use now. He visualized a blackboard divided in half. On the left was the section he called "The Past," which was completely filled with information from childhood. On the right was the section labeled "The Rest of My Life," which was a blank slate. He couldn't see any usable skills from the past to bring into the present and future. When I asked him to ask the blackboard what it would take to be able to fill up the right side, he immediately had the answer. "First I need to know what my needs are in order to gain access to the rest of my life. I'll make another section and call it 'Needs.' I'll put it in the middle. Once I list my needs, I'll discover opportunities."

It's useful to rethink the ways we think about ourselves. This involves modifying the words we use to portray ourselves or our feelings. For example, earlier I spoke of the difference between shame and embarrassment. Feelings of shame may be an automatic response, a habit. Feeling embarrassed doesn't carry the emotional charge of feeling ashamed. Try thinking of a situation as embarrassing rather than shameful or humiliating. Often a feeling of embarrassment is all that's warranted. The situation doesn't call for any more than that. Try repeating to yourself, "I'm only feeling embarrassed."

In the same vein, if you make a mistake you don't have to tell yourself you're a failure. Okay, so you screwed up—maybe you misspoke or made a misstep, a miscalculation, an omission, an oversight. But this doesn't mean you're a freak or a failure. You don't have to wrap yourself in unwarranted innuendo. There's almost always something to learn from the experience. Remind yourself that there is no failure, there is only feedback.

As we saw in chapter 13, relabeling can work wonders. Another way to make use of this ability is to practice relabeling your emotions. Relabeling your emotions provides another opportunity for change. For example, you could relabel "feeling anxious" as "feeling excited." You'll have a much different outlook if you're excited by anticipation than if you're anxious about your performance. Can you think of it as "creative tension"?

You could also think about relabeling "defective" to "vulnerable." Vulnerability is much more versatile. And it can be a strength when it includes openness, honesty, and caring sensitivity. What about relabeling "nosy" to "curious," "sneaky" to "astute," "obstinate" to "tenacious," or "difficult" to "spirited"? You get the idea.

One of my favorite relabeling stories is about a college student who experienced himself as defective because he was too shy to join class discussions or ask questions. He never said a word in class. If the class was expected to give oral presentations, he'd make sure he was "out sick" when it was his turn. He came into therapy because he was torturing himself with worry that the whole class was aware of his silences. He wasn't sure which situation was more mortifying: speaking or not speaking.

I wondered if perhaps he was safeguarding his thoughts in class—after all, he was a very private person. Maybe he was keeping his best thoughts private and taking his time until he felt ready.

He considered this for a week then returned to the next session with an observation of his own. "That reminds me of a story my parents used to tell about my childhood. I didn't walk until I was eighteen months old I'd just sit and watch people, waiting until I was ready. Then, when the time was right, I stood up and walked. I never tottered, never lurched, never stumbled. I just walked!" Once he recognized he had his own style of doing things, and once he began to think of himself as "private" rather than "shy," something happened. Three weeks later he stood before the class and gave a required short report. I guess he was ready.

You, too, might try to shed some of those old labels and rewrite new ones for yourself. Disidentify with the old images and be open to new ways of seeing yourself. One way you can practice relabeling previously identified "weaknesses" with strengths is through visual imagery. Do you remember the scene in *The Yellow Submarine* where the cartoon characters of the Beatles were running back and forth across the hall, from room to room? Using a similar idea, visualize two sets of rooms on each side of a hallway. You can close your eyes if you want. The rooms on one side of the hallway all contain behaviors that have been previously labeled as "Not Okay." Think of these rooms as storage areas, containing every possible type of storage container—closets, shelves, bins, boxes, and file cabinets. Imagine yourself rummaging through these strengths, seeing what is usable, and desirable. Give yourself several minutes to sort through, and select these strengths, noticing their shapes and colors. Perhaps you will choose one, then refold it and put it away for now, moving on to another one because you like its energy better. Let this be a process of sorting, choosing, and selecting. Some traits you will decide to take with you, some you will decide to leave behind. You'll find each trait has an energy all its own. Try borrowing this energy you have found and admired, and walk with it across the hall to another room, bringing it to another part of yourself that can appreciate it and make use of it. In this new space you have made for it you might discover this energy begins to change, transforming into something even more useful and precious to you.

Recovery is recovering something you already have. Sometimes we overlook our assets. We forget how solid and strong our underpinnings are. We forget how much we have to fall back on, to work with, to use in new and different ways. It's like giving a new look to a worn sofa by recovering it in a new and vibrant fabric. Perhaps you can recover yourself in the same way.

---

**Recovery is recovering something you already have.**

---

Sometimes this means looking at skills that already exist in one area of your life and transferring them to another area. Doris provided a good example of this. As soon as I heard her message on the voice mail at work, I knew she was "in charge" there—not at all like the picture of helplessness she painted when she described her relationship with her teenager. So we identified her work skills: managing, listening, responding, defining, problem solving. Then she began borrowing from that quite capable "work compartment" of her life and transferring those skills into use at home with her daughter. Things got better.

But things don't always consistently stay better. We all backslide once in a while. Try not to get thrown by stumbling blocks that occasionally appear in the form of overreactions. Can you begin to think of old behaviors as old friends? After all, they grew up with you. And like old friends, they may come back to pay you a surprise visit once in a while.

---

**Think of old behaviors as if they are old friends paying a surprise visit once in a while.**

---

These occasional visits are markers, reminders of how far you have come along your road of changing. My clients and I call it the "Oh Shit Thing." It comes from a story one woman told me: She got upset with herself for taking something personally and slipping back into an old overreacting behavior. When she realized it had been nearly four months since the last outburst, she was actually delighted. "Oh, shit," she said, "Here it is again. Well, I *used* to do this every day!"

Think about taking two or three steps forward and one step back. Sometimes that's the only way to achieve progress. There you are, moving along into some new behaviors and out of the blue, you get whacked on the head with an overwhelming feeling or overreaction that flares up like a match. Sure, it seems like you are taking a step backward, but remember, once you do a new behavior, it's added to your repertoire.

---

**Each time it feels you're taking a step backward, remember it's the backward motion that could propel you forward into new behavior.**

---

So a step backward won't take long to recover from, because you've already visited that new place and you can get there again easily. Also remind yourself that each time it feels you are taking a step backward, it is the backward motion that could propel you forward into new behavior.

This process is like having your own tool shop with each tool hanging on the wall, carefully outlined, so it's easy to get to it when you need it. One man said, "I can make a special tool after the fact. Each time, I ask myself, 'What did I learn from this experience?' and the next time it's hanging on the wall waiting for me!"

---

**Once you practice a new behavior it's added to your repertoire.**

---

In the introduction I described how old behaviors are like a slow-motion version of trick birthday-cake candles in the way they seem to die down for varying lengths of time, then unexpectedly flare up again. I remind you of that image again here, in the hope that after reading this book, you can better understand how these flare-ups can be useful. I hope you can see the possibilities for taking the best part of them, transforming them into new skills, and using them in creative and resourceful ways. Rather than letting your history lead to negative reactions, let it become a positive resource to you.

## Redirect Your Energy

One final suggestion: There's no doubt you are a master of being supersensitive to your world and taking things personally. Why stop there? Why not *use* this information in order to take better care of yourself? You can redirect the energy you spend on watching others for cues and give it back to yourself in the form of quality personal attention.

This is how to go about it. Early in the book I defined taking things personally as taking information as if it were directed at you (even though it might not have been). Why not make an effort to really get to know yourself by directing energy to yourself—noticing your own cues, honoring your intuition, and getting to know and appreciate yourself? Why not personalize things so they work for you in your own unique way? In other words, try taking *yourself* personally. You've spent years paying far too much attention to your "inner censor," why not turn your attention to respecting your "inner sensor" for a change? Why not hone your imperfections, recognize your vast resources, and explore new ways of engaging with the world around you? By opening up your heart and mind to all aspects of your world, you are taking things in—in a personal and intimate way. This, too, is taking things personally.

---

Instead of worrying about your "inner censor," why not put your energy into developing your "inner sensor"?

---

One woman, trained in massage, knows about unblocking energy and moving it around. Whenever she wants to move from a negative place into a positive place, she visualizes a honeycomb. The energy takes the form of warm, thick, sweet, amber-colored liquid, constantly moving through the interconnected tunnels. As the energy flows, a wondrous transformation takes place. She notices how the negative messages of childhood take on new qualities as they flow from space to space. As the energy changes from life-depleting to life-sustaining, it provides sustenance, allowing room for her needs and wants, and encouraging clear boundaries. Then the energy develops new vitality, permitting choices and enhancing good communication. And it keeps on moving, flowing.

Moving and flowing. That's the answer, isn't it? Whenever you feel helpless, afraid, immobilized, dazed, numbed, or stunned, when it becomes hard to think or act, try to move. Move your fingers or your toes. Try to get some energy flowing. Once you do even a small amount of movement you are no longer stuck.

Suppose you find yourself feeling like a scared little child again, sitting paralyzed on the sofa. Maybe it seems like you've been living in a cartoon, things don't seem real to you, you're not a part of time. If you can remember to move your finger back and forth, then your arm, you have just made a choice to reconnect with your body. Another way to reconnect is to self-soothe. By gently touching yourself, stroking your hand or your arm or your shoulder, you activate energy. You have just brought time back into the picture.

Once you create an option you won't feel so stuck. Once you open up just a little, and let the energy flow, you are empowering yourself. As you develop a stronger sense of who you are, you'll find you won't tend to personalize messages as much. With a more defined sense of yourself and adequate self-determination, you can embrace an environment that begins to feel welcoming and accepting. And this energy will spread, growing into self-acceptance and creativity, filling you with a new experience of yourself in relationship to others.

## Follow the Signposts

So let's review ways to go about transforming self-rejection into self-acceptance: not an easy task for sure. Hopefully, in the preceding pages you have discovered some new perspectives and ideas that can help you take one step at a time, along your path. Here are some signposts to use in your journey. Feel free to photocopy this list and put it up on your refrigerator or mirror.

- Ask yourself, "Am I taking this personally?"

- Ask yourself, "Am I trying to read someone's mind?"

- Ask yourself, "Am I expecting someone to read my mind?"

- Remind yourself that certain beliefs may have seemed true in childhood but they are not true now. Try to disidentify from them.

- Make sure you're not blowing things way out of proportion by catastrophizing or overgeneralizing beliefs about yourself.

- Walk alongside yourself. Notice as much as you can. Observing gets the flow going and opens up space for choices.

- Keep reminding yourself that you have choices.

- Empathize—put yourself in the other person's shoes.

- Hypothesize, but don't analyze, pathologize, or therapize.

- Practice making eye contact.

- Practice saying "thank you" to compliments.

- Don't presume—check things out with the other person.

- Check in with yourself about your boundaries; Whose feelings belong to whom?

- Remind yourself there is a difference between needs and neediness.

- Practice asking yourself what you want or need each day and from whom you want it.

- Practice asking directly for what you want or need.

- Ask about the other person's needs.

- Remember that *allowing* vulnerability is a strength. It's very different from *feeling vulnerable*.

- If you're uncomfortable in a situation, you can leave—taking a time-out is just fine. Even counting to ten helps a lot.

- Ask yourself, "What's different this time? How is it different? What can I learn from this?"

- Try rejecting rejection. Just ignore it for a change.

In writing this book I wanted to replicate the same process I use doing therapy. I wanted to gather information and present it to you so things would begin to fit together in new and different ways.

In the course of doing therapy, my clients and I work as a team, interweaving the "then" with the "now," by first recognizing the problem, then looking for its source, and ultimately doing something about it. The best way I know to convey this process is by using one of my favorite metaphors—reweaving a tapestry. Approaching psychotherapy is much like looking at your life experience as if it's a tapestry. Through the ages tapestries have been used to tell colorful stories. There is the Bayeux Tapestry, depicting the Norman Conquest, and the Unicorn tapestries from the fifteenth century with their background of a thousand flowers. The tapestry of your life tells a unique story as well.

As you survey it, you'll find many sections are intact, solidly woven, and sturdy. But it's not perfect. Some parts most likely became worn over the years, perhaps a little frayed. There are some weakened places here and there, maybe even a few holes. It would be a shame to reject the whole tapestry because part of it is tattered or torn, when in fact, much of the surrounding areas are durable and vital. Even though a few holes might be bigger than others, they can all be filled in, they're all restorable.

Sometimes it's hard to know where to start. Sometimes it seems like an overwhelming project. But all you have to do is to locate one small piece of thread and follow it. It will lead to others. It's a matter of gathering together the stitches, a little here and a little there, connecting those parts of yourself, restoring form and order. And while you're at it notice the colors and the textures, too. Discovering and reclaiming parts of yourself is similar to gathering in different colors; you can choose a blue or a gold or a red or a purple or a green. Your experiences of growing up in your family of origin are like the various textures, all contributing to the character of the overall arrangement. Remember, too, that the energy can also be directed outward. Each thread is capable of linking you to other people, forming an interlocking pattern.

Most importantly, you don't have to put that tapestry together in exactly the same way it was before. Now you have options. Here is an opportunity to redesign the tapestry of your life experiences. You can choose to work from the center to the perimeter, filling in spaces and adding a new border if you want. Or you can work from the outside toward the center, choosing to add blocks of new color or new texture. You can even add a different pattern to the center. You can weave in the ability to recognize what you need and even the capacity to ask for it. You can intertwine the art of empathizing. You can add a sense of clearer boundaries. You can incorporate some self-confidence and self-acceptance. You can take yourself seriously by honoring your uniqueness, by reminding yourself that this is *your* tapestry and you can reweave it any way you want. And as you gather in those strands, reclaiming parts of yourself, giving them form, shape, color, texture, richness, and vibrancy, you will be gathering energy toward your heart. Use this renewed energy to notice how the edges of *your* tapestry touch the world around you, and how you're touched in return.

As you continue to weave your tapestry, acknowledge and honor your past as well as your present. This enlightenment can be used as a resource to help you make choices along the way that broaden your experience of life. As one of my clients said, "I'm working hard to accept life on life's terms and accept myself in the process."

# Notes

## Introduction

2 As psychotherapist and researcher ... : Elaine Aron, *The Highly Sensitive Person* (1996, Secaucus, N.J.: Birch Lane Press), 28–30: "... sensitive children come with a built-in tendency to react more strongly to external stimuli." She goes on to describe how sensitivity is created by the balance of two systems in the brain—the *behavioral activation* system, which takes in messages from the senses and sends out orders to the limbs, and the *behavioral inhibition* system, which moves us away from things, making us cautious, attentive to danger, and watchful for signs. Why not, Aron asks, recognize the positive benefits of this second system and call it the *automatic-pause-to-check* system?

3 Adult Attention Deficit ... : Although Adult Attention Deficit Disorder can only be diagnosed by a trained professional in the field, there are many books available on the subject. Here are three that may be helpful in understanding the scope of the problem: Ed Hallowell and John Ratey, *Driven to Distraction* (1994, New York: Random House); Kate Kelly and Peggy Ramundo, *You Mean I'm Not Lazy, Crazy or Stupid: A Self-Help Book for Adults with Attention Deficit Disorder* (1993, New York: Fireside Books); M. Susan Roberts and Gerald J. Jansen, *Living with ADD: A Workbook for Adults with Attention Deficit Disorder* (1997, Oakland, CA: New Harbinger Publications).

4 As Harvey Mackay writes ... : Harvey Mackay, *Sharkproof* (1993, New York: HarperBusiness), 31–34.

5 Then, a few years ... : NIA (Neuromuscular Integrative Action), a healing process of connecting the body, mind, and spirit through guided movement, was first introduced in 1983 by Debbie and Carlos Rosas. (800) 762-5762.

# Chapter 1

18  But, as Judy Tatelbaum observes . . . : Judy Tatelbaum, *You Don't Have to Suffer: A Handbook for Moving Beyond Life's Crises.* (1989, New York: Harper & Row), 55–61.

25  Gershen Kaufman, *Shame: The Power of Caring* (1985, Cambridge, MA: Shenkman Books, Inc.), 8.

# Chapter 2

29  According to Susan Jeffers . . . : Jeffers, *End the Struggle,* 62–63.

31  As Sheldon Kopp . . . : Sheldon Kopp, *If You Meet the Buddha on the Road, Kill Him! The Pilgrimage of Psychotherapy Patients* (1972, Ben Lomond, CA: Science and Behavior Books, Inc.), 2.

# Chapter 3

37  As Judy Tatelbaum . . . : Tatelbaum, *You Don't Have to Suffer,* 55–61.

37  Sometimes we may find . . . : Stephen B. Karpman, "Fairy Tales and Script Drama Analysis" (1968 *Transactional Analysis Bulletin,* VII, No. 26), 39–43.

38  The classic "martyr mother" . . . : From conversations with Dr. Stephen Karpman, 1996.

39  I thought I had . . . : An excellent discussion of how codependents engage in the Drama Triangle is given by Melody Beattie in *Codependent No More* (1987, New York: Harper/Hazelden), chapter 8.

45  The best way to do this . . . : Lonnie Barbach and David Geisinger, *Going the Distance: Finding and Keeping Lifelong Love* (1993, New York: Plume), 86.

46  Lonnie Barbach and David Geisinger, *Going the Distance.*

# Chapter 4

55  Disappointments also develop . . . : Clifford Sager, *Marriage Contracts and Couples Therapy* (1976, New York: Brunner/Mazel), 85–88.

57  In the fantastic world . . . : Selma Fraiberg, *The Magic Years* This is a charming account of the magical world of young children. (1959, New York: Charles Scribner's Sons).

63  Don Juan, the Seducer: Alice Miller, *Thou Shalt Not Be Aware* (1984, New York: Farrar, Straus, Giroux), 79–82.

65  As Susan Jeffers observes . . . : Susan Jeffers, *End the Struggle and Dance with Life* (1996, New York: St. Martin's Press), 74.

65  Now is a gift . . . : "The I Can" cards, ©1985 G2BE Publishers, Inc.

68  Psychologist Janet Wolfe addresses this . . . : Janet Wolfe, *What to Do When He Has a Headache* (1993, New York: Penguin), 15, 26.

71  Susan Jeffers writes . . . : Susan Jeffers, *Feel the Fear and Do It Anyway* (1987, New York: Fawcett), 111.

# Chapter 5

76 "Those who love me . . .": This theory of double binds is put forward by D. Spiegel in "Dissociation, Double Binds and the Posttraumatic Stress in Multiple Personality Disorder" (1986, In B. G. Braun (ed.), *Treatment of Multiple Personality Disorder*, Washington, D.C. : American Psychiatric Press).

87 When this ambivalence surfaces . . . : Lillian Rubin, *Intimate Strangers* (1983, New York: Harper & Row), 65.

# Chapter 6

94 Dr. Bruce Perry of the Baylor College of Medicine. . . . quoted from an article by J. Madeleine Nash, *Time Magazine*, February 3, 1997, p. 55. "Experience is the chief architect of the brain." says Dr. Perry. The article goes on to say, "Because the brain develops in sequence, with more primitive structures stabilizing their connections first, early abuse is particularly damaging . . . these early experiences of stress form a kind of template around which later brain development is organized, the changes they create are all the more pervasive."

96 In *Intimate Worlds* . . . : Maggie Scarf, *Intimate Worlds* (1995, New York: Random House).

96 Many observers have commented. . . : Allan Schore, *Affect Regulation and the Origin of the Self: The Neurobiology of Emotional Development.* (1994, Hillsdale, NJ: Lawrence Earlbaum Associates), 71–91. This comprehensive discussion of mutual gazing between infant and parent includes discussions of ideas by D. W. Winnicott and expanded on by Heinz Kohut and others, including "mutual gazing," "mutuality," "reflecting back," and "the mirror role of the mother." Daniel Stern's ideas on "attunement" between mothers and their infants is also discussed in detail.

96 The human soul . . . : A. H. Almaas, *The Point of Existence* (1996, Berkeley, CA: Diamond Books).

97 This reciprocal nature . . . : Mary Main, Nancy Kaplan and Jude Cassidy, Security in Infancy, Childhood, and Adulthood: A Move to the Level of Representation, (*Monographs of the Society for Research in Child Development, 50*, 1985) 79–80.

Mary Main and Ruth Goldwyn, "Predicting Rejection of Her Infant From Mother's Representation of Her Own Experience: Implications for the Abused-abusing Intergenerational Cycle," *Child Abuse and Neglect*, 8 (1984): 203–217.

98 According to British psychiatrist . . . : John Bowlby, *A Secure Base: Parent-Child Attachment and Healthy Human Development* (1988, New York: Basic Books), 11.

98 Researchers find that whether children . . . : M. Ainsworth, M. Blehar, E. Waters, and S. Wall, Patterns of Attachment: *A Psychological Study of the Strange Situation.* (1978, Hillsdale, NJ: Erlbaum); Mary Main

and Ruth Goldwyn, "Predicting Rejection of Her Infant from Mother's Representation of Her Own Experience: Implications for the Abused-abusing Intergenerational Cycle," *Child Abuse and Neglect* 8 (1984): 203–217; Bryon Egeland, L. Alan Sroufe, and Martha Erickson, "The developmental consequence of different patterns of maltreatment, *Child Abuse and Neglect* 7 (1983): 459–469; Margaret Ricks, "The Social Transmission of Parental Behavior: Attachment Across Generations," *Monographs of the Society for Research in Child Development* 50 (1985): 211–227.

98   Depending on how responsive. . . . Mary Ainsworth coined the terms secure, avoidant, and anxious-ambivalent based on the work of John Bowlby. M. Ainsworth, M. Blehar, E. Waters, and S. Wall. *Patterns of Attachment: A Psychological Study of the Strange Situation* (1978, Hillsdale, NJ: Erlbaum).

98   A fourth attachment style—insecure-disorganized/disoriented . . . : Mary Main, Nancy Kaplan and Jude Cassidy, Security in Infancy, Childhood, and Adulthood: A Move to the level of Representation, (*Monographs of the Society for Research in Child Development* 50, 1985) 79–80.

Recent research regarding adult attachment styles is presented in Michael Sperling and William Berman (editors), *Attachment in Adults: Clinical and Developmental Perspectives* (1994, New York: The Guilford Press).

99   For more information on recent . . . : Cindy Hazan and Phillip Shaver looked at how these attachment styles are also present in romantic love. (Romantic love conceptualized as an attachment process.) *Journal of Personality and Social Psychology*, vol. 52, pp. 511–524, (1987). They based their work on three attachment styles conceptualized by John Bowlby and Mary Ainsworth.

99   Bowlby makes a distinction . . . : Bowlby, *A Secure Base: Parent-Child Attachment and Healthy Human Development*, 26–29.

99   Psychologist/anthropologist . . . : Ronald P. Rohner, *The Warmth Dimension: Foundations of Parental Acceptance-rejection Theory.* (1986, Beverly Hills, CA: Sage Publications), 19–21.

101  . . . Dr. Harlow's and his experiments . . . : Harry Harlow, "The Development of Affectional Patterns in Infant Monkeys." (1961, in B.M. Foss (editor), *Determinants of Infant Behavior* (Vol 1), New York: Wiley).

102  As Judith Viorst writes . . . : Judith Viorst, *Necessary Losses* (1987, New York: Fawcett), 23.

103  Psychiatrist John Bowlby describes some . . . : Bowlby, "The Making and Breaking of Affectional Bonds," *British Journal of Psychiatry* 130 (1977): 206.

103  Based on the work . . . : The psychological maltreatment definitions used in this chapter are the product of the National Psychological

Maltreatment Consortium and the American Professional Society on the Abuse of Children (APSAC) Task Force on Psychological Maltreatment chaired by Stuart N. Hart, Ph.D.and Marla Brassard, Ph.D.

Practice guidelines are discussed in American Professional Society on the Abuse of Children *Psychosocial Evaluation of Suspected Psychological Maltreatment in Children and Adolescents,* 1995, and in Stuart N. Hart, Marla R. Brassard, and Henry C. Karlson, "Psycho- logical Maltreatment" (1996, in J. Briere, L. Berliner, J. Bulkley, C. Jenny, and T. Reid (editors), *The APSAC Handbook on Child Maltreatment,* New-bury Park, CA: Sage Publications), 72–89.

The Office for the Study of the Psychological Rights of the Child, Director, Stuart N. Hart, Ph.D. (317) 274-6805 or 6801. 902 West New York Street. Indianapolis, IN 46240.

Two excellent books discussing the concepts of psychological maltreatment are: Marla R. Brassard, Robert Germain, Stuart N. Hart. 1987. *PsychologicalMaltreatment of Children and Youth.* New York: Pergamon Press and James Garbarino, Edna Guttmann, Janis Wilson Seeley. 1986. *The Psychologically Battered Child.* San Francisco: Jossey-Bass.

105  My own research . . . : Elayne Savage, *Perception of Childhood Parental Acceptance or Rejection: How It Relates to Adult Intimacy* (1989, unpublished dissertation).

107  The young black man . . . : This article first appeared in the *Baltimore Evening Sun,* May 6, 1993, entitled "Don't Tell Me I'm Imagining It!" by Elayne Savage.

114  When parents try to live their lives vicariously . . . : is from an article that first appeared in the *San Francisco Chronicle,* May 16, 1996, entitled "Motivation Versus Manipulation," by Elayne Savage.

114  Jay North, the actor who played . . . : Rick Sandack, "After the Laugh Track Fades" (1993, *Real People* magazine, distributed by the Los Angeles Times Syndicate).

# Chapter 7

119  And let's not forget . . . : Elaine Aron's book, *The Highly Sensitive Person* describes a case study of fraternal twins raised in the same household. The boy is highly sensitive and the girl is not (23–27).

119  This trait of sensitivity is related to children's temperaments and how their parents perceive them. Dr Jim Cameron, Director of The Preventive Ounce, offers a questionnaire that helps parents understand their childrens temperaments (ages infancy–six years). You can check their web site: www.preventiveoz.org or contact them at 510-658-8359 (Oakland, CA).

121  Her initial idea . . . : Mary Main, and Ruth Goldwyn. *Child Abuse and Neglect,* 8, pp 203–217, 1987.

121  Parent-infant expert Selma Fraiberg describes . . . : Selma Fraiberg, Edna Adelson, and Vivian Shapiro, "Ghosts in the Nursery: A Psychoanalytic Approach to the Problems of Impaired Infant-Mother Relationships" (1975, *Journal of the American Academy of Child Psychiatry*, Vol. 14, 387–421.

125  Pat Conroy, author of . . . : Julian Guthrie, "High Tide in the Low Country" (July 16, 1995, *The San Francisco Examiner Magazine*).

126  Parents who have experienced anxious attachment . . . : Bowlby, *Separation: Anxiety and Anger*. (1973, New York: Basic Books) and *A Secure Base: Parent-Child Attachment and Healthy Human Development*. (1988, New York: Basic Books).

127  But for girls . . . : These studies about preadolescent girls contain many kinds of themes of rejection of the self and rejection by others and can be found in The American Association of University Women, *Shortchanging Girls, Shortchanging America: A Call To Action* (1991, Washington, D.C.: The American Association of University Women); Carol Gilligan, *In A Different Voice: Psychological Theory and Women's Development* (1982, Cambridge: Harvard University Press); Emily Hancock, *The Girl Within* (1989, New York: Fawcett Columbine); Peggy Orenstein, in association with the American Association of University Women, *School Girls: Young Women, Self-Esteem, and the Gender Gap*. (1994, New York: Anchor); Mary Pipher, *Reviving Ophelia* (1994, New York: Ballantine).

128  Robert Johnson, in . . . : Robert A. Johnson, *Owning Your Own Shadow* (1991, San Francisco: HarperSan Francisco), 7–8.

128  Maggie Scarf describes . . . : Excellent discussions of projective identification are in Maggie Scarf, *Intimate Partners* (1988, New York: Ballentine Books), 186; Scarf, *Intimate Worlds*, (1995, New York: Random House) 76–77; and Judith Viorst, *Necessary Losses* (1986, New York: Fawcett), 214–215.

129  Scarf notes that . . . : Scarf, *Intimate Partners*, 185.

129  Scarf goes on to say . . . : Scarf, *Intimate Partners*, 200.

129  In *The Missing Piece* . . . : Claudia Black and Leslie Drozd, *The Missing Piece—Solving the Puzzle of Self* (1995, New York: Ballantine Books).

130  The legacy of . . . : Amy Tan, *The Joy Luck Club* (1989, New York: Ivy Books).

130  . . . raised hopes and failed . . . : ibid., 144.

130  . . . something so large . . . : ibid., 54.

130  People rise to . . . : ibid., 20.

130  Why do you have to . . . : ibid., 101–102.

131  I often do a genogram . . . : Genograms have various forms—there is no right from wrong way. For more information on how to draw genograms and how they are used in systems therapy, a good reference is Monica McGoldrick and Randy Gerson, *Genograms in Family Assessment* (1985, New York: W. W. Norton & Company).

## Chapter 8

135  Mealtimes in some families are like ...: Lewis Carroll, *Alice's Adventures in Wonderland*, Chapter VII, A Mad Tea-Party (1865, New York: J. J. Little & Ives Company), 64.

139  For further information ...: Thomas Cash, *The Body Image Workbook* (1997, Oakland, CA: New Harbinger Publications); Geneen Roth, *Feeding the Hungry Heart* (1982, New York: Signet); Geneen Roth, *Appetites: On the Search for True Nourishment* (1996, New York: Dutton); Debra Waterhouse, Like Mother, Like Daughter: *How Women Are Influenced by Their Mother's Relationship With Food and How to Break the Pattern* (1997, New York: Hyperion); Marion Woodman, *The Owl Was A Baker's Daughter* (1980, Toronto: Inner City Books).

## Chapter 9

143  ... placing a psychological blight ...: is from Julius Segal and Herbert Yahraes, *A Child's Journey: Forces That Shape the Lives of Our Young* (1978, New York: McGraw-Hill), 248. Many of my ideas on child development have come from this book.

146  Girls don't express ...: Mary Pipher, *Reviving Ophelia*, 68.

148  According to Mary Pipher, "scapegoating ...": Pipher, *Reviving Ophelia*, 68.

151  Parents are often alarmed ...: Stephen P. Bank and Michael D. Kahn, *The Sibling Bond* (1982, New York: Basic Books, Inc.), 198–201.

## Chapter 10

158  When parents aren't ...: I heard the term "cookie lady" in Claudia Black's workshop, San Francisco, 1984.

158  Lillian Rubin, *The Transcendent Child* (1996, New York: BasicBooks).

158  Conversation with Lillian Rubin, 1996.

159  Another researcher has found ...: Rohner, *The Warmth Dimension*, 131–136.

164  Self-soothing is an absolutely ...: Nancy Napier, *Re-creating Your Self* (1990, New York: W.W. Norton), 157–176.

## Chapter 11

166  ... seven categories of personal ...: John Friel and Linda Friel, *Adult Child's Guide to What's "Normal"* (1990, Deerfield Beach, FL: Health Communications, Inc.), 29–31.

167  Having boundaries is like ...: Pia Mellody and A.W. Miller, *Facing Codependence* (1989, San Francisco, CA: HarperSan Francisco), 11.

172  [overreact] to outside forces and underreact to inside forces ...: Friel and Friel, *Adult Child's Guide*, 16.

174  Alice Miller states . . . : Alice Miller, *Thou Shalt Not Be Aware* (1984, New York: Farrar, Straus, Giroux), 79–82.

175  In the same vein . . . : David Viscott, *Emotionally Free: Letting Go of the Past to Lore in the Moment* (Chicago, IL: Contemporary Books), 145–150.

175  Claudia Black, *Repeat After Me* (1985, Denver, CO: M.A.C. Publishing), 83–92.

176  There are several techniques . . . : Mellody, *Breaking Free* (1989, New York: Harper Collins), 320.

176  Mellody also describes . . . : Mellody, *Breaking Free*, 330.

## Chapter 12

182  The studies mentioned . . . : Gilligan, Hancock, Orenstein, Pipher.

183  Go Away a Little . . . : Lillian Rubin, *Intimate Strangers*.

182  Elaine Aron, *The Highly Sensitive Person*, 11.

185  Steve Bhaerman and Don McMillan. *Friends and Lovers: How to Meet the People You Want to Meet* (1986, Cincinnati, OH: Writer's Digest Books), 49.

186  The answer will always . . . : Patricia Fripp, San Francisco.

## Chapter 13

189  Some of the best descriptions of ambivalence I've come across are in Susan Page's *If I'm So Wonderful,Why Am I Still Single?* 1990. New York: Bantam Books; and Maggie Scarf's *Intimate Partners* New York: Ballantine; and Judith Viorst's *Necessary Losses* New York: Fawcett 1986.

193  This growth process . . . : Portia Nelson, "Autobiography in Five Short Chapters," from Black, *Repeat After Me*.

194  Jeffers, *Feel the Fear*, 118.

194  Abraham Maslow, "Self-Actualization and Beyond," *Challenges in Humanistic Psychology* (1967, in James F. T. Bugental (ed.), New York: McGraw Hill), 282.

198  Sheldon Kopp, *If You Meet the Budda on the Road, Kill Him!* 34–38.

## Chapter 14

200  Maybe you learned . . . : The process of dissociation is described very well in Lenore Terr, *Unchained Memories* (1994, New York: Basic Books), 70–71.

# Bibliography

Ainsworth, M. D., M. C. Blehar, E. Waters, and S. Wall. 1978. *Patterns of Attachment: A Psychological Study of the Strange Situation*. Hillsdale, NJ: Erlbaum.

Almas, A. H. 1996. *The Point of Existence*. Berkeley, CA: Diamond Books.

Aron, Elaine. 1996. *The Highly Sensitive Person*. Secaucus, N.J.: Birch Lane Press.

Bank, Stephen P., and Michael D. Kahn. 1982. *The Sibling Bond*. New York: Basic Books.

Barbach, Lonnie, and David Geisinger. 1993. *Going the Distance: Finding and Keeping Lifelong Love*. New York: Plume.

Beattie, Melody. 1987. *Copdependent No More*. New York: Harper/ Hazelden.

Bhaerman, Steve, and Don McMillan. 1986. *Friends and Lovers: How to Meet the People You Want to Meet*. Cincinnati, OH: Writers Digest Books.

Black, Claudia. 1985. *Repeat After Me*. Denver, CO: M.A.C. Publishing.

Black, Claudia, and Leslie Drozd. 1995. *The Missing Piece—Solving the Puzzle of Self*. New York: Ballantine Books.

Bowlby, John. 1973. *Separation: Anxiety and Anger*. New York: Basic Books.

Bowlby, John. 1988. *A Secure Base: Parent-Child Attachment and Healthy Human Development*. New York: Basic Books.

Brassard, Marla R., Robert Germain, and Stuart N. Hart. 1987. *Psychological Maltreatment of Children and Youth*. New York: Pergamon Press.

Briere, J., L. Berliner, J. Bulkley, C. Jenny, and T. Reid (editors.). 1996. *The APSAC Handbook on Child Maltreatment.* Newbury Park, CA: Sage Publications.

Burns, David. 1992. *Feeling Good.* New York: Avon Books.

Carroll, Lewis. *Alice's Adventures in Wonderland.* New York: J. J. Little & Ives Company.

Carter, Steven and Julia Sokol. 1995. *He's Scared, She's Scared.* New York: Dell.

Cash, Thomas. 1997. *The Body Image Workbook.* Oakland, CA: New Harbinger Publications.

Fraiberg, Selma. 1959. *The Magic Years.* New York: Charles Scribner's Sons.

Friel, John, and Linda Friel. 1990. *Adult Child's Guide to What's "Normal."* Deerfield Beach, FL: Health Communications, Inc.

Garbarino, James, Edna Guttmann, and Janis Wilson Seeley. 1986. *The Psychologically Battered Child.* San Francisco: Jossey-Bass.

Gil, Eliana. 1992. *Outgrowing the Pain: A Book for and about Adults Abused as Children.* New York: Dell.

Gilligan, Carol. 1982. *In A Different Voice: Psychological Theory and Women's Development.* Cambridge, MA: Harvard University Press.

Goleman, Daniel. 1995. *Emotional Intelligence.* New York: Bantam.

Hallowell, Ed and Ratey, John. 1994. *Driven to Distraction.* New York: Random House.

Hancock, Emily. 1989. *The Girl Within.* New York: Fawcett Columbine.

Herman, Judith Lewis. 1992. *Trauma and Recovery.* New York: Basic Books.

Jeffers, Susan. 1987. *Feel the Fear and Do It Anyway.* New York: Fawcett.

———. 1996. *End the Struggle and Dance with Life.* New York: St. Martin's Press.

Johnson, Robert A. 1991. *Owning Your Own Shadow.* San Francisco: Harper SanFrancisco

Kaufman, Gershen. 1985. *Shame: The Power of Caring.* Cambridge, MA: Shenkman Books, Inc.

Kelly, Kate and Ramundo, Peggy. 1993. *You Mean I'm Not Lazy Crazy or Stupid: A Self-Help Book for Adults with Attention Deficit Disorder.* New York: Fireside Books.

Kopp, Sheldon. 1972. *If You Meet the Buddha on the Road, Kill Him! The Pilgrimage of Psychotherapy Patients.* Ben Lomond, CA: Science and Behavior Books, Inc.

Kupers, Terry. 1993. *Revisioning Men's Lives: Gender, Intimacy, and Power.* New York: Guilford Press.

Mackay, Harvey. 1993. *Sharkproof.* New York: HarperBusiness.

Maslow, Abraham. 1967. "Self-Actualization and Beyond." In James F. T. Bugental (editor), *Challenges in Humanistic Psychology.* New York: McGraw-Hill.

McGoldrick, Monica, and Randy Gerson. 1985. *Genograms in Family Assessment.* New York: W. W. Norton & Company.

Mellody, Pia, and A. W. Miller. 1989. *Breaking Free.* New York: Harper-Collins.

Miller, Alice. 1984. *Thou Shalt Not Be Aware.* New York: Farrar, Straus, Giroux.

Napier, Nancy. 1990. *Re-creating Your Self.* New York: W. W. Norton.

Orenstein, Peggy (in association with the American Association of University Women). 1994. *School Girls: Young Women, Self-Esteem, and the Gender Gap.* New York: Anchor.

Page, Susan. 1990. *If I'm So Wonderful, Why Am I Still Single?* New York: Bantam.

———. 1997. *How One of You Can Bring the Two of You Together: Breakthrough Strategies to Resolve Your Conflicts and Reignite Your Love.* New York: Broadway.

Pipher, Mary. 1994. *Reviving Ophelia.* New York: Ballantine.

———. 1994. *Hunger Pains.* New York: Ballantine.

Roberts, M. Susan and Jansen, Gerald J. 1997. *Living with ADD: A Workbook for Adults with Attention Deficit Disorder.* Oakland CA: New Harbinger Publications.

Rohner, Ronald P. 1986. *The Warmth Dimension: Foundations of Parental Acceptance-Rejection Theory.* Beverly Hills, CA: Sage Publications.

Roth, Geneen. 1982. *Feeding the Hungry Heart.* New York: Signet.

———. 1996. *Appetites: On the Search for True Nourishment.* New York: Dutton.

Rubin, Lillian. 1983. *Intimate Strangers.* New York: Harper & Row.

———. 1996. *The Transcendent Child.* New York: Basic Books.

Sager, Clifford. 1976. *Marriage Contracts and Couples Therapy.* New York: Brunner/Mazel.

Scarf, Maggie. 1988. *Intimate Partners.* New York: Ballentine Books.

———. 1995. *Intimate Worlds.* New York: Random House.

Schore, Allan. 1994. *Affect Regulation and the Origin of the Self: the Neurobiology of Emotional Development.* Hillsdale, NJ: Lawrence Earlbaum Associates.

Segal, Julius, and Herbert Yahraes. 1978. *A Child's Journey: Forces That Shape the Lives of Our Young.* New York: McGraw-Hill.

Sperling, Michael, and William Berman (editors). 1994. *Attachment in Adults: Clinical and Developmental Perspectives.* New York: The Guilford Press.

Stern, Daniel. 1987. *The Interpersonal World of the Infant.* New York: Basic Books.

Tan, Amy. 1989. *The Joy Luck Club.* New York: Ivy Books.

Tatelbaum, Judy. 1989. *You Don't Have to Suffer: A Handbook For Moving Beyond Life's Crises.* New York: Harper & Row.

Terr, Lenore, M.D. 1994. *Unchained Memories.* New York: Basic Books.

Viorst, Judith. 1986. *Necessary Losses.* New York: Basic Books.

Viscott, David. 1992. *Emotionally Free: Letting Go of the Past to Love in the Moment.* Chicago: Contemporary Books.

Waterhouse, Debra. 1997. *Like Mother, Like Daughter: How Women Are Influenced by Their Mother's Relationship With Food and How to Break the Pattern.* New York: Hyperion.

Wolfe, Janet. 1993. *What to Do When He Has A Headache.* New York: Penguin.

Woodman, Marion. 1980. *The Owl was a Baker's Daughter.* Toronto: Inner City Books.

# More New Harbinger Titles

**DYING OF EMBARRASSMENT**
Provides clear, supportive instructions for coping with social anxiety and social phobia. *Paperback, $12.95*

**NO MORE BUTTERFLIES**
Offers step-by-step skills for overcoming shyness, stagefright, interview anxiety, and fear of public speaking. *Paperback, $12.95*

**THE TAO OF CONVERSATION**
Critical skills for open exploration of ideas, nondefensive problem solving in relationships, and making productive decisions in professional life. *Paperback, $12.95*

**MESSAGES**
An indispensable resource for anyone who wants to communicate more effectively. *Paperback, $13.95*

**THE ANXIETY & PHOBIA WORKBOOK**
This comprehensive guide is the book therapists most often recommend to clients struggling with anxiety disorders. *Paperback, $17.95*

**AN END TO PANIC**
A state-of-the-art treatment program for overcoming panic disorder. *Paperback, $17.95*

Call **toll-free 1-800-748-6273** to order. Have your Visa or Mastercard number ready. Or send a check for the titles you want to New Harbinger Publications, 5674 Shattuck Avenue, Oakland, CA 94609. Include $3.80 for the first book and 75¢ for each additional book to cover shipping and handling. (California residents please include appropriate sales tax.) Allow four to six weeks for delivery.

*Prices subject to change without notice.*

# Other New Harbinger Self-Help Titles